MAMMOTHS

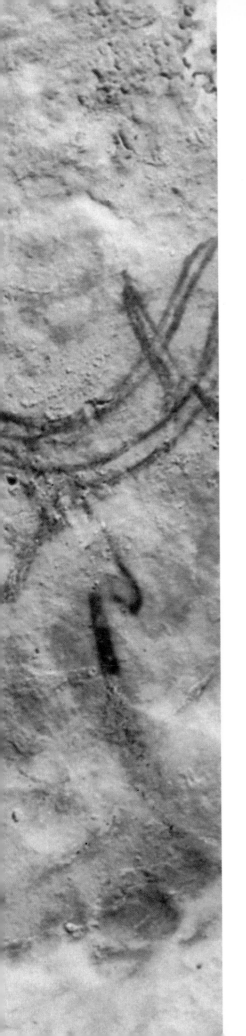

MAMMOTHS

Adrian Lister
and
Paul Bahn

Foreword by Jean M. Auel

BOXTREE

For Barbara and Stanley Lister
and for Guy Bahn

BOXTREE
First published in Great Britain in 1995 by
Boxtree Limited
Broadwall House, 21 Broadwall, London SE1 9PL

A Marshall Edition
Developed, edited and designed by
Marshall Editions, 170 Piccadilly, London W1V 9DD

1 3 5 7 9 10 8 6 4 2

ISBN 0 7522 1604 X

Editor **Antony Mason**
Art editor **Ruth Prentice**
Research **Liz Ferguson**
Picture research **Richard Philpott**

Printed and bound in Italy by New Interlitho

A CIP catalogue entry for this book is available from the British
Library.

Page 1: *A carving of a mammoth* made of mammoth bone – probably
a patella (kneecap) or a vertebra – was discovered at Avdeevo, in Russia.
This site dates to between 22,000 and 12,000 years ago.

Pages 2–3: *A mammoth forms part of a scene* with other animals,
including an ibex, drawn on the ceiling of the cave at Rouffignac in
southwestern France. Some authorities have suggested that this drawing
may not date to the Ice Age, but the details of the mammoth are strong
arguments for its authenticity.

Above: *A series of posters* have been issued this century in Russia, offering
rewards for reports of mammoth carcasses in Siberia.

CONTENTS

FOREWORD

Since few of us will ever have the opportunity to go to Africa or India to see elephants in their natural environment, it is only at zoos or circuses that we can gaze in wonder at these fantastic creatures – the largest to walk the Earth. But at one time, early relatives of elephants roamed the northern continents and grazed in places that are now the busy streets of major cities. Imagine how wonderful it would be to see those huge exotic animals, clothed in fur and sporting magnificent tusks.

In *Mammoths* Adrian Lister and Paul Bahn have given us the chance, or at least the next best thing to it. How I wish this readable book had been available when I was trying to find information about woolly mammoths for my books of Ice Age fiction, instead of having to search through dozens of highly technical books and papers.

Currently, in the popular perception – and in toy stores – mammoths are lumped together with dinosaurs as extinct animals. As the reader of this book will discover, dinosaurs died off 65 million years ago, and mammoths arose in tandem with humans around four or five million years ago. With all the attention that is currently being paid to extinct dinosaurs, it's time these equally intriguing behemoths got their share. *Mammoths* has set the record straight.

Professionals, science teachers, curious adults and, though it is not specifically written for them, even children – anyone who is interested in learning the details of how these fascinating animals fit into the overall picture – will welcome this book. Within its pages, readers will discover how the European woolly mammoths were uniquely adapted to their cold world, and the differences between them and the American variety. They will learn that mammoths were cousins of the African and Asian elephants, not their ancestors. They will find out how we have come to know so much about mammoths, including their behaviour.

A woolly mammoth skull unearthed at Ilford, near London, shows the distinctive twist of the mammoths' enormous tusks.

In this comprehensive and beautifully illustrated volume, each of the frozen specimens found in the ice and permafrost of the north is described, dispelling a few myths along the way. For example, except for dogs and other carnivores, no one is known to have actually eaten frozen mammoth meat, although it is deep red in colour like beef. Scientists have extracted their DNA and are using it, along with careful study of their physical characteristics, to tell whether mammoths were more closely related to Asian elephants or the African variety.

From the paintings and engravings made by our own Ice Age ancestors, we perceive how they saw these massive and inspiring animals that shared their frozen world, and how important mammoths were to more than their survival. They lived in dwellings constructed of mammoth bones, and burned bones for fuel. They made tools from cleavers to needles to boomerangs out of mammoth tusks, and created art from them as well. But their art was more than carved objects. Early modern humans created music from mammoth bones, and probably used them in joyous celebration and ceremony.

In weaving together all the various strands of this fascinating story, Lister and Bahn have performed a great service for all of us. We have learned about more than the life of the mysterious mammoth, we have learned something about ourselves as well.

A horse made of mammoth ivory, found at Vogelherd in Germany, was carved some 30,000 years ago, and is one of the oldest sculptures in the world.

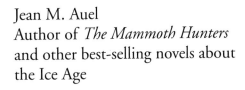

Jean M. Auel
Author of *The Mammoth Hunters*
and other best-selling novels about
the Ice Age

INTRODUCTION

"Round a bend in the path, the towering skull appeared, and we stood at the grave
of the diluvial monster. The body and limbs still stuck partially in the masses of
earth with which the corpse had been precipitated in a big fall from the bank of ice.
We stood speechless in front of this evidence of the prehistoric world, which had
been preserved almost intact in its grave of ice throughout the ages. For long we
could not tear ourselves away from the primeval creature, the mere sight of which
fills the simple children of the woods and tundra with superstitious dread."

These words of Eugen Pfizenmayer, a zoologist from the Russian Imperial Academy of Sciences, describing his dramatic encounter of 1901 on an expedition within the Arctic Circle, capture the special excitement and awe of finding a perfectly preserved frozen mammoth. We have both long been fascinated by mammoths, and through our research have been lucky enough to experience the thrills of excavating mammoth remains which had lain buried for thousands of years, and of seeing with our own eyes the depictions of these extinct animals left by our distant ancestors. It is this excitement and these experiences that we wish to share with readers through the pages of this book.

Among prehistoric creatures there is, we believe, no other species about which so many fascinating facts are known. Yet while dinosaur books abound, there has until now been no popular book devoted to all aspects of the mammoth – its life, death and preservation and its interactions with prehistoric people. In *Mammoths* we have attempted to redress this balance, drawing on the latest discoveries and research, including our own work and that of many friends and colleagues. Our text is complemented by specially created illustrations that dramatically set the mammoths in their Ice Age habitats.

The book presents the mammoth story in a logical sequence, and begins by placing the animals in their evolutionary context, looking back at their origins and their links with similar creatures, notably the elephants, their nearest living relatives. This opening

A carving of a mammoth
in mammoth ivory was found
at Předmostí in the Czech
Republic. It is probably about
26,000 years old.

The carcass of the baby woolly mammoth known as Dima was found in Siberia in 1977. Virtually complete, baby Dima is probably the most celebrated of all the Siberian mammoth finds.

chapter also traces the migration of mammoths across the globe – a story that started in Africa some three million years ago and ended in places as far apart as Great Britain, California and the island of Wrangel in the Arctic Ocean.

Chapter two tells how mammoth remains are preserved, discovered and unearthed. Here readers can join Pfizenmayer and the "mammoth hunters" of old as well as the modern excavations that reveal new pieces of evidence that help to fill in the mammoth story. From single teeth in gravel pits to carcasses preserved entire and deep frozen in the permafrost, each has an important place in the record as a whole.

In chapter three we show how the information from mammoth remains is used to reveal everything we know about the mammoth as a living animal – its appearance and adaptations, its behaviour and social life. Teeth and bones, skin and hair of mammoths – male and female, young and old – are used to help create pictures of the way these prehistoric creatures went about their daily lives.

Unlike the dinosaurs, mammoths coexisted with our early human ancestors, and chapter four is devoted to this relationship, beginning with the remarkable depictions of mammoths by the people of the Ice Age.

Following this we reveal the many different ways in which humans used the animals' bones and tusks – for home building, for tools and ornament, and for ritual burial.

The final chapter investigates whether and how people may have hunted mammoths, questions how far this predation might have caused the extinction of the species, and looks at the role of climate in the mammoths' ultimate demise. Here we describe the last living mammoths known to have survived on Earth – the miniature mammoths of Wrangel Island, which were probably still alive some 4,000 years ago, when Egyptian civilization was already established. In conclusion we look at current attempts to "resurrect" the mammoth through robotics, and at DNA analysis which, although exciting in its own right, is unlikely, at least in the fore-seeable future, to produce a living mammoth.

But if we cannot entertain the hope of seeing mammoths alive, we can go a long way toward breathing life into their flesh and bones. This has been made possible by the efforts and discoveries of archaeologists and paleontologists, together with the beautiful images left to us by the many prehistoric artists who saw these extraordinary animals in the flesh.

ORIGINS

THE ANCESTRY OF THE MAMMOTHS CAN BE TRACED *back through time to about fifty-five million years ago. The last dinosaurs had become extinct about ten million years before the emergence of a group of mammals we know as the proboscideans, which soon evolved protruding tusks and extended, trunklike noses. Some fifty million years later, the first mammoths arose from this ancestral line.*

Although they were related to modern elephants, mammoths were not their ancestors but came from a separate branch of the family tree. The first mammoths walked and browsed in the tropical woodlands of Africa, but later migrated into Europe and Siberia and eventually reached North America. With the increasing cold of the Ice Age, mammoths in northern latitudes became transformed, through evolution, into the familiar woolly mammoths, which were highly specialized for survival in Arctic temperatures. In North America, by contrast, a rather different species, the Columbian mammoth, evolved. And the isolated environments of islands also led to their own peculiar transformations: dwarf mammoths, some of which seem to have been the very last mammoths on Earth.

Living relatives of the mammoth, today's elephants are the last survivors of a formerly widespread and diverse group of animals spanning 55 million years of evolution.

EUROPE'S FIRST MAMMOTHS

A group of male ancestral mammoths browses in a lush, forested area of southern Europe about 1.5 million years ago. This species, *Mammuthus meridionalis*, was the direct descendant of tropical ancestors which had migrated north out of Africa a million or more years previously.

M. meridionalis   M. trogontherii   M. primigenius M. columbi

Mammuthus meridionalis was the ancestral mammoth from which two separate lines evolved: M. trogontherii *(the steppe mammoth) and* M. columbi *(the Columbian mammoth).* M. primigenius *(the woolly mammoth) descended from* M. trogontherii.

Unlike their ultimate descendants, which were primarily grass-eaters, ancestral mammoths were adapted to feeding mostly on trees and shrubs. They ate the fruit and bark as well as the leaves. Like modern elephants, these animals almost certainly had a direct impact on their environment through their habit of stripping the bark from trunks and even knocking whole trees over.

At first sight, these ancestral mammoths look more like the elephants of today. Not yet adapted to the cold of the Ice Age, they lack the hairy coat of their descendants. However, several features mark them out as mammoths, in particular the single-domed head and the beginnings of a spiral twist to the tusks. Their ears were probably similar in size to those of the modern Asian elephant.

Europe in the Early Pleistocene enjoyed a mild climate for much of the time, and the forests included many species of animals and plants whose closest relatives now live farther south. One example is the porcupine, which today is found in North Africa and the Middle East.

MAMMOTHS OF THE STEPPES

A group of steppe mammoths, *Mammuthus trogontherii*, migrates along a river valley in central Europe around 600,000 years ago. The steppe mammoth was the largest of all the mammoths, big males reaching a height of 14 ft (4.3 m) at the shoulder and weighing at least 10 tons.

The steppe mammoths' habitat *included large areas of grassy vegetation like the modern steppes – hence the species' name. Grass provided the bulk of its fodder. However, trees and shrubs were to be found along river valleys and in other sheltered areas, and their leaves and branches supplemented the mammoths' diet.*

Steppe mammoths probably showed *the first signs of the development of a thick coat, the reduction in size of the ears and tail and other features later seen in the woolly mammoth. Given the habits of modern elephants, it is fair to assume that mammoth groups came together to migrate once or several times each year to search for new feeding grounds.*

Mammoths were not the only species of elephant in the European Pleistocene. The straight-tusked elephant Palaeoloxodon antiquus (left), probably related to the Asian elephant Elephas, equalled the steppe mammoth in size. It generally lived in warmer, more forested areas than the mammoth, but the two sometimes coincided where there was both grassland and trees.

Many other large animals thrived in this steppe habitat. One was the broad-antlered moose. Some 7 ft (2 m) high, it was the largest deer ever to evolve. Its huge antlers spread out sideways from its head.

M. trogontherii (the steppe mammoth) was an evolutionary link between the earlier M. meridionalis (the ancestral mammoth), from which it arose, and the later M. primigenius (the woolly mammoth), which was its descendant.

M. meridionalis   M. trogontherii   M. primigenius   M. columbi

ADAPTED FOR THE COLD

With its hairy coat, sloping back and huge tusks,
the woolly mammoth, *Mammuthus primigenius*,
has become a symbol of the Ice Age. This scene
is set in England around 50,000 years ago – the
middle of the last Ice Age and the heyday of
the woolly mammoth.

M. meridionalis   M. trogontherii   M. primigenius   M. columbi

M. primigenius *(the woolly
mammoth) was descended from*
M. trogontherii *(the steppe mammoth),
which had in turn evolved from*
M. meridionalis *(the ancestral
mammoth).*

The woolly mammoth probably arose in Siberia, but soon came to occupy a vast range, stretching from Ireland to the east coast of North America. Living south of the ice sheets, it inhabited a landscape of rich, grassy vegetation largely devoid of trees. Sharing this habitat were other now extinct species, such as the woolly rhinoceros and giant deer.

A light snowfall has obscured the **vegetation,** *and one mammoth is using its tusks to clear the snow, revealing its grassy food. Contrary to the popular image of the mammoth habitat, snow was rarely heavy over much of its range.*

At close quarters, **the woolly mammoth,** *with its huge tusks apparently curving over its head, presented an imposing sight to any smaller animals, including humans. The details of its appearance, such as its small ears, pointed trunk tip and the length of its hair, are known from whole carcasses found in Siberia. The woolly mammoth represents the end point in a series of adaptations to the Ice Age habitat.*

***Dugongs,** which inhabit the coasts around Southeast Asia and the Indian Ocean, are among the closest living relatives of mammoths and today's elephants. They have small tusks formed from the incisor teeth, but these usually remain hidden beneath the lips.*

Mammoths rank with the dinosaurs as the most celebrated of prehistoric animals. The dinosaurs, however, were reptilelike animals and were extinct by 65 million years ago, while mammoths were mammals and did not appear until about 4 million years ago, lasting until only a few thousand years before the present. Mammoths are therefore very much closer to us in time and, indeed, coexisted with our human ancestors.

With the demise of the dinosaurs, the "Age of Mammals" began. Mammals had been in existence for a long time before that – their earliest remains date as far back as 200 million years – but during their early history they had remained as small, shrewlike animals living in the shadow of the dinosaurs. With the departure of the dinosaurs, mammals rapidly diversified into the many varied groups known today, as well as others that are now extinct. By about 50 million years ago, most of the major living mammalian groups had begun their evolution. These groups, known as orders, include the rodents, the carnivores, the whales, the primates, the bats and so on.

The mammoth was a member of the mammalian Order Proboscidea. This name comes from the Greek *proboskis* and refers to the characteristic trunk. Today, only two species of proboscideans remain – the African and Asian elephants. However, the Proboscidea were previously much more diverse – remains of up to 160 different species have been found worldwide.

The story of the evolution of the Proboscidea has been worked out by the study of fossils, and also of the remaining living species. Among other mammals, it seems that the closest living relatives of the Proboscidea are the Order Sirenia. These are the

sea cows, manatees and dugongs: large, barrel-shaped, slow-moving aquatic mammals which feed on sea grasses around tropical coasts. At first sight, they seem unlikely relatives of elephants, but at the time of their common ancestry, about 60 million years ago, both groups were small, land-living (perhaps amphibious) mammals, which had not yet acquired their specialized adaptations.

Detailed anatomical observation reveals their relatedness: for example, sirenians and elephants share a peculiar division at the top of the heart, and in both groups the mammary glands are between their forelegs instead of farther back as in most mammals. Somewhat more distantly related to both proboscideans and sirenians are hyraxes – small,

***Tree-dwelling hyraxes** from Africa may bear little resemblance to elephants, but they have a number of physical features in common which suggest a shared ancestry. These include the anatomy of their ear and leg bones.*

Amebelodon

herbivorous creatures of tropical Africa. Similarities of the ear and leg bones have suggested distant relatedness to elephants, and in recent years this has been corroborated by molecular studies of proteins and genes.

TUSKS AND TRUNKS

The earliest true proboscideans arose about 55 million years ago, in the area of the former Tethys Sea, roughly where the Mediterranean is today. Lacking a trunk, and with small, hippolike tusks, many of the early forms (such as the piglike Moeritherium) were amphibious. Some, among a group known as the barytheres, became very large and ponderous.

"Many distant ancestors of the mammoths had four tusks"

The earliest proboscideans to show evidence of a trunk and tusks were the deinotheres, which arose about 40 million years ago, and all later proboscideans bear these distinguishing traits. The trunk is formed by a fusion of the nose and upper lip; where it joins the skull there is a large, broad, keyhole-shaped nasal opening. The existence of this feature allows us to deduce the presence of a trunk in fossil forms of proboscideans; the trunk itself never appears in ancient fossils since it contains no bones. The tusks are greatly enlarged incisors – originally biting teeth near the front of the mouth. In some species, such as *Deinotherium*, the lower incisors formed the tusks. In others, such as the mammoths and the living elephants, it is the upper incisors. Many fossil proboscideans had both upper and lower tusks – a total of four in all.

The heyday of the Proboscidea was in the period of time known as the Miocene – between about 24 and 5 million years ago. Many different species evolved, broadly known as mastodonts, but grouped into several distinct families. The mammutid family included the American mastodon *Mammut*, which survived until about 10,000 years ago. This species therefore came to coexist with the mammoths, although it was only a distant cousin whose family history had taken a separate course 25 million years previously. Other families included the "shovel-tuskers" such as *Amebelodon*, with enormously expanded, flattened lower tusks as well as a pair of smaller upper ones.

One particularly significant group of Miocene Proboscidea was formed by the stegodons of Southeast Asia and Africa, because it was from this group that the true elephants are believed to have arisen. Stegodons had long, straight tusks, and their molar teeth (the back, grinding teeth) show the beginnings of the ridged form that characterizes those of elephants.

Deinotherium

The ancestry of the mammoth can be shown in a simplified family tree. The hyrax and dugong, closest living relatives of the mammoth and elephants, are nonetheless separated from them by more than 50 million years of proboscidean evolution, starting with Moeritherium *and followed by up to 160 fossil species, only a few of which are shown here. Each group's time of origin is approximate and is estimated from its earliest fossil dates together with its degree of evolutionary advancement. For example,* Deinotherium *is first known from rocks about 25 million years old, but its primitive features suggest that its line diverged much earlier.*

Millions of years ago

80

70

HYRAXES

60

SEA-COWS

50

Moeritherium

PRIMITIVE PROBOSCIDEANS

40

Phiomia

30

MASTODONTS

20

Ambelodon

10

THE PROBOSCIDEAN FAMILY TREE

Tracing the Ancestry of the Mammoth

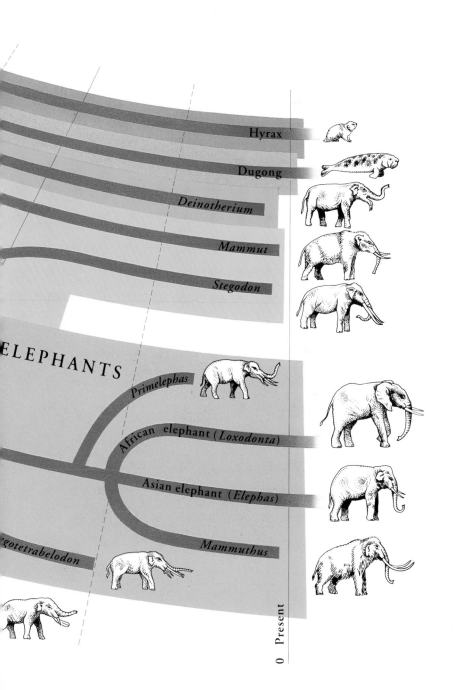

Hyrax

Dugong

Deinotherium

Mammut

Stegodon

ELEPHANTS

Primelephas

African elephant (*Loxodonta*)

Asian elephant (*Elephas*)

gotetrabelodon

Mammuthus

0 Present

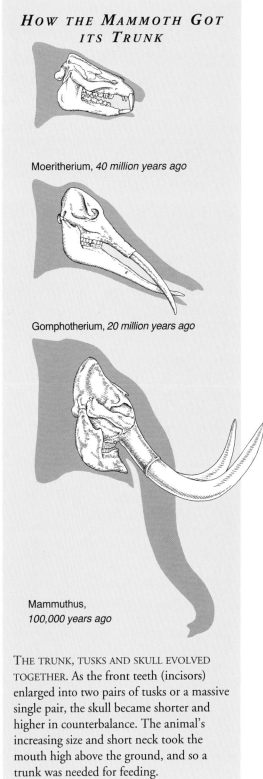

HOW THE MAMMOTH GOT ITS TRUNK

Moeritherium, *40 million years ago*

Gomphotherium, *20 million years ago*

Mammuthus, *100,000 years ago*

THE TRUNK, TUSKS AND SKULL EVOLVED TOGETHER. As the front teeth (incisors) enlarged into two pairs of tusks or a massive single pair, the skull became shorter and higher in counterbalance. The animal's increasing size and short neck took the mouth high above the ground, and so a trunk was needed for feeding.

OUT OF AFRICA

The true elephants, including the two living species and the mammoths, form a family within the Proboscidea known as the Elephantidae. The crucible of elephant evolution appears to have been in Africa, for it is there that the earliest fossil representatives, and the evidence of the beginnings of diversification into different forms, are found. Only later did the elephants leave Africa to colonize other parts of the world.

Two distinctive features of mammoths and other elephants, in contrast to their predecessors, are the absence of enamel around the tusks and their ridged molar teeth *(see p.25)*. The tusks are composed of solid dentine, the hard tissue at the core of the incisor teeth. The earliest fossil forms with these features – and therefore the earliest true elephants – are the four-tusked *Stegotetrabelodon* and smaller *Primelephas*, which lived in Africa about 6 million years ago. About 4 or 5 million years ago, still in Africa, the elephant line split into three main branches.

The first branch, *Loxodonta*, produced the living African elephant, *L. africana*. This lineage has remained in Africa since its origin. The second branch, *Elephas*, eventually gave rise to today's Asian elephant, *E. maximus*. The fossil record shows that this line first diversified into a number of species in Africa before one of them migrated

SPECIES	**Woolly mammoth** *Mammuthus primigenius*	**American mastodon** *Mammut americanum*
HEIGHT	9–11 ft (2.75–3.4 m)	8–10 ft (2.4–3 m)
WEIGHT	4–6 tons	4–5 tons
BACK SHAPE	sloping	straight
FUR	dense	probably dense
HEAD	high single dome	low single dome
EAR	very small	unknown
TUSKS	curved and twisted	sometimes two pairs
TRUNK TIP	1 short, 1 long "finger"	unknown
TAIL	short	medium

Elephants are the closest living relatives of the mammoth. Like today's elephants, the earliest mammoths evolved in a tropical climate – in contrast to the woolly mammoth, which acquired various adaptations to survive in an Arctic habitat.

MASTODONTS AND ELEPHANTS

| African elephant
Loxodonta africana | Asian elephant
Elephas maximus |
|---|---|
| 10–11 ft (3–3.4 m) | 8–10 ft (2.4–3 m) |
| 4–6 tons | 3–5 tons |
| saddle-shaped | humped |
| very sparse | sparse |
| low single dome | double dome |
| large | medium |
| gently curved | gently curved |
| 2 equal "fingers" | 1 "finger" |
| long | long |

north and east into India and Southeast Asia, where it evolved into the Asian elephant still found there.

The third main branch of the elephant family was the line that was to lead to the mammoths (*Mammuthus*). It appears likely that all three branches split at around the same time, and it remains unclear whether the mammoth line is more closely related to the Asian or to the African elephant. Features of the skull and teeth suggest affinity to the Asian elephant. However, preserved fragments of the genetic code (DNA) *(see pp.138–39)* imply

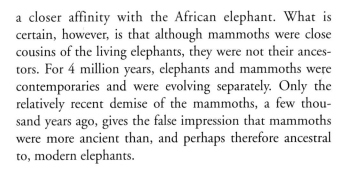

a closer affinity with the African elephant. What is certain, however, is that although mammoths were close cousins of the living elephants, they were not their ancestors. For 4 million years, elephants and mammoths were contemporaries and were evolving separately. Only the relatively recent demise of the mammoths, a few thousand years ago, gives the false impression that mammoths were more ancient than, and perhaps therefore ancestral to, modern elephants.

"Mammoths and elephants roamed the Earth at the same time – they were close cousins"

Fossils of the earliest representatives of the mammoth line, which lived about 4 million years ago, were first identified in the 1920s. Named *Mammuthus subplanifrons*, they are found in South Africa and in Kenya and other countries in East Africa. Their remains are recognized as belonging to *Mammuthus* on the basis of features such as the spirally twisting tusks that are unique to mammoths. From the sediments in which they were found, and from plant fossils discovered with them, it is clear that they were living in a tropical environment, very different from that of their ultimate and most famous descendants, the woolly mammoths.

M. subplanifrons is known to have survived until about 3 million years ago. Some time after this another mammoth species appeared in North Africa and was probably its descendant. Named *Mammuthus africanavus*, it seems to have been relatively small, with tusks that diverged more widely from the skull than is usual in other species of *Mammuthus*. This has led some paleontologists to suppose that it was an evolutionary "dead end", since the feature is not found in later species.

Probably the world's oldest mammoth fossil, this fragment of molar of Mammuthus subplanifrons *was found in the Afar Depression of Ethiopia in deposits more than 4 million years old. It is 5 in (13 cm) long, which represents about half the complete tooth.*

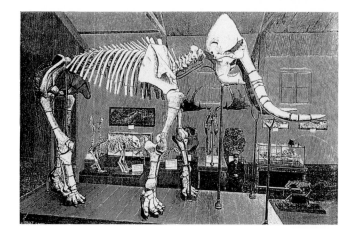

MAMMOTHS MOVE NORTH

Between about 3 million and 2.5 million years ago, the first mammoths appeared in Europe. Their remains have been found at sites such as Montopoli, near Florence in Italy, and in coastal deposits known as Red Crag in Suffolk, England. Some scientists have suggested that their route from Africa was via the western Mediterranean at the Strait of Gibraltar. However, although previously bridged by land, the seaway may well have already existed by this time. A more probable route was therefore through the Middle East and Turkey. These populations were derived either from *Mammuthus africanavus* or, more likely, directly from late representatives of *M. subplanifrons*.

The seemingly long distances of such migrations become plausible when the timescale is taken into account. An average spread of only 3 miles (5 km) per year would achieve the 3,600 miles (6,000 km) from East Africa to northwestern Europe in 1,200 years – a very short period in the history of life on Earth. The migration into Britain presented no problems because the English Channel did not exist until half a million years ago.

The early European mammoth fossils were first studied in 1825 by the Italian paleontologist Filippo Nesti, who did not recognize their affinity with mammoths and gave them the species name *Elephas meridionalis*. Nowadays the fossils are classified as *Mammuthus meridionalis*.

Following the original discovery, the remains of *M. meridionalis* have been found in many other countries of Europe, including European Russia. Several complete skeletons have

The world's largest mammoth thigh bone, from an ancestral mammoth, is 5 ft (1.5 m) long. It was eroded out of a coastal cliff at Mundesley in Norfolk, England, during the 19th century and was recovered from the beach.

been collected in the Florence area over the past hundred years or so, and in the 1980s 15 individual skeletons were excavated at a lignite mine at Pietrafitta in central Italy. Isolated skeletons are known from other localities, such as Durfort in central France and Nogaisk in southern Russia, but, as with all fossil proboscideans, the most abundant finds are isolated teeth. For example, the British zoologist Sir Richard Owen wrote in 1846 that as many as 2,000 molars of *"Elephas" meridionalis* had been dredged from submarine deposits off the village of Happisburgh in Norfolk, England, in just 13 years.

From these finds a picture of *M. meridionalis* and its habitat can be pieced together. Complete skeletons reveal an animal considerably bigger than a modern elephant – about 13 ft (4 m) high and probably weighing around 10 tons. The tusks were robust and showed the characteristic mammoth twist. Plant and other fossils found with the remains show that *M. meridionalis* was living in a time of mild climate, generally as warm as or slightly warmer than Europe experiences today. Deciduous mixed woodland provided its habitat and food, which comprised mostly tree-browse: oak, ash, beech and other familiar European trees, as well as some that are now exotic to the region, such as hemlock, wing nut and hickory.

Judging from its climatic context, *M. meridionalis* probably lacked the dense fur of later mammoths and would have looked at first sight more like a typical elephant. However, the curved tusks and the rather pointed top of the head marked it out as a mammoth. Alongside it lived numerous other exotic animals such as porcupines, comb-antlered deer, zebralike horses, small rhinoceroses and primitive pigs and cattle.

A skeleton of an ancestral mammoth, Mammuthus meridionalis, *was exhibited in the Paris Museum of Natural History in 1893. Excavated at Durfort in central France, it was the most complete specimen known at the time and formed the basis of early reconstructions of the ancestral mammoth.*

THE WOOLLY MAMMOTH

Mammuthus meridionalis survived for approximately 2 million years, but toward the end of its reign, about a million years ago, climatic changes were accelerating. These brought about shifts of adaptation in many mammalian species, including the mammoths. As global cooling intensified, much of the warm, forest habitat of the ancestral mammoth reverted to a more open, grassy landscape. It was almost certainly this change of conditions that led to the progressive evolution toward the familiar woolly mammoth, highly specialized for the Ice Age world.

Clear changes are seen in mammoth fossils dating to between 750,000 and 500,000 years ago, enough to identify a separate species. This was *Mammuthus trogontherii,* also known as the steppe mammoth because some of the best fossils were found associated with plant remains indicating a grass-dominated habitat.

> *"Mammoths moved into the open steppes around 600,000 years ago"*

Some populations still lived in warm, wooded areas, as the discovery of a complete skeleton of *M. trogontherii* at West Runton in eastern England in 1990 revealed. This skeleton was found in a peaty deposit about 600,000 to 700,000 years old, with woodland plants that suggest a mild and forested habitat similar to that of the ancestral *M. meridionalis.* But other evidence shows that around this time *M. trogontherii* had also started to appear in cooler and more open habitats. Numerous fossils of these

Mammuthus trogontherii, the steppe mammoth

EVOLUTION OF MAMMOTH SKULLS AND TEETH

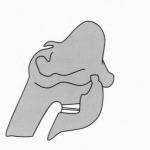

THE TRANSITION FROM THE FOREST-DWELLING ancestral mammoth *Mammuthus meridionalis* to the cold-adapted woolly mammoth *M. primigenius* involved a number of changes, such as the development of thick fur *(see pp.70–71)* and the reduction in the size of the ears and tail. One of the clearest pointers to this process of adaptation is the fossil teeth, always a good indicator of diet. Some 2.5 million to 1.5 million years ago, the ancestral mammoth had molars *(right)* with comparatively low crowns and a small number of thick enamel ridges (usually no more than 12 to 14 on the back molar). This relatively modest chewing power was sufficient for a woodland diet consisting mainly of the soft leaves of trees and shrubs.

Later fossils, which trace the transition to *M. trogontherii* and thence to *M. primigenius,* have progressively higher tooth crowns and more enamel ridges, around 18 to 20 in the back molars of *M. trogontherii,* and up to 26 in *M. primigenius.* This was linked to the shift to a grassy diet, which required more chewing power and wore down the teeth more rapidly – due to the minute silica particles in grass leaves and to the tendency of the animal to pick up grit when feeding. Parallel, if less pronounced, changes occurred in the North American branch leading to *M. columbi.*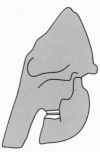

At the same time, there were changes in the skull and jaws. Partly to accommodate the higher-crowned teeth, the upper and lower jaws deepened. The top of the skull grew taller, providing a greater area of attachment for tendons and muscles running to the back. These acted to hold up the skull in counterbalance to the increasing weight of the tusks. The mechanical effort involved in moving such a weighty apparatus up and down was further assisted by the shortening of the skull from front to back, while the tusk sockets were now directed downward rather than forward. The result was the high but short skull which characterizes both the woolly and Columbian mammoths *(top, left).*

In the evolution from ancestral mammoth (above left) *to woolly mammoth* (above right)*, the skull became higher and the face and jaw more compressed front to back.*

The modern Arctic tundra is restricted to the northern latitudes and is now home to large herds of caribou. In the Ice Age this species ranged as far south as Spain in Europe and Tennessee in North America.

animals have been found in deposits in Germany and elsewhere, with evidence of a grassy, steppelike habitat. Compared to those of the ancestral mammoth, their teeth had changed, reflecting the shift in diet: they have more enamel ridges to cope with tough, grassy food, and a higher crown to allow for greater wear through life.

Recently discovered fossils from the Kolyma region of northeastern Siberia suggest that this evolutionary change may have begun there, where the effects of the Ice Age were felt earlier and also more severely than in Europe. *M. trogontherii* may, therefore, have originated in these northern regions about a million years ago and then, at about 750,000 years ago, moved into Europe as cold climates started to spread southward. It replaced its ancestor *M. meridionalis*, which became extinct.

The steppe mammoth *M. trogontherii* can be regarded as a kind of evolutionary intermediate between the warmth-loving, forest-dwelling ancestral mammoth *M. meridionalis* and the cold-adapted, grass-eating woolly mammoth. After the *M. trogontherii* stage, the mammoth's evolution accelerated and, by 250,000 years ago, the true woolly mammoth *Mammuthus primigenius* had emerged in Europe. As in the previous change, the fossil record shows a period of transition, with some more "primitive" populations still inhabiting milder areas of southern Europe and even spreading north during interglacials. For example, mammoths found in 1992–94 in deposits at Stanton Harcourt near Oxford, England, are dated to a temperate phase about 200,000 years ago and associated with vegetation and fossils of mollusc and insect species typical of a mild climate *(see pp.58–59)*.

Eventually, however, these populations died out and were superseded by "advanced" woolly mammoths, fully tolerant of the cold climate and treeless vegetation of the

THE ICE AGE

THE PLEISTOCENE PERIOD, WHICH BEGAN about 1.7 million years ago and lasted until only 10,000 years ago, saw convulsive changes in climates and habitats around the globe. This period is often referred to as the Ice Age, although the term is sometimes restricted to the episodes of cold climate within it, such as the "last Ice Age", 100,000–10,000 years ago.

Taking England as an example, the mean summer temperature was commonly about 50°F (10°C), or 10°F (6°C) colder than today's, and the mean winter temperature about 16°F (-9°C), or 24°F (13°C) colder. These periods of cold were punctuated by warm episodes called interglacials, when the climate became similar to that of today. The warm periods were generally much shorter than the cold ones, coming only every 100,000 years or so, and lasting a few thousand years or tens of thousands of years at most. The Earth is currently in an interglacial period, which has been termed the Holocene or postglacial. The diagram *(right)* shows only major cycles of cold and warm; there were also many shorter fluctuations. During the coldest episodes, the polar ice sheets expanded to cover areas far to the south of glaciers today, and winter temperatures in England fell to 0°F (-18°C) or lower, similar to those of western Siberia today. The alternation of warm and cold is thought to be due to minor variations in the Earth's orbit.

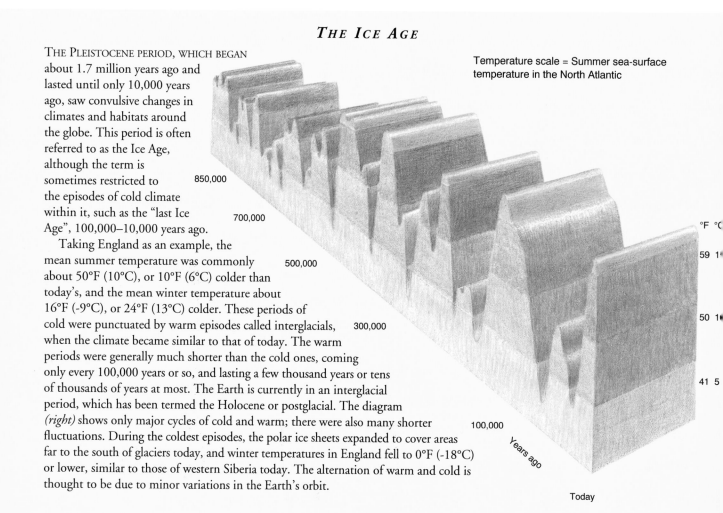

Temperature scale = Summer sea-surface temperature in the North Atlantic

850,000

700,000

500,000

300,000

100,000

Years ago

Today

°F °C

59 1

50 1

41 5

Mammuthus primigenius,
the woolly mammoth

Ice Age. There is fossil evidence that the transformation, as previously, had first occurred in northeastern Siberia, with a subsequent southward spread into Europe. Certainly by 100,000 years ago, the beginning of the last Ice Age, the mammoths had taken up residence right across the vast expanse of largely treeless vegetation that extended from the British Isles to eastern Siberia.

The environment of the woolly mammoth for much of the last Ice Age was quite rich. Although the climate was generally too cold for trees, clear skies producing longer hours of sunlight and moderate precipitation promoted abundant vegetation, comprising a mixture of the plant species now living in the Arctic tundra with those of a more grassy, steppelike nature. Other inhabitants included now extinct forms, such as the woolly rhinoceros and cave bear, as well as various species still known today, such as reindeer, musk oxen, horses and bison.

The world 18,000 years ago, at the peak of the last Ice Age, *was very different from that of today. Ice extended in Europe as far south as central England, and in North America to below the Great Lakes. South of the ice there was a vast expanse of meadowlike grassy vegetation, named "mammoth steppe" after its most famous inhabitant, the woolly mammoth. Farther south was a mosaic of parklands and open woods, which in North America was home to the Columbian mammoth* Mammuthus columbi. *Elsewhere, the vegetation was similar to modern steppes, deserts, subtropical savannas and tropical forests, although their ranges were different from those of today. Mammoths did not live in these areas.*

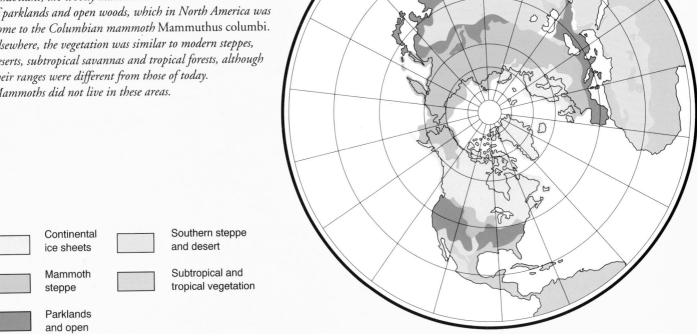

- Continental ice sheets
- Mammoth steppe
- Parklands and open woodlands
- Southern steppe and desert
- Subtropical and tropical vegetation

THE AMERICAN MAMMOTH

Watched by a pair of coyotes, a small family of Columbian mammoths feeds in the rolling landscape of the Black Hills of South Dakota, 25,000 years ago. This species, *Mammuthus columbi*, was exclusive to North America. Its range extended to Mexico – farther south than any other mammoth species since the original migration from Africa millions of years before.

M. meridionalis   M. trogontherii   M. primigenius   M. columbi

The American branch of the mammoth family, M. columbi, *evolved from populations of* M. meridionalis *(the ancestral mammoth), which entered the New World about 1.5 million years ago. In Eurasia the same ancestor evolved into* M. primigenius *(the woolly mammoth).*

In the northern part of its range, the Columbian mammoth may occasionally have encountered its woolly cousin migrating from its more northerly territory. Here, male Columbian and woolly mammoths are pictured confronting each other. The woolly mammoth is distinguished by its smaller size and heavier coat.

The Columbian mammoth was up to 13 ft (4 m) in height and weighed an estimated 10 tons. The details of its external appearance are in part speculative but, since the animal lived in a more southerly habitat, it is likely that its coat was much less developed than the woolly mammoth's. The tusks, however, were every bit as imposing; those of the females and young shown in the foreground are relatively modest compared to the massive pair carried by full-grown males.

INTO THE NEW WORLD

Mammoths first spread into North America about 1.5 million years ago. This was during the reign of *Mammuthus meridionalis* in Europe and Asia. The route to North America was eastward. The northeastern tip of Asia (the Chukotka region of Siberia) and the northwestern tip of America (Alaska) are today separated by 60 miles (100 km) of sea, but during each Ice Age sea levels fell by about 300 ft (100 m) because so much of the world's water was locked up in the ice caps. At such times the Bering Strait between Siberia and Alaska became dry land, forming part of a region known as Beringia, and animals could migrate across this land link between the two continents.

Only a single fossil tooth of *M. meridionalis*, from the Vilui River basin, attests to its presence in eastern Siberia. However, even without this fossil it is clear that the early mammoths must at some time have expanded into Beringia, for this was the only route into North America, and their remains – beginning around 1.5 million years ago – have been found on that continent. The migration presumably occurred during a phase of relatively mild climate, for *M. meridionalis* was essentially a warmth-adapted species, and Beringia was in the Arctic. Once in the New World, the ancestral mammoths soon spread to the south, for early remains have been found in southern Alberta, Florida and elsewhere.

The evolution from *M. meridionalis* was somewhat similar to that occurring at the same time in Eurasia. This is an interesting example of parallel evolution – the independent development of similar features in two parts of a lineage that have become separated geographically. Nonetheless, the end result was not identical. While in Europe the evolution led to the woolly mammoth *M. primigenius*, in America it gave rise to the so-called Columbian mammoth *Mammuthus columbi*.

 Landmass during Ice Age

 Mammoths and humans migrate to America

 Horses and camels migrate to Asia

At times of low sea level, during the Ice Age, Asia and America became linked by land (above). *Species that had evolved in the Old World spread into the New. This included mammoths, bison, wapiti and humans. Traffic in the opposite direction was more limited, but included horses* and camels. *These species did not all cross at the same time, but during successive episodes of land connection. At these times the area was not just a land bridge but formed a large territory in its own right, in which many animal and plant species evolved and flourished.*

The Columbian mammoth was larger than its woolly cousin and probably did not have such a dense covering of fur. It was adapted to a more open and cooler habitat than its ancestor *M. meridionalis*, but not to such an extreme degree as the woolly mammoth. In its adaptations to a changing diet it progressed about as far as *M. trogontherii* had in Europe, typically with around 20 enamel ridges in its last molars. But whereas in Eurasia *M. trogontherii* had evolved farther to produce the woolly mammoth, the Columbian mammoth remained at roughly this level of adaptation until its extinction at the end of the Pleistocene. It occupied much of what is now the United States, and even extended south into Mexico, but did not live in the Arctic regions of Canada, in other words, not as far north as the woolly mammoth in Eurasia.

The Columbian mammoth was part of the rich and varied mammal fauna of the Pleistocene in North America, much of which is now extinct *(see p.124–25)*. Its remains have been found together with such exotic species as the giant armadillo, sabre-tooth cat, the giant ground sloth and "yesterday's camel", as well as its distant relative the American mastodon and large numbers of more familiar animals such as horses and buffalo.

Many American fossils have been named "Imperial Mammoth" *Mammuthus imperator*, but it is not certain if these are the same species as *M. columbi*, or an earlier stage in its evolution. Additionally, some researchers believe that certain populations of the American mammoth lineage evolved beyond the *M. columbi* stage, producing a more advanced species, *Mammuthus jeffersonii*. However, the existence of *M. jeffersonii* as a species distinct from *M. columbi* is uncertain. The name *jeffersonii* was coined by the American paleontologist Henry Fairfield Osborn, the leading expert on fossil elephants in the early 20th century.

He named it after President Thomas Jefferson who, more than a century earlier, had had a particular interest in mammoths and mastodons, which he believed might still be living in the American West.

About 100,000 years ago there was a second wave of mammoth migration, but this time it involved the woolly mammoth. Like its ancestor *M. meridionalis* more than a million years previously, the woolly mammoth migrated across the dry Bering Strait from the Siberian part of Beringia into North America. Fossils of woolly mammoths dating from this time onward are common in Alaska, Canada and the northern part of the United States. The woolly mammoth took up the same range of latitudes and habitats in America as it occupied in the Old World. To the south, the Columbian mammoth was already established, so the two species more or less divided the continent between them.

Although woolly and Columbian mammoths have each been found at hundreds of fossil localities, few sites contain both. However, at Hot Springs in South Dakota *(see pp.52–53)*, some woolly mammoth fossils were found in the same sinkhole as numerous Columbian mammoth skeletons. This site is in the region of overlap between the ranges of the two species. However, it is not clear whether both were there at the same time, or whether woolly mammoths entered the area at a time of cooler climate when the Columbian mammoths had retreated south.

Mammoths never reached South America or southern Asia, nor did they re-enter Africa after the original dispersal. But they came to cover most of Europe, northern Asia and North America.

Mammuthus columbi,
the Columbian mammoth

MAMMOTHS IN MINIATURE

On several islands around the world, mammoths of greatly reduced body size evolved. Pictured here is *Mammuthus exilis* – a dwarfed version of the Columbian mammoth, *M. columbi* – which lived on the California Channel Islands between 30,000 and 12,000 years ago.

Santa Barbara
Los Ange

San Miguel
Santa Rosa
Santa Cruz

California Channel Islands

*A **flock of geese,** each bird some 2–3 ft (60–90 cm) in height, graphically illustrates the small size of the island mammoths. The Californian dwarfs were typically 4–6 ft (1.2–1.8 m) high at the shoulder, less than half the height of their mainland ancestors and contemporaries. They may have weighed only about 1 ton, compared to the 10 tons of the average Columbian mammoth. In other respects they were probably similar, with short fur and a typical mammoth body form, but a relatively large head.*

During the Ice Age, sea levels were low enough to connect some of the smaller California Channel Islands, but not to link them to the mainland 20 miles (30 km) or so away, so the original, colonizing mammoths must have arrived by swimming. Remains of at least 50 dwarf individuals have been discovered, most of them on Santa Rosa. A complete skeleton was found there in 1994. Some bones of larger mammoths have also been found, but it is uncertain whether these represent stages in a single dwarfing process or successive waves of immigration.

Even on the mainland, mammoths varied in body size between areas and at different times, largely because of the quality of feeding available. None, however, became as small as those stranded on small islands, where the food supply was strictly limited, especially in times of seasonal shortage. Island inhabitants were unable to migrate to richer feeding grounds, so smaller animals that could survive with less food were at an advantage.

ISLAND DWARFS AND GIANTS

ISLANDS HOLD A SPECIAL PLACE IN THE STUDY OF EVOLUTION. Populations of animals and plants in isolation from their mainland relations often evolve into new species unique to an island or archipelago. Famous examples include the finches and giant tortoises of the Galápagos Islands in the Pacific, studied by Charles Darwin in the 1830s.

The founding members of an animal population may reach an island in one of two ways. First, the island may once have been connected to the mainland but, with rising sea level or subsidence of land, may have become isolated along with its cargo of animals and plants. Second, the island may always have been isolated by sea, but animals may have reached it by swimming, drifting, rafting on flotsam, flying in the case of birds and bats or, for some small organisms, being carried by birds.

One of the most common evolutionary responses to island life is an increase or decrease in body size. Fossils excavated on islands show that, during the Pleistocene, many populations of large mammals isolated on islands became dwarfed. In the Mediterranean, for example, there were diminutive antelopes in the Balearic Islands, dwarf hippopotami on Cyprus and elsewhere, and miniature deer on many islands including Sicily and Crete. On Indonesian islands other species of deer became dwarfed, as did isolated populations of stegodon – a proboscidean distantly related to mammoths. Even today similar phenomena can be observed, for example in the key deer – populations of white-tailed deer on islands off the coast of Florida.

The key deer of Florida – a modern example of island dwarfing – have half the body weight of mainland white-tailed deer.

Large mammals probably become dwarfed by a combination of limited food resources and an absence of predators. Conversely, many small mammals – rodents and shrews, for example – as well as some cold-blooded animals such as the Galápagos giant tortoises, often increased in size on islands. In their case, lack of predators may have reduced the need for small size. Other evolutionary forces, such as the advantage of large size in competing for mates, then took over. Evidence suggests that these processes of adaptation may occur comparatively quickly – within a few thousand years or less.

DWARF MAMMOTHS

Fossil evidence suggesting the existence of dwarf mammoths has been found in at least three island locations.

The earliest case seems to have produced the most extreme result. Caves in Sicily and Malta have yielded many bones of an elephantlike mammal only 3 ft (1 m) high in the adult, and named *Elephas falconeri*. These remains are believed to be at least 500,000 years old and date to a time when Sicily and Malta were joined as one island. Although the dwarf remains, with their single-domed skull and curved tusks, look superficially like a mammoth, this may be a result of dwarfing, and the teeth suggest that the species evolved from the straight-tusked elephant *Palaeoloxodon antiquus*.

"Some adult dwarf mammoths were no taller than a goat"

On the other side of the world, in the California Channel Islands, a dwarfed species of mammoth appropriately named *Mammuthus exilis* evolved from the American lineage *M. columbi (see pp.32–33)*. Research indicates that there has not been a land bridge from the Channel Islands to the California mainland in recent geological history. The founding Columbian mammoths must therefore have arrived by swimming the 21 miles (35 km) or so from the mainland, plausible given the strong swimming powers of elephants.

The most recent discovery of dwarf mammoths was announced by three Russian scientists in 1993. The remains come from the extremely remote island of Wrangel in the Arctic Ocean 125 miles (200 km) north of Siberia. Partially eroded tusks, teeth and leg bones were found lying on the surface of the tundra or buried in shallow stream gravel. On the basis of the small teeth, it has been estimated that the animals stood about 6 ft (1.8 m) high, compared to 10–11 ft (3–3.4 m) in typical woolly

The rugged coast of Wrangel Island, in the Arctic Ocean off northeastern Siberia, rings the treeless environment that once supported a population of dwarf mammoths. Isolated from the mainland, mammoths survived here longer than anywhere else on Earth.

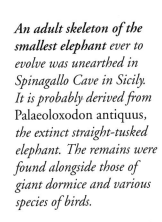

1 Wrangel Island

2 Malta/Sicily

3 California Channel Islands

Dwarf mammoths evolved independently on at least three islands across the globe. In each case, these mammoths were descended from normal-sized animals from the adjacent mainland.

mammoths. Radiocarbon dates on the fossils indicate that the dwarfs lived only 7,000 to 3,700 years ago *(see p.137).*

Larger, normal-sized mammoth remains, with radiocarbon dates of 12,000 years ago and older, were also found on the island. On the basis of these, it is possible to plot the process of dwarfing. Some 12,000 years ago, Wrangel was connected by dry land to the Siberian part of Beringia and shared its population of mammoths. At the end of the last Ice Age, sea levels rose and Wrangel, with its population of mammoths, became isolated. By 7,000 years ago, the mammoths had become fully dwarfed, so the maximum amount of time taken for the process can be estimated at 5,000 years. This represents approximately 500 generations of mammoths – one of the shortest evolutionary transitions found in a fossil record.

What was the cause of dwarfing in the island mammoths? Most researchers agree that it is related to restricted food resources and the absence of predators. On a limited area of terrain, food is at a premium and small-bodied individuals that can make do with less should be favoured by natural selection. This would be particularly felt during times of winter shortage, when the opportunity for migrating to richer feeding grounds is denied to island inhabitants. The absence of wolves and other predators would have contributed to this process. Small islands cannot hold sufficient numbers of herbivorous mammals to support carnivore populations. In this situation, some adaptive reasons for large size – predator avoidance and defence – disappear. Also, with no predators to keep down their numbers, herbivore populations expand to the point at which they are in direct competition for food – augmenting the pressure for frugality and size reduction.

An adult skeleton of the smallest elephant ever to evolve was unearthed in Spinagallo Cave in Sicily. It is probably derived from Palaeoloxodon antiquus, the extinct straight-tusked elephant. The remains were found alongside those of giant dormice and various species of birds.

MAMMOTHS UNEARTHED

MAMMOTH REMAINS ARE BY NO MEANS RARE. OVER *the centuries they have been found on four continents and in a wide variety of locations: in the frozen wastes of Siberia and Alaska, in the tarpits of Los Angeles, on the bed of the North Sea, in gravel pits, caves and coal mines. Their bodies have been revealed in every possible condition and range from specimens with hair, hide, flesh, blood and internal organs to skeletons and mere fragments of teeth and bones. They have been found by all kinds of people – ivory collectors, hunters, miners, bulldozer drivers, boat crews and people out walking the dog.*

Such discoveries were once a source of dread and superstition, but gradually scientists have been able to use these finds to build up a thorough picture of this great creature of the past. By carefully piecing together the evidence presented by mammoth finds it has been possible to learn about the animal's life, its numerous causes of death, and the conditions leading to its varied states of preservation.

A mammoth skeleton is carefully excavated at the Hot Springs site in South Dakota, where up to 100 mammoths met their deaths in a sinkhole some 26,000 years ago.

THE DEATH OF BABY DIMA

Baby mammoth Dima struggles to free himself from silty water in a Siberian pond some 40,000 years ago. His mother anxiously tries to approach the youngster as other group members hasten to the scene. Dima perished, but was rediscovered in 1977, providing scientists with the most complete mammoth carcass ever recovered.

__Having fallen into a pool of soft mud,__ Dima was probably pulled in even deeper by his own struggles. Eventually he died either from exhaustion or by suffocation in the mud. The following spring, mudflows buried him deeper, protecting his body from thaw and decay. Pockets of ice formed as ice lenses.

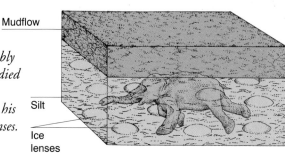

Mudflow

Silt

Ice lenses

Dima was less than a year old at death, and may have been in poor physical condition, as indicated by his lack of fat and the parasite remains found in his gut. His body had not decayed and was untouched by scavengers, so it is unlikely that he died lying on the surface. Theories about how he died include drowning in water, or falling down a crack in the frozen ground. The most likely scenario, however, is that he was trapped in saturated mud.

The size and poor condition of Dima ensured rapid freezing and account for the exceptional preservation of his body. The ice veins in the surrounding silt drew moisture out of his body, resulting in a shrivelled mummy – rather as with meat left too long in the freezer.

Until only a few centuries ago, any large bones discovered in the fields or caves of Europe were usually assumed to be the remains of giants, and were often displayed as curiosities in castles, palaces, town halls, churches and monasteries. Among the best known is a mammoth thigh bone – engraved with its date of discovery (1443) and the motto of Emperor Frederick III – which for about three centuries hung in the "Giant's Portal" of Vienna's Cathedral of St. Stephen. In 1577 a collection of mammoth bones sparked a heated theological debate in Switzerland. When it was proposed that they should be given a Christian burial in a cemetery, a doctor studied them closely and declared them to be the bones of a giant, 18 ft (5.5 m) tall, who deserved no such courtesy, being a heathen.

"In the distant past mammoth bones were assumed to be the remains of giants"

Eventually, the true nature of such remains dawned on a few scholars. For example, in 1696 a skeleton found at Tonna, in the Grand Duchy of Gotha, Germany, was declared by the Gotha medical college to be an elephant-shaped freak of nature, but a historian to the dukes of Saxony examined it and correctly identified it as that of an extinct elephant.

This interpretation, however, presented a difficulty: if such remains belonged to elephants, which today live in warm southern countries, how could they possibly be found in northern Europe? Until the mid-18th century any finds in Italy were attributed to animals brought north in Roman times: for example, it was known that Hannibal, as well as Pyrrhus, king of Epirus (in modern Greece), had used elephants against the Romans. But with more northerly finds scholars could only assume that the climate in these countries used to be warmer than it is now, or that drowned elephants had been carried north by the biblical Flood.

In 1796 the great French anatomist Georges Cuvier put forward the proposition, on the basis of comparative anatomy, that the remains were those of fossil elephants similar to, but quite distinct from, those existing today. The mammoth was in fact among the first extinct animals to be discovered and studied. In 1799 it was given a name: *Elephas primigenius*.

Meanwhile, in North America, numerous bones believed to belong to elephants (actually those of mastodons) had been found in the 18th century in the salty bog soil of Big Bone Lick in Kentucky. The French Baron de Longueuil acquired a tusk, several molars and a thigh bone, and shipped them back to France. At this time American scholars followed Thomas Jefferson in believing that there was no such thing as an extinct animal: if the bones existed, then so must the living animal. This is reflected in the first name given to the species: *Incognitum* (unknown). It was Cuvier, once again, who demonstrated that although the mastodon was related to the elephant, it was quite distinct from both the African and Asian forms and from the Eurasian mammoth.

WHAT'S IN A NAME?

THE ORIGINS AND MEANING OF THE WORD MAMMOTH REMAIN OBSCURE. Some claim that it is derived from the Hebrew "behemoth", the name for a primeval creature mentioned in the Old Testament of the Bible (Job, 40: 15–24). An animal of enormous size and strength, with curved horns or tusks, the behemoth was believed to consume huge amounts of grass and water, and had a mild and peaceful nature. An alternative view traces the name to various northern languages. The most plausible candidate is Estonian, in which *maa* means earth and *mutt* means mole, linking the name to the widespread belief that the animal burrowed beneath the ground (see p.42).

Whatever its origin, the word appears to have been introduced into Europe in 1618–20 by Richard Johnson, who reported on the *maimanto* tusks found by the Samoyeds of Siberia. By the 18th century the term "mammoth", in its various forms, had spread into virtually every European language.

First attempts to draw a mammoth on the basis of its bones and carcass produced fanciful beasts resembling unicorns or oxen, or an enormous bird with the tusks for talons. Even after the existence of extinct elephants had been established, reconstructing their appearance was still a puzzle: the tusks, for instance, were sometimes assumed to point downward rather than up.

Many mammoth remains are found in yedoma, *rounded hills of silt composed of up to 80 percent ice. Warm, rainy weather causes them to erode rapidly, making it difficult to stop the frozen site thawing before the arrival of mammoth specialists.*

SIBERIAN CARCASSES: MAMMOTHS IN THE FREEZER

The bodies of animals – primarily mammoths, but also other species such as woolly rhinoceroses – have been emerging from the Siberian permafrost since the end of the Ice Age. Siberians and Eskimos believed the mammoth to be a living animal because, on seeing its remains – including flesh and blood – exposed by rivers and thawing, they assumed it was some kind of gigantic mole that occasionally came to the surface like a whale, but which died immediately on exposure to sun- or moonlight. This explained neatly why nobody ever saw one alive.

The distribution of these frozen remains, unsurprisingly, corresponds to that of the permafrost, nature's deep freeze; hence they are found only north of 60° latitude, and mostly above the Arctic Circle. Ever since the late Pleistocene (and in some places for at least a million years), the ground here has been frozen to a depth of up to 1,500 ft (500 m), and in the brief summer only the top 5 ft (1.5 m) thaw out.

No single catastrophic event can account for all these remains and there is no real evidence that any of the animals slowly froze to death: many specimens appear healthy, with full stomachs. Some clearly died of asphyxia, either by drowning or by being buried alive in a mudflow or when the ground above them caved in. Some probably got bogged down in marshy places, while others may have crashed through thin river ice or into concealed, snow-filled gullies.

Such accidental deaths and burials may explain why the Siberian carcasses are predominantly mammoths and rhinos: these were heavy-footed giants, whose sheer size would make it especially dangerous for them to graze at the soft edges of a gully or river bluff and hard for them to extricate themselves when trapped. Often the animals, alive or dead, were then enveloped by solifluction – water-saturated sediments that slid downhill, then froze around them.

It is the build-up of layers of ice in the sediments around the bodies that accounts for the perfect preservation of these "mummies": the ice desiccated the soil and dehydrated the

carcasses as the moisture was drawn into the surrounding layers of ice and crystallized. However, by no means all bodies are intact in the permafrost, since many animals seem to have been exposed to predators and the elements for some time before being buried and, therefore, had largely decomposed prior to preservation.

Most of the preserved carcasses in Siberia are dated to two periods: before 30,000 years ago, and between 13,000 and 10,000 years ago. The intervening millennia have yielded only skeletal material. One possible explanation for this is that these periods had a slightly milder climate (the coldest period was 15,000 to 25,000 years ago). With more water available to create mudflows, carcasses would have become covered more quickly and hence have been more effectively preserved.

In 1806 the site was visited by Mikhail Adams, a botanist attached to the Russian Academy of Sciences, who found the mammoth still *in situ*, although decomposed and mutilated. Shumakhov claimed that it had once been so fat that its belly hung down below its knees. The local Yakuts had fed some of its flesh to their dogs, and the carcass was surrounded by tracks of bears, wolves, wolverines and foxes. As a result, the skeleton was almost entirely defleshed, but was still complete except for one foreleg.

Adams carefully gathered up the skeleton, as well as large quantities of hair and skin. This included much of the skin of the head, including the right ear *(see p.72)*. The skin from the side on which the animal had been lying was well preserved: it was dark grey and covered with reddish wool and coarse long black hair. Everything was sent to St. Petersburg, including the curving 10-ft (3-m) tusks, which Adams had managed to repurchase.

In 1808 the Adams mammoth skeleton was reassembled, with the few missing bones replaced by plaster and wood copies. It was the first ever mammoth skeleton to be mounted. Over 16 ft 6 in (5 m) long and 10 ft (3 m) tall, it was a male which had died at the age of about 45 years.

THE ADAMS MAMMOTH

In 1799 Ossip Shumakhov, a Tungus ivory collector and hunter, noticed a shapeless mass among the blocks of ice at the edge of a swamp by the mouth of the Lena River. The following year it had become further disengaged from the earth, and by the end of 1801 one entire side and a tusk of a mammoth were visible. His wife and friends believed it to be an omen of calamity, since the old men had heard that a similar find had once led to the death of the discoverer's whole family. Shumakhov nonetheless determined to profit from his find by selling the enormous tusks. By the end of 1803 the huge mass of this intact mammoth had fallen onto a bank of sand, and the following year Shumakhov cut off the tusks and sold them to a merchant.

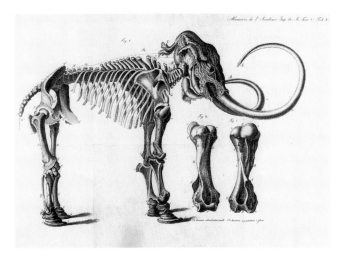

The skeleton of the Adams mammoth *was reassembled in St. Petersburg in 1808 and samples of its skin and hair were sent to many European and American museums. The location of the find and the animal's tooth structure led Cuvier to his pioneering conclusion that it was a cold-adapted, extinct local species rather than a victim of the Flood.*

THE BERESOVKA MAMMOTH

An expedition which set out from St. Petersburg in 1901 led by Dr. Otto Herz and Eugen Pfizenmayer, zoologists from the Imperial Academy of Sciences, was responsible for the most thoroughly documented recovery of a frozen mammoth. The previous year the governor of Yakutsk had reported the discovery of a mammoth in an almost perfect state of preservation, frozen in a cliff along the Beresovka River, a tributary of the Kolyma, 745 miles (1,200 km) west of the Bering Strait and 62 miles (100 km) inside the Arctic Circle. A Lamut deer hunter had first spotted a huge mammoth tusk, weighing about 175 lb (80 kg), and then, below it, the head of a second mammoth protruding from the ground, with one smaller tusk of about 65 lb (30 kg).

The hunter sold the two tusks in Kolyma, but did nothing else to the carcass on account of Lamut superstition about such mammoth finds. The buyer reported the find and the Russian finance minister assigned 16,300 roubles for an expedition to examine and secure the specimen. It reached the mammoth after a four-month journey (*see box*). Pfizenmayer gave a graphic description of their first impressions: "Some time before the mammoth body came in view I smelt its anything but pleasant odour – like the smell of a badly kept stable heavily blended with that of offal. Then, around a bend in the path, a towering skull appeared, and we stood at the grave of the diluvial monster....We stood speechless in front of this evidence of the prehistoric world, which had been preserved almost intact in its grave of ice throughout the ages."

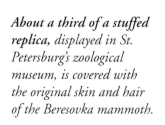

About a third of a stuffed replica, displayed in St. Petersburg's zoological museum, is covered with the original skin and hair of the Beresovka mammoth.

THE JOURNEY TO A MAMMOTH

ON MAY 3 THE HERZ–PFIZENMAYER EXPEDITION LEFT St. Petersburg. It was to cross more than one-third of the Earth's circumference, without leaving the Tsar's empire. The first stage was the easiest, travelling by train to Irkutsk, which was reached on May 14. From Irkutsk, the party proceeded by carts and boats to Yakutsk, which was reached on June 14. The next 2,000 miles (3,200 km) was accomplished on foot and on horseback. At Srednaia Kolymsk the expedition had to stock up with provisions: not only food but also tools to break frozen ground, mosquito nets, gloves and a collapsible boat which could also serve as a tent. A guide and interpreter were also hired. The party finally reached the Beresovka mammoth on September 9, after a journey of four months.

Dr. Otto Herz and Eugen Pfizenmayer removed about 287 lb (130 kg) of flesh from around the mammoth's hindquarters; this was wrapped in cow and horse hides and allowed to freeze again in the open to preserve it. Skin was cut from the abdomen – 507 lb (230 kg) of it – as well as from the head, which included the cheeks, right eyelid and lips.

Most of the internal organs had rotted away before freezing could preserve them. The stomach was badly decayed and torn, but 26 lb (12 kg) of food fragments were recovered, confirming that the animal did not die of hunger.

The dissection of the Beresovka mammoth was completed by October 11, and the remains were packed into 27 cases and placed on 10 sleighs, drawn by reindeer. During the long, arduous journey back to Yakutsk the temperature sometimes descended to -54°F (-48°C); sleighs disintegrated on the

The mammoth was later identified as a male, aged about 35 to 40, and about 29,000 to 33,000 years old. Herz and Pfizenmayer believed it had died in this position, on the spot, having probably broken through a thin layer of earth into an ice fissure. Falls of earth had buried and suffocated it. Death by asphyxiation was indicated by the erect penis, which was 34 in (86 cm) long and 7 in (18 cm) in diameter. The animal still had food in its mouth, confirming its rapid demise. The pelvis, right shoulder blade and several ribs were broken, suggesting to Herz that it had fallen with great violence into a crevasse. Later

Most of the head skin and the trunk had been eaten by bears and wolves. The left foreleg was still bent, as if the animal had attempted to lever itself out of the crevasse.

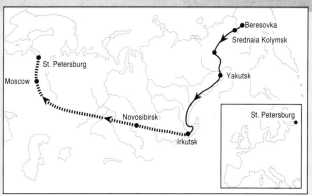

unsurfaced roads, and reindeer broke legs on hidden tree stumps. For the 1,865-mile (3,000-km) journey from Yakutsk to Irkutsk horses were used. The party finally reached St. Petersburg on February 18 – after just under 10 months of travel by rail and boat, 4,000 miles (6,400 km) by sleigh and 2,000 miles (3,200 km) on horseback, and six weeks of excavation in the harshest conditions.

The mammoth's body was reassembled in St. Petersburg. Tsar Nicholas II and his wife Alexandra visited the still-reeking specimen: the Tsar listened to the explanations with interest, while his wife stood with her handkerchief pressed to her nose.

investigators came to the conclusion that the mammoth had not died in situ, however, but had moved within a landslide which had resulted from the thawing of ice under the tundra. This might account for the broken bones. The death of the Beresovka mammoth probably occurred in the autumn, when the surface soil was still mobile after the summer thaw, but temperatures were dropping, allowing rapid freezing of the buried mammoth.

The carcass had to be cut into pieces because it could not be thawed intact from the frozen ground, nor could its great bulk have been transported whole to St. Petersburg. The job of recovering the carcass was made particularly unpleasant by the stench. However, it appealed greatly to animals – in fact the mammoth had been discovered because the Lamut hunter's dog had been enticed by the smell.

A timber structure was built around the carcass, which was still frozen since there was a layer of ice underneath it. Two stoves were used to accelerate the thawing. Herz stands on the left, with Pfizenmayer next to him. A suitable emblem was designed for the flag that flies overhead.

The Shandrin mammoth, found embedded in loam and gravel, is at least 43,000 years old. Unfortunately, it was washed out with a motorized pump which pulverized the chest organs and destroyed any intact pieces of skin on the ribs. The intestines, however, formed a well-preserved mass in the permafrost.

LATER SIBERIAN FINDS

Between 1901 and 1903 a Russian expedition to the Liakhov Islands recovered a small adult male mammoth, 8 ft (2.4 m) tall and 14 ft (4.25 m) long. It was presented to the Jardin des Plantes in Paris in 1914, shortly before an edict forbade any piece of mammoth to leave Russia permanently; it is thus the only full Siberian skeleton outside its native land.

In 1908 Eugen Pfizenmayer set out to recover a mammoth on the Sanga-Yurakh River, in Yakutia. He reported that the locals were astonished to find him in good health, in view of the legends that anyone who disturbed a mammoth could not escape misfortune. The earlier death of Herz had confirmed their suspicions. The Sanga-Yurakh specimen proved to be a disappointment since most of it had been eaten by foxes and both tusks were missing. However, its trunk was almost complete: no trunk had ever been recovered from earlier finds. The animal was a female about 60 years old and is thought to have died in winter at least 29,500 years ago when it became stuck in silt on the river bank.

The next major find was that of the Taimyr mammoth, discovered in 1948 by geologists in permafrosted peaty soil in the valley of the Mammoth River, in the northwest Taimyr Peninsula. A small adult male, aged about 50–55 and radiocarbon dated to about 11,500 years ago, it was found with

some soft tissue, skin and hair. The skeleton is remarkably complete – almost all of the bones were recovered except for a few from the toes and tail. The Taimyr mammoth was, therefore, used in 1990 as the type-specimen for the species Mammuthus primigenius, the woolly mammoth.

In the summer of 1972 a mammoth was excavated on the bank of the Shandrin River, a tributary of the Indigirka. It turned out to be the almost complete skeleton of an old

MAMMOTH REMAINS WERE UNEARTHED sporadically throughout the 19th century, and in 1860 the Academy of Sciences produced a leaflet that offered a reward of 100 roubles to anyone who discovered and reported a complete skeleton, and an additional 50 roubles if the Academy was satisfied with the find. Discoverers could sell the tusks to anyone they wished. If the meat and hide were present, the reward was to be 300 roubles (later increased to 1,000).

However, many local Siberians remained unenthusiastic, feeling that the reward was not worth the trouble that such a find would bring – either because of the misfortune which, superstition told them, would ensue, or on account of the digging and carrying which they would be called upon to do. This attitude was largely the product of the Adams expedition, during which the Yakuts had been forced to work and provide haulage, which they deeply resented. As a result, many later finds were kept secret. Rather than report it, one police chief ordered all the pieces of a mammoth find to be thrown into the sea. The 1,000 roubles were paid only once, for the Dima carcass *(see pp.48–49)*, together with a silver medal.

In 1910 a new law was passed, designating all mammoth remains as national property and obliging discoverers to report them: but of course it was unenforceable. Posters and leaflets, such as the one above, continued to be printed by the Academy at irregular intervals – in 1924, 1938 and 1973 – to encourage people to look out for and report finds. But even today, probably

only a small fraction of finds are reported. According to Siberian geologists, work at the gold mines uncovers frozen corpses every year, but since the arrival of scientists can delay and complicate the mining, most are lost to science. In 1983 a group of Siberian construction workers claimed to have fed their dogs with meat from an unearthed frozen mammoth rather than report it to the authorities. Such an attitude is ironic, since a whole preserved mammoth could now fetch up to a million dollars on the international market.

On the rare occasions when the Academy of Sciences is notified, it is still difficult, even today, to mount a properly organized expedition of qualified specialists – archaeologists, biologists, microbiologists, taphonomists (specialists in organic remains), geologists – and send them rapidly to the back of beyond. Most bodies or skeletons remain intact for only a few days after their appearance, before they are torn to bits by carnivores, decompose in the summer sunshine, are covered by a landslide or are carried away by floodwater or ice.

There are innumerable creeks and lakes in the vast area of northern Siberia, so it is almost certain that hundreds, if not thousands, of frozen mammoths have emerged from their shores over time. Yet barely a dozen of these are known to science. The few preserved carcasses that have been recovered are, therefore, enormously precious, providing science with a unique glimpse of a vanished species.

but not particularly large male dating to at least 43,000 years ago. The animal's position, lying on its stomach with its legs pointing forward, is characteristic of dying elephants, so this specimen may simply have had a natural death, probably in the late summer. Its great importance lies in its viscera: the gastrointestinal tract was cut into segments and enabled scientists to reconstruct for the very first time the abdominal organs of a mammoth – the spleen, pancreas, kidneys, intestines and so on. The stomach contained 641 lb (291 kg) of plant material *(see pp.74–75)*.

In 1977, the year of Dima's discovery *(see pp.48–49)*, a small female mammoth 10–14 years old was found in a hill

on the right bank of the Yuribei River, on the Gydanskij Peninsula, while a third specimen, the Khatanga mammoth, was discovered by a reindeer herder in alluvial sands on the left bank of the Bolshaya Rassokha River. It was an adult male, about 40 years old, and has recently become one of the first mammoths from which DNA (genetic material) has been successfully extracted *(see pp.138–39)*.

A mammoth calf, since named Mascha, found in 1988 on the Yamal Peninsula, is the westernmost frozen specimen yet discovered. This baby female, aged only 3–4 months, was probably washed out of a frozen deposit during the last Ice Age, then carried away by a flood before being refrozen.

***Only a handful of the mammoths** found in Siberia are as complete as Mascha, seen here lying where she was found. The carcass was spotted by a passing boat on the bank of a tributary of the River Ob. A laceration to the back of her right hind foot – with shredded, blackened fibres of sinew – may have been the cause of death.*

THE BABY MAMMOTH DIMA

In June 1977 Alexei Logachev, a bulldozer driver, made the most remarkable find of modern times when he spotted a mammoth calf on Kirgilyakh Creek, a tributary of the Berelekh River in the Magadan region. He received the 1,000 roubles reward for the discovery.

Gold is found at the bottom of valleys, in the sediments of the rivers that flowed here before the Ice Age climate became too cold and dry. To reach them, gold-miners need to remove the solifluction deposits, which they do by hosing the permafrost layers with water jets. It was during such an operation that the mammoth was uncovered.

The complete frozen carcass lay on its left side under 6 ft 6 in (2 m) of frozen silt. Unfortunately, the bulldozer blade cut off part of the right side. This mammoth, named Dima after a local stream, was a male aged about 6–12 months, about 3 ft (90 cm) tall and 3 ft 8 in (110 cm) long and dates to around 40,000 years ago. Its emaciated body was well preserved, including all the internal organs, and is the most complete mammoth yet to be recovered. It included parts of the woolly covering on the ears, trunk and body, although only the hair on the feet remained after the subsequent embalming process. Lots of wool was found frozen into the ice below the body. When alive, the baby mammoth would have

Alaska has yielded a number of important frozen carcasses of Ice Age species, including parts of horses, an entire musk ox, and the head and legs of a bison. However, few frozen mammoths have yet been found, although their remains – such as this woolly mammoth skull unearthed near McGrath – are abundant and have been reported for over a century.

weighed 220–250 lb (100–115 kg). However, the dehydrated carcass weighs only 134 lb (61 kg).

His main diet was probably still mother's milk, though the slightly worn milk molars indicate that he had started to feed on vegetation too. The colon contained 7½ lb (3.4 kg) of plant detritus, but there are no plant remains in the small stomach, which contains only 2 oz (50 g) of dark silt together with some of Dima's own hair. These facts, together with the lack of layers of fat, indicate poor condition. Death was by falling into a pool or crevasse or becoming stuck in a bog or mudflow. The following year Dima was further buried by mud and rock flowing down in the spring thaw.

It has also been suggested that Dima died in a situation from which a normal infant could have escaped. But Dima was sickly, as evidenced by his heavy load of parasites, and

lacked the strength to extricate himself. Young animals are frequent victims of such incidents, and the presence of his mother would have kept predators and, after death, scavengers, at bay. The strange contents of Dima's stomach – earth and hair – can also be explained, since trapped animals tend to become delirious and will feed on anything within reach, even mutilating themselves when in pain.

Dima was flown to Leningrad (St. Petersburg), and soon became a worldwide media sensation. Following chemical treatment, it was possible to carry out a full study of his anatomy, including a close inspection of his internal organs, a biochemical examination of the muscles and brain, and a study of his blood vessels and cells *(see p.73)*. Dima has subsequently been exhibited in Europe, North America and Japan and has been insured for $12 million.

ALASKAN FINDS

The explorer Otto von Kotzebue, on a voyage of discovery in 1815–18, wrote about quantities of mammoth teeth and bones exposed by melting ice in Alaska. Since then there have been countless finds of bones, teeth and tusks, but very few flesh remains, although these appear occasionally.

As in Siberia, it was the start of gold-mining that sharply increased the number of discoveries, since the diggers have to thaw and wash away layers of soil with high-pressure jets to reach the gold-bearing levels, and their work extends over large areas. In places there are huge hydraulic operations, which strip off the sun-softened soil, while drag lines scrape away the underlying gravel down to bedrock.

Alaska's most famous find was made in August 1948 at Fairbanks Creek, where the face, trunk and one foreleg of a mammoth calf were recovered. The skin was almost hairless; it was embalmed and sent to the American Museum of Natural History in New York, where it was preserved in commercial glycerine and displayed in a freezer *(see p.31)*. In life this baby, nicknamed Effie, would have weighed around 220 lb (100 kg). It has been dated to 21,300 years ago.

Like most of the best-preserved frozen carcasses, the baby male mammoth Dima appears to have died in August, or the early autumn. The work teams and bulldozer crews involved in his discovery were specially rewarded for accepting the loss of a few days of gold mining and tolerating the influx of scientists, reporters and curious onlookers attracted to this remarkable find.

MAMMOTH CEMETERIES

The idea of an "elephants' graveyard" – where elephants choose to go to die – is a myth. But it is a myth that contains a grain of truth, for in Africa and Asia there are a number of distinct places, mostly dried-out waterholes or riverbeds, where accumulations of elephant bones are found. The places mark the spot where elephants have died natural deaths, either singly or in groups, through drought or some catastrophe such as a flash flood.

There are, likewise, a number of places, especially in Siberia, where large numbers of mammoth bones have accumulated, but the explanation for this is probably somewhat different. Over thousands of years individual mammoths died while walking along river valleys, or by falling through ice, and their bones were eventually brought together by flowing waters in gullies, backwaters and oxbow lakes.

"The bones of at least 156 mammoths lay in the banks of the Berelekh River"

The greatest accumulation known is on the Berelekh River, a tributary of the Indigirka. The Berelekh meanders between gently sloping hummocks of permafrost that are constantly being eroded by the river and by thawing. Mammoth bones have been washed out of these hummocks for centuries and redeposited on the riverbed. Between 1970 and 1980 a total of 8,830 mammoth bones from a minimum of 156 individuals was collected by expeditions to the site.

A mammoth tusk from the base of the bone layer gave a radiocarbon date of 12,240 years ago, while scraps of skin and ligament from another spot were dated to 13,700 years ago. These results provide some idea of the possible time span represented by this accumulation. The Berelekh "cemetery", therefore, is probably the product of numerous individual accidents that occurred over many centuries – the

Thousands of mammoth bones have accumulated at the Berelekh "cemetery". Modern expeditions use hoses to free the bones from the frozen soil. To add to the physical hardships of this task, the area swarms with large and voracious mosquitoes.

"Elephants' graveyards" in Africa result from natural deaths on the spot, usually around a dried-out water source. Siberian mammoth "cemeteries", by contrast, are accumulated in river backwaters or by later erosion out of silty yedoma deposits (centre).

result of animals becoming stuck in fluid mud or falling through thin ice and drowning.

A Paleolithic site, dating to about 10,700 years ago, has been found 390 ft (120 m) downstream, containing stone tools as well as some tusk fragments clearly taken from the accumulation of bones. One shaft of tusk, 3 ft 1 in (94 cm) long, bore a remarkable engraving of a mammoth with extremely long legs *(see p.98)*. The occupants might have been able to use some of the fresher meat from the mammoth site, and certainly used bones and tusks as tools, but it is unlikely that they played any major role in the accumulation of mammoth remains, especially since the biggest concentration of bones seems to pre-date this site by two millennia.

In the summer of 1988 a different kind of mammoth cemetery was discovered on the left bank of the Seva River in southeastern Bryansk Province, south of Moscow, when a bulldozer excavating a sand quarry picked up several bones. The following year a compact bone layer was encountered, containing between 10 and 15 mammoths. Careful excavation at the "Sevsk cemetery" resulted in the recovery of about 4,000 fragments from at least 35 individuals.

This area used to be a marshy river floodplain. Its rich food resources probably attracted the animals, which may have been trapped by flooding. The carcasses seem to have been brought here during a period of high water and quickly buried under alluvial deposits. Although far fewer bones were found here than at Berelekh, this is the largest natural mammoth cemetery known in Europe. The site's importance, however, lies not in the number of animals but in the fact that much of the material comprises large articulated parts of skeletons. Seven almost intact skeletons of all ages, including three babies, were recovered. These may all have been members of a single herd, and even of a single family.

The Sevsk mammoths seem to have died within a brief period and were instantly covered, in full or in part, by the river sand. Their remains have been radiocarbon dated to 13,950 years ago.

Several of the Sevsk skeletons were almost complete (right), with a high proportion of young animals (45 percent were under 10 years of age). At Berelekh, by contrast, the bones were not found as skeletons, and only 30 percent were less than 10 years old, corresponding to a different mode of accumulation.

NATURAL MAMMOTH TRAPS

The most spectacular accumulation of Columbian mammoth fossils was found at a former sinkhole (*see box opposite*) at Hot Springs, a small town in South Dakota, in the middle of the North American continent. So far, about 50 individual mammoths have been discovered, but this list is growing each year, and it is estimated that at least 100 met their end in the sinkhole.

According to radiocarbon dating, these Columbian mammoths died around 26,000 years ago. It is thought that the trap was operative for about 300 to 700 years before it finally filled up with sediment. The individual mammoths are spread throughout the sediment indicating that they did not enter at the same time but at intervals. This means that even 100 or so preserved skeletons represent only an occasional fatal incident – the entrapment of one animal every several years on average. Most were young adult males, caught at their most adventurous age.

There have been further intriguing finds at Hot Springs. Excavation in 1975 revealed a mammoth molar that appeared different from the others: it looked rather like a tooth of a woolly mammoth, unlike all the other mammoth remains from the site, which were of Columbians. However, the researchers did not dare conclude that woolly mammoths were present on such skimpy evidence. Then, toward the end of the 1987 archaeological season, the partial skull of a woolly mammoth was unearthed, with its teeth in place.

This is one of the very few sites where both species have been found at the same location, but this does not necessarily mean that the two coexisted *(see p.31)*. Both of the woolly mammoth specimens were found rather high in the deposits, perhaps indicating that the woolly mammoths entered the area briefly at a time when the range of the Columbians had receded toward the south. Radiocarbon dating of the finds may resolve this question, demonstrating whether the woolly mammoths were contemporary with, or later than, the Columbian mammoths.

The Hot Springs site has now been roofed over in recognition of its exceptional scientific importance. Some 50 mammoth skeletons have so far been unearthed there. The state of preservation of the bones is outstanding: they include delicate hyoid (tongue) bones, which have survived in place, and even bile stones (like human kidney stones).

*Building contractors first discovered
the site at Hot Springs, South
Dakota, in 1974, when levelling the
ground for a housing development.
Excavations at the site still continue.*

Similar traps existed wherever mammoths lived. At Condover in Shropshire, England, a woman walking her dog around a gravel pit in 1986 spotted some large bones. The result was the recovery of the skeletons of four or five woolly mammoths, dating to between 12,700 and 12,300 years ago – the first evidence that the species survived in Britain after the retreat of the ice.

They lie within a kettle hole, a feature formed as a result of large, buried blocks of ice being left by a retreating glacier. As the block melted, overlying sediments collapsed, forming a crater which subsequently filled up with more sediment. The Condover kettle hole was 33 ft (10 m) deep at its centre,

but at the end of the Ice Age its sides were not steep. It is therefore most likely that the mammoths entered it in search of food or drink and became mired in mud at the bottom.

The 400 bone fragments found there come from one adult male, aged about 28, and at least three juveniles aged between 3 and 6 years. They were probably not a family group, as juvenile elephants stay with their mother, not their father, while males of this age generally roam alone or in bachelor groups. So the Condover site probably represents occasional deaths over several centuries. The carcasses must have lain exposed after death, since hatched fly puparia and the remains of dung beetles were found in the bones' cavities.

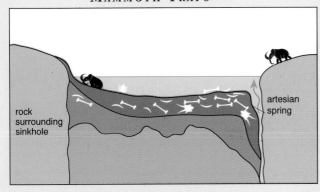

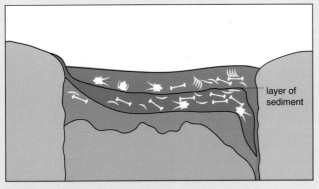

MAMMOTH TRAPS

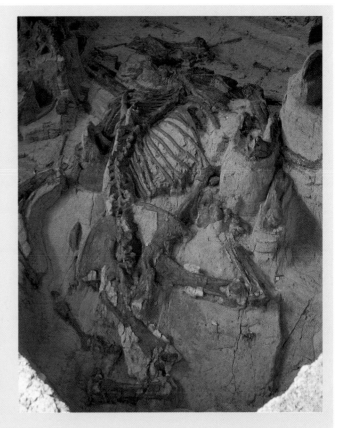

THE EXCAVATIONS AT HOT SPRINGS IN SOUTH DAKOTA show that the mammoths had become trapped in a geological formation known as a sinkhole – a crater about 130 ft (40 m) long, with steep, slippery sides. The mammoths may have been attracted by the warm waters, or were probing the pond's edge for vegetation or water, then either ventured or slipped into the pool. Once inside, the animals would have been unable to escape

and would eventually have died of starvation or drowning. The skeleton of one mammoth, known as Murray (above), lies sprawled against the side, presumably showing how he collapsed in the effort to struggle free. An artesian spring kept the sinkhole wet; meanwhile, erosion of sediment from the sides covered the mammoth bones for posterity. Kettle holes, formed by the melting of glacier ice, trapped mammoths in a similar manner.

DEATH IN THE TARPITS
A Columbian mammoth trumpets with fear as it fails to
extricate itself from an asphalt seep, while hungry predators
look on. This scene is set 30,000 years ago at the tarpits of
Rancho La Brea, now in downtown Los Angeles. These natural
traps have provided a unique window on late Pleistocene life.

*The accumulated results of 30,000 years of entrapment
at La Brea have so far produced some 100 tons of fossils, and
more than 600 species of animals and plants. Mammals
include wolves, big cats, bison, horses, camels, bears and the
Shasta ground sloth* (Nothrotheriops, left), *which measured
8 ft (2.4 m) from head to tail.*

Mammal and bird bones, insect carapaces and wood have been perfectly conserved by asphalt impregnation in the La Brea tarpits. The bones are contained in layers of tar alternating with bands of sand or silt, which were periodically deposited over the tar seeps by streams or winter rains. The remains of herons and pond turtles are testimony to the presence of water bodies nearby.

The La Brea fossils are dominated by the remains of carnivorous species, which came to feed on trapped animals and themselves became caught in the tar. A sabre-tooth cat (Smilodon) feeds on a still-exposed mammoth carcass, while another approaches from the left. Dire wolves (Canis dirus) gather excitedly at the scene, while scavenging condors circle overhead or wait in a nearby tree.

THE LA BREA TARPITS

Mammoths have also been preserved in what is now the heart of Los Angeles, California. Off Wilshire Boulevard are the famous tarpits of Rancho La Brea (*brea* is the Spanish word for tar). These tarpits have been known for centuries and were formerly mined for their natural asphalt. Thousands of tons were extracted before 1875, when it was first noticed that the tar contained fossil remains.

Since then, over 100 tons of fossils, 1.5 million from vertebrates, 2.5 million from invertebrates, have been recovered, often in densely concentrated tangled masses. The creatures found range from insects and birds to giant ground sloths, but a total of 17 proboscideans – including mastodons and Columbian mammoths have been recovered, most of them from Pit 9, the deepest bone-bearing deposit, which was excavated in 1914. Most of the fossils date to between 40,000 and 10,000 years ago, though the single human find – a woman – dates to about 9,000 years ago.

> ## "Mammoth remains have been discovered in the heart of Los Angeles"

The asphalt at La Brea seeps to the surface, especially in the summer, and forms shallow puddles that would often have been concealed by leaves and dust. Unwary animals would, therefore, become trapped on these thin sheets of liquid asphalt, which are extremely sticky in warm weather. Stuck like flies on flypaper, the unfortunate beasts would die of exhaustion and hunger, or fall prey to predators which often also became stuck.

As the animals decayed, more scavengers would be attracted and caught in their turn. Carnivores greatly outnumber herbivores in the collection: for every large herbivore, there is one sabre-tooth cat, a coyote and four dire wolves. The fact that some bones are heavily weathered and carry fly

***Major excavations were undertaken at the Rancho** La Brea tarpits in the early decades of this century and established the true significance of this remarkable site. They were found to contain the remains of scores of species of animals from the last 30,000 years of the Ice Age.*

puparia shows that some corpses remained above the surface for weeks or months. Bacteria in the asphalt would have consumed some of the soft tissues, and the asphalt itself would dissolve what was left, at the same time impregnating and beautifully preserving the saturated bones which are now dark brown or black and shiny.

No soft tissue survived at La Brea, but it may, in certain circumstances, be preserved by crude oil. At Starunia in Poland the subsoil is filled with veins of paraffin. The site is best known for its preserved rhinoceros carcasses, but in 1907 a mammoth was found at a depth of 140 ft (43 m). There had been some decomposition before the tissues became embalmed, but this was still a mammoth "in the flesh" – the only one outside the permafrost regions – because it had been naturally pickled in a petrochemical seep associated with salt deposits and surrounded by the mineral wax ozocerite. The skeleton was well preserved and the skin still supple, but the hair had become firmly stuck to the surrounding sediments.

The scene at La Brea today (above) *contrasts vividly with that 80 years ago* (top). *Life-size figures of Columbian mammoths in and around the tar illustrate one of the many dramas that occurred in this natural trap. Remains of various animals found at the site can be seen in the Los Angeles Natural History Museum.*

RIVER AND LAKE DEPOSITS

While frozen carcasses and natural traps provide the most spectacular source of mammoth remains, the most common and most widespread discoveries are made in a more mundane context: deposits of gravel, sand or clay being dug up for industrial use or excavated for building foundations or pipelines. These fossils, which fill our museums, are generally isolated teeth, partial tusks and occasional leg bones. The nature of the sediment gives a clue to the ancient environment of deposition – gravels representing fast-flowing rivers (sometimes bringing meltwater directly from a glacier), sands and silts indicating quieter stretches of rivers, and clays implying still lakes.

> ### "Countless isolated teeth and bones lie scattered across the whole range where mammoths once lived"

The preservation of isolated bones and teeth in river deposits can be explained as follows. In some cases an animal died by the waterside, and would probably already have been partially scavenged and broken up when, perhaps due to a rise in the river level, it was washed into the water. In other cases the animal may have died while attempting to cross a river, as sometimes happens to elephants in Africa today. In either case, the carcass – or parts of it – would have been further broken up as it was transported downstream before settling, and decay would then have caused additional separation before some elements were finally buried. In lakes, partial or complete carcasses were washed in by rivers, or floated in from a bank if the water level rose. Generally, molars and tusks survive best because their enamel and dentine are harder and denser than bone.

One British gravel pit, near Stanton Harcourt in Oxford-shire, has recently yielded some important finds of this type.

The excavations at Stanton Harcourt, near Oxford, England, have so far uncovered 34 mammoth tusks. During the excavation season of 1993 one of these, encased in plaster, proved so heavy that it had to be lifted from the site by a Royal Air Force helicopter.

The skeleton of a mammoth about 200,000 years old was excavated in 1964 at Aveley on the Lower Thames, east of London. It lay directly above that of a straight-tusked elephant, Palaeoloxodon antiquus, which had occupied the site when it was more heavily forested earlier in the interglacial period.

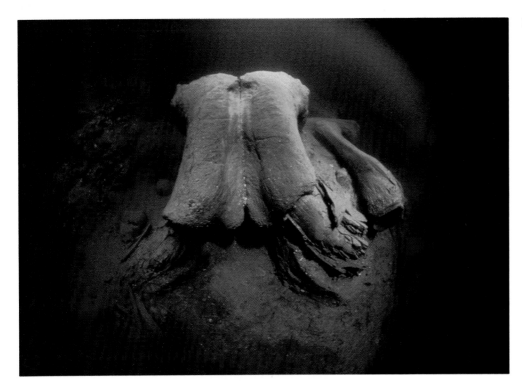

The skull of a Columbian mammoth, lying in a bed of silt in the Aucilla River, Florida, was photographed by scuba divers from the underwater archaeology team that recovered it.

The disused 5-acre (2-ha) gravel pit is to become a garbage dump, but about 200,000 years ago this was an area of grassy meadows through which flowed the ancient River Thames. Animal bones, which appear to have accumulated naturally at a bend in the river, include the remains of aurochs, bison, fish, frogs and at least 34 mammoth tusks. The presence of acorns and hazelnuts indicates that the animals represented in the finds lived during an interglacial period, when the climate was similar to that of today or slightly warmer. The mammoths were an early variety of *Mammuthus primigenius*, the woolly mammoth, which may not yet have been fully adapted to cold conditions.

Occasionally, a complete skeleton is found in this type of deposit. Specimens that have been mounted include skeletons from the Aa River in northern France, Steinheim and Ahlen in Germany, and Mátra in Hungary. An exceptionally complete skeleton was discovered by a 16-year-old boy while walking in a wood which had grown over former lake sediments, near Siegsdorf in Bavaria. He found the first rib in 1975, but the complete skeleton was not finally excavated until 1985, a task which entailed the removal of 777,000 cubic ft (22,000 m³) of earth and clay deposit by bulldozers. The specimen appears to be the largest known woolly mammoth of the last Ice Age. Now carefully reassembled and

Five complete mammoth skeletons were retrieved from the Aucilla River, Florida, in the 1960s, they were lifted bone by bone from the riverbed 40 ft (12 m) beneath the surface.

mounted, and christened Oscar, it stands 11 ft (3.4 m) high, with tusks up to 8 ft 6 in (2.6 m) in length. It has been dated by the electron spin resonance technique to around 48,000 years ago.

Finds of otherwise complete mammoth skeletons often lack one crucial element: the skull. This may well be because, full of gases that result from decay, it became detached from the carcass and floated off. (This still occurs with modern elephant corpses in African lakes and rivers.) Sometimes the toughest parts survive, such as the back of the skull, tusks and teeth, while the thin, porous bones of the rest of the skull have disintegrated. This is the case in several of the skeletons described above, including those from Condover, Steinheim and Siegsdorf, whose mounted skulls have been reconstructed in plaster or resin.

CAVES AND DUNG DEPOSITS

Mammoth remains are found in caves for several reasons. Most often, they were carried in by humans or predators. For example, juvenile mammoth remains were accumulated in Friesenhahn Cave in Texas by the extinct scimitar cat, and in Kent's Cavern, England, by the spotted hyena *(see p.88)*. Many of the mammoth bones bear the tooth marks of these predators or scavengers.

Occasionally, mammoths entered the caves themselves to escape bad weather, give birth, or in search of water or salt. A striking indication of this is the presence of quantities of mammoth dung in dry caves in the American Southwest. These have provided detailed evidence of the mammoths' diet *(see pp.75–76)*. In the Chinese province of Inner Mongolia, 7 lb (3 kg) of mammoth dung was recovered in 1980 from an open-cut coal mine, together with bones of two mammoths. Mammoths are by no means rare in China and have been found at more than 150 localities.

FISHING FOR MAMMOTHS

Perhaps the most unexpected source of mammoth bones is the bed of the North Sea. The first finds were recorded in the 19th century, but over the past 50 years a wealth of fossilized mammal remains has been trawled from the seabed. At times during the Ice Age, when the sea level was 330 ft (100 m) lower than today, the North Sea was an area of dry land. During those periods, animals would have died there and been deposited in rivers and lakes in the usual way.

Most of the remains recovered are from the typical fauna of the last Ice Age in Europe (110,000 to 10,000 years ago),

The skull of a woolly mammoth was found in 1994 by divers 40 ft (12 m) under water in a former gravel pit at Bergharen in the eastern Netherlands. It was embedded in river gravels laid down during the last Ice Age.

Fossils are often found in fishing nets dragged over the seabed of the North Sea. This mammoth tooth, lying at the centre of a haul of flatfish and miscellaneous debris, was one such catch.

Bones recovered from the North Sea have often been blackened by mineralization, but to preserve them they merely require desalinating by soaking in fresh water. An average "catch" from a six-week trawl (right) includes bones of reindeer and bison as well as mammoths.

and include bison, horses, woolly rhinos, reindeer and giant deer; but proboscideans are common, especially woolly mammoths. A few remains of the ancestral mammoth, and even a form of mastodont, both more than a million years old, have also been recovered. The bones are all separate, but are well preserved.

Nets designed to catch flatfish (sole, turbot, plaice) trawl across the uneven seabed, and the beams at the front rake up the fish so that they pass back into the net. At the same time they dredge up – and sometimes break – the fossils that have been laid bare by currents. The bones come from depths of 65–165 ft (20–50 m). Each haul takes about an hour and covers 6 miles (10 km).

A six-week fishing trip can produce several hundred fossils, and over the past 43 years a fishing trip has been organized for one day a year by the people of Leiden in the Netherlands specifically to bring up a catch of fossils. Amateur fossil hunters haunt the ports, awaiting the return of the boats with their bones.

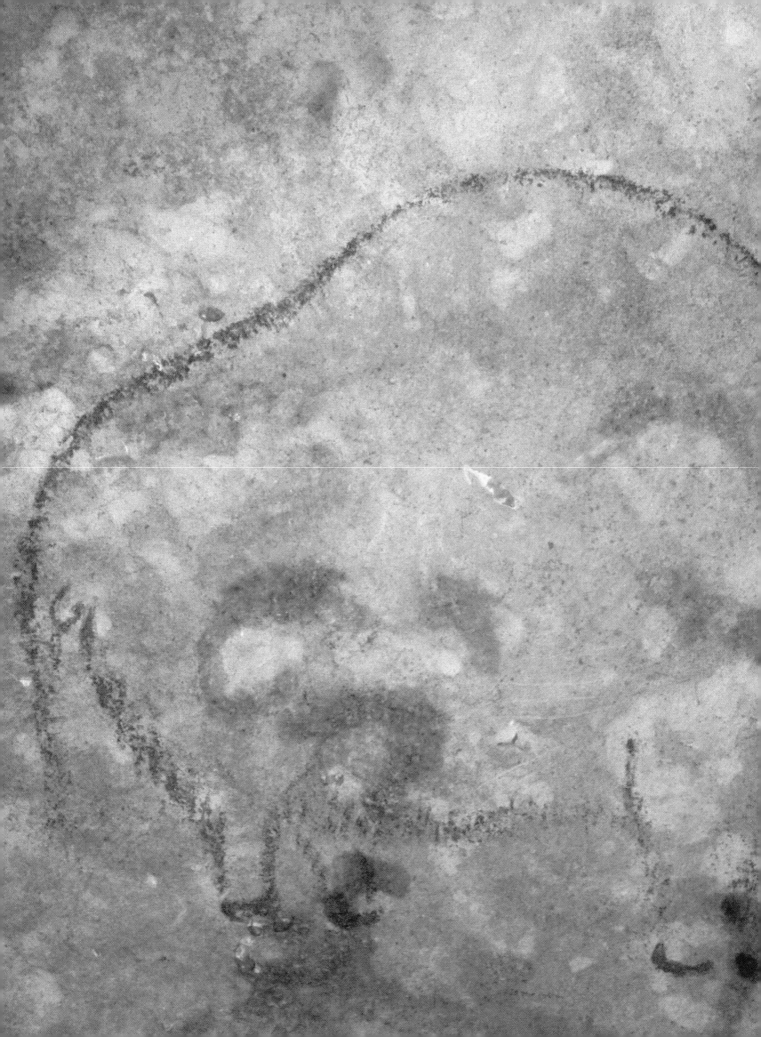

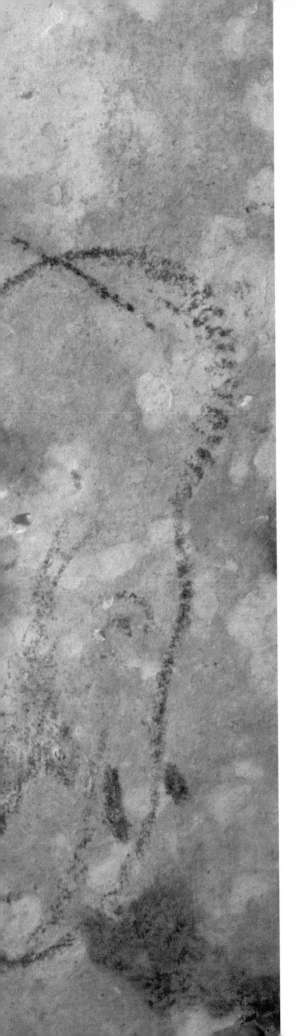

THE NATURAL HISTORY OF MAMMOTHS

MORE IS KNOWN ABOUT THE APPEARANCE AND way of life of the mammoths than about any other extinct prehistoric animal. Almost all other fossil species are represented only by their bones and teeth. But for the mammoth – thanks to the preservation of remains frozen in the far north and dried in caves farther south – there is flesh, hair, stomach contents and even dung. In addition, our human ancestors left us a record of the mammoths they saw, in cave paintings and other art forms. By combining these sources of information with deductions based on what is known about modern elephants, it is possible to arrive at a genuine "natural history" of the mammoths that is more complete than those we have for many animal species still alive today.

Prehistoric naturalists have bequeathed us this mammoth drawing at Rouffignac Cave in France. It conveys the mammoth's woolly coat, domed head, tail and even its anal flap. The convex back and small tusks suggest a juvenile animal.

FUELLING THE BULK

Eating took up a great deal of the mammoth's life. The large Columbian mammoth, shown here, needed some 500 lb (225 kg) of fresh food a day, and so was almost continually foraging. This scene is set about 15,000 years ago on the Colorado Plateau in the southwestern United States, where the mammoths' feeding habits to some degree played a part in shaping the local vegetation.

After eating the bark which it stripped with its tusks, a mammoth pushes over a small tree to gain access to the upper foliage. The tusks could also be used for digging up plants by the roots.

A female pulls up a bunch of grass by curling her trunk around the stems, while a youngster pulls a few stalks from her mouth. Two mammoths are drinking from a stream, sucking up water with their trunks and then squirting it back into their mouths.

With its thousands of small muscles, the trunk was capable of delicate operations. The two long projections at the tip acted like a "finger and thumb" to pick flowers, buds or grass stems. Possibly these evolved as an adaptation to feeding on the short grasses of the Ice Age, as compared to the tall tropical grasses eaten by modern elephants, which use mainly the "trunk curling" method.

All mammoths were completely vegetarian. The precise composition of their plant food varied with the local conditions, since both the Columbian and the woolly mammoth occupied a wide range of habitats. However, grass was almost always the staple, supplemented by flowering herbs, shrubs and parts of trees as available.

Many other herbivorous species shared the local forage: here, a group of now extinct American camels grazes on the other side of the stream.

Not Without Enemies
Defending themselves from predators was a relatively
easy task for mammoths, with their powerful trunk,
deadly tusks and huge body. Nonetheless, a group
of mammoths needed to remain vigilant, since
pack-hunting carnivores could occasionally pick
off a youngster or ailing adult.

*In this scene, set in Alaska during the last Ice Age, a pack of
wolves harries a small group of woolly mammoths. As relatively
small predators, wolves would rarely have troubled mammoths,
and certainly could never have taken an adult in its prime. This
pack, however, by distracting and confusing a small mammoth
group, may have been attempting to capture – most likely without
success – the baby being held back and protected by its mother.*

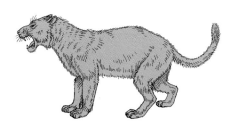

Large carnivores such as lions and hyenas are today restricted to tropical areas. This is not because of climate, but because only in the tropics does abundant large herbivore prey remain. In the Pleistocene many more herbivorous mammals still lived in the northern continents and were preyed upon by hyenas and various large cats which are now extinct, including the lion Panthera leo atrox (left) and the sabre-tooth and scimitar-tooth cats.

With a body weight measured in tons, mammoths were extremely strong animals, and a healthy adult could deal with a challenge from almost any other creature. A sideways or downward swipe with the tusks would stun or kill an aggressor and, by lowering the head, the points of the tusks could be used for stabbing. The trunk, as in living elephants, was extremely powerful and could kill a predator by breaking its back. Finally, an attacker would have to avoid being jumped on or trodden on.

This faded painting of a mammoth in red ochre is one of seven from Kapova Cave in the southern Urals of Russia, dating to about 14,000 years ago. The distinctive shape of the animal's domed head can be seen to the left, while behind it are the shoulder hump and sloping back.

The most striking feature of the mammoths was their sheer scale. They were big animals, the biggest in their environment, and quite accurate estimates of their size can be obtained from their mounted skeletons, with a little added for flesh. That said, most mammoths were not in fact larger than living elephants. In the woolly mammoth, adult males generally stood between about 9 and 11 ft (2.7 and 3.4 m) at the shoulder. This size compares quite closely with the living African elephant, the world's largest land mammal, in which heights of 10–11 ft (3–3.4 m) are common in males. As is the case with living elephants, female mammoth skeletons are noticeably smaller and more lightly built than males. Woolly mammoth females probably averaged 8 ft 6 in–9 ft 6 in (2.6–2.9 m) in height. Using elephants as a guide, a body weight of up to 6 tons in male woolly mammoths can be calculated – about 80 times the weight of an adult human of 170 lb (77 kg).

"The Columbian mammoth weighed the equivalent of 130 adult humans"

Despite its great size, the woolly mammoth, *Mammuthus primigenius*, was in fact smaller than its immediate ancestors, and so does not represent the continuation of an evolutionary trend toward greater size. Skeletons of the ancestral mammoth *M. meridionalis* indicate an animal that was generally about 13 ft (4 m) high, while the peak of size was attained with *M. trogontherii*, in which individuals reached over 14 ft (4.3 m). The reasons for the reduction in size to *M. primigenius* are unknown. In the American lineage this was less evident: *M. columbi* had a shoulder height of up to 13 ft

(4 m), and a weight of about 10 tons, equivalent to around 130 average adult humans.

The outline of the mammoth's body was distinctive: it is shown consistently enough in dozens of Ice Age depictions to indicate that the shape given was genuine and not the result of an individual artist's imagination. The depictions present a relatively large head, with a high dome on top. The neck, although short, forms a very clear division between the head and the back. The shoulder has a distinctive, high hump, behind which the back slopes markedly from front to rear. Preserved skeletons show that the sloping back was due mostly to a decrease in the length of spinal vertebrae, rather

FROM BIRTH TO OLD AGE

LIKE ELEPHANTS, BUT UNLIKE MOST OTHER MAMMALS, MAMMOTHS continued to grow well into adult life. About 3 ft (90 cm) high and 200 lb (90 kg) at birth, their height had doubled and weight increased 15-fold by the age of 10. Growth then continued slowly but progressively, females not ceasing growth until around 25 years old, males not until around 40 years old. Life expectancy was about 60 years for the woolly mammoth, but was probably higher for the larger Columbian mammoth.

Baby

5 years

10 years

Baby mammoth Dima shows several characteristic woolly mammoth features, such as the very short tail. The X-ray of his skeleton reveals how the domed skull and shoulder hump had not yet formed, and shows limb bones with free ends, allowing space for growth in length.

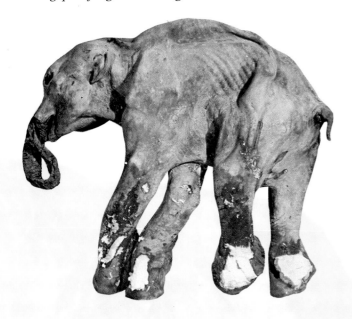

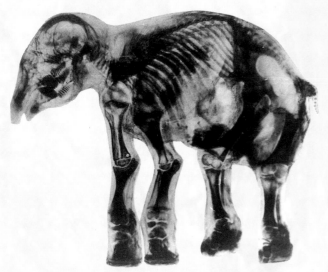

than to any difference in the length of front and back legs.

Skeletons and frozen carcasses of young animals give clues to the mammoth's growth (the age of these individuals can be determined from their teeth, *see p.78*). At the Sevsk site near Moscow, skeletons of mammoths only two months old were found. They are about 2 ft (60 cm) in height, although this is a little smaller than average for their age. Most mammoths probably weighed about 200 lb (90 kg) at birth.

The famed frozen mammoth Dima (*see pp.48–49*) was 6 to 12 months old at death and was about 3 ft (90 cm) high. He shows that the shoulder hump and sloping back developed later in life: in infants the back formed a convex arch rather like a modern adult Asian elephant's. Studies of bone development indicate that the ends of the limb bones did not fuse to the main shaft until about 40 years old in males and 25 in females, so the shafts were still lengthening up to that age.

Many features of the woolly mammoth show striking adaptations to an Arctic climate. There is much less information available for its American contemporary, the Columbian mammoth, and for the earlier species in Eurasia, since soft tissues are not preserved,

40 years (female)

40 years (male)

The skeleton of a male woolly mammoth of around 30 years old was discovered at Condover, England, in 1986. It had a femur (thigh bone) 4 ft (120 cm) long. The head of the bone is shown in actual size in the background. The two ends are still separate from the shaft, indicating that the animal would have continued growing for several years had it not died.

The coarse, wiry outer hairs of a woolly mammoth (shown left in actual size) *were up to 3 ft (90 cm) long, while the inner hairs* (below right) *were much shorter and finer, forming a dense underwool. The orange colour of these 12,000-year-old samples from Siberia is probably not natural, but the result of long burial.*

but it is likely, given their warmer habitat, that these adaptations were less developed.

The furry coat of the woolly mammoth is known from many Siberian carcasses. The most common colour is orange, but it varies on different specimens from blond to brown or almost black. Although many modern reconstructions show the mammoth with an orange coat, it is likely that the predominance of this colour in preserved hair is largely the result of loss of natural pigment during long burial. Dark brown seems the most likely general colour, although no doubt there was variation. Dark brown is also the coat colour of the living musk ox, which in some ways is the closest modern equivalent to the mammoth, being a large herbivore with shaggy coat that lives under Arctic conditions.

The mammoth's fur consisted of long, coarse outer guard hairs beneath which were shorter, thinner hairs forming an underwool. The guard hairs were typically about one-fiftieth of an inch (0.5 mm) in diameter, about six times thicker than a typical human hair and twice as thick as those of an Asian elephant. In their preserved state, at least, they are springy and transparent, resembling fishing line. The hairs of the underwool were much thinner and shorter – about 1–3 in (2.5–8 cm) long – but they were more densely packed and formed an effective insulating layer.

All parts of the body were covered with fur ranging in length from a few inches to over 3 ft (90 cm). The head, including ears and trunk, was clothed in relatively short hair a few inches long, although it was longer under the chin and neck and on the sides of the trunk, from which hung a clear fringe, noted by Ice Age artists. Hair on the upper body was 1 ft (30 cm) or so long, but from the flanks and belly hung the longest hair, up to 3 ft (90 cm) long, forming a "skirt" reminiscent of the living musk ox or the Tibetan yak.

The upper leg bore fur up to 15 in (38 cm) in length, and several frozen carcasses show that even on the feet the

The living musk ox is the most northerly land mammal in the world and is now restricted to Arctic Canada. Its long, shaggy coat of brown hair, shed annually, recalls that of the woolly mammoth.

Living elephants have hair over much of their body, most notably on the head and hanging from the end of the tail. The potential of elephants and their relatives to produce a furry coat, shown clearly in this baby Asian elephant, was developed to the greatest degree in the woolly mammoth, as an adaptation to much colder conditions than the tropical habitat of the modern species.

hair was 6 in (15 cm) long, falling to the ends of the toes. It is likely that the woolly mammoth changed coats between winter and summer, shedding its heaviest fur in spring. Since most of the frozen carcasses are probably of animals that died in autumn – when the soil was still mobile but the falling temperature allowed fast freezing – much of the evidence of the mammoth's fur may be based on its winter coat.

Little evidence is available on the coat of the Columbian mammoth of North America. However, in Bechan Cave in Utah, noted for its impressive deposit of mammoth dung *(see pp.75–76)*, quantities of hair were discovered, including coarse material identical to that of woolly mammoths from Siberia. Since Bechan Cave is in the southwestern United States, the hair almost certainly pertains to *M. columbi*, and indicates that that species was not naked, although the density and distribution of its fur is unknown.

The mammoth's skin was between ½ and 1 in (1.25 and 2.5 cm) thick, no different from that of living elephants. In the case of the woolly mammoth, a thick fat layer 3–4 in (8–10 cm) deep lay beneath the skin, as seen in the carcasses from Beresovka and the Liakhov Islands. This would have contributed to heat insulation, although fat layers are known to be less effective in this function than a hairy coat.

In addition to the fur and fat layer, there were several other features of the woolly mammoth that were probably

A frozen carcass of a woolly mammoth, discovered in the Liakhov Islands off northern Siberia in 1901, included a complete foot. Although twisted and dehydrated, it still shows its horny nails, dark coat colour and long hair reaching down to the toes. If the mammoth's skin contained sebaceous (oil) glands, the coat would have had a glossy sheen, but the presence of such glands has yet to be verified.

The head of the Adams frozen mammoth (below left), excavated in 1806, still retains some of its dried flesh and skin. The left side shows, at the top left of the picture, the perfectly preserved oval-shaped ear, only 15 in (38 cm) long. The tusks emerge from their sockets at bottom right.

adaptations to a cold climate. Most obvious among these are the small size of the ears and tail. In living elephants the large ears act as a radiator and are flapped in hot weather to help the animal lose heat. The woolly mammoth, living in a cold climate, had the opposite problem, and the small size of its ears and tail helped to prevent the loss of body heat. Even more significant, there was a danger of frostbite on these thin, exposed organs, which their small size and hairy covering would have minimized.

The woolly mammoth's ears, preserved on three adult carcasses, were surprisingly similar in shape to human ears. They were about 15 in (38 cm) long and 7–11 in (18–28 cm) across, with a total area of only one-fifteenth that of an African elephant. In the case of baby Dima, the ear was less than 5 in (13 cm) long.

In living elephants the ears are used not only for hearing and heat loss, but also to intimidate rivals or predators, the ears being held out from the body during a mock charge. Given the reduced size, this function was presumably less significant in the woolly mammoth.

Only in the Beresovka carcass and baby Dima is a complete tail preserved. For Otto Herz, leader of the

Beresovka expedition *(see pp.44–45)*, the discovery of the tail was a moment of triumph. He measured its exposed length as just 14 in (36 cm). The Beresovka skeleton shows that this relatively short length results from the fact that the tail contains only 21 vertebrae, compared to 28 to 33 in modern elephants. Several Ice Age depictions illustrate this feature, showing the fleshy part of the tail extending only a short distance down the leg, in contrast to living elephants where it hangs well below the "knee".

Several carcasses also show, however, that the short, fleshy part of the tail was extended by long, coarse hairs that were up to 2 ft (60 cm) in length and twice the thickness of normal guard hairs. These hairs, hanging in bunches from the tail, would have compensated for the shortness of the fleshy part of the tail and ensured that the mammoth retained an effective fly-swat. Again, this feature can be perceived in Ice Age art, especially the engraving from La Madeleine *(see p.97)* and drawings from Rouffignac.

At the base of the tail was a broad flap of skin covering the anus. This has sometimes been regarded as a further adaptation to the cold, but it is also present in living elephants that inhabit a tropical climate. The anal flap of the mammoth was faithfully recorded by several prehistoric artists *(see p.62)*.

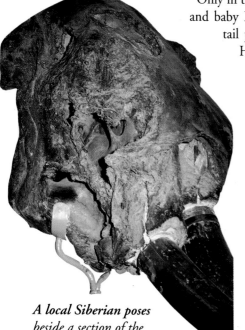

A local Siberian poses beside a section of the Beresovka mammoth, found in 1901. Its short tail, at the top of the picture, has at its base the anal flap. The 3-ft (86-cm) long penis projects toward the bottom left.

LOOKING INSIDE THE MAMMOTH

THE MUMMIFICATION OF CARCASSES in the permafrost was so effective that not only organs but also tissues and cells are extraordinarily well preserved. The very latest non-destructive scientific techniques have been applied to the most recent finds of intact mammoths. For example, Japanese investigators led by N. Suzuki of Tokyo Jikei University have produced a three-dimensional picture of Mascha's skull *(see p.47)* by computer tomography: a scanner provides colour images of cross-sectional "slices" through the body, allowing detailed internal views without opening it. Dima's heart *(above)* is still in excellent condition, and the Japanese anatomists have likewise been able to produce coloured images of "slices" of the organ, as well as a three-dimensional computer image through tomography. Despite some shrivelling and wrinkling of the tissues, all of the heart's essential internal structure could still be seen.

Dima's preserved carcass also provided scientists with a unique chance to investigate such details as blood cells after more than 40,000 years of burial in the permafrost. Under a scanning electron microscope, red and white cells are indistinguishable from those of living mammals. Microscopic studies also revealed parasitic flies and protozoa in Dima's gut.

In America, similar studies have been carried out on both mammoths and mastodons. In 1976 two U.S. scientists reported on the tissues of the mammoth face from Alaska dating to 21,300 years ago *(see p.31)*. Although the skin was dry and leathery, the hair was well preserved, and the eyes survived as globoid structures filled with a soft, white, cheesy material.

More recently an almost complete mastodon skeleton from the Burning Tree site in Ohio, dating to about 11,500 years ago, was found to contain the remains of the animal's last meal in its stomach as well as bacteria within the stomach contents. These microbes were clearly associated with the food, since there were none in the surrounding peat, and they must have helped to digest the mastodon's food. It is uncertain whether these bacteria are the original inhabitants of the animal's stomach or their descendants.

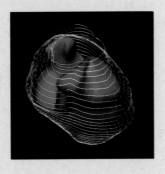

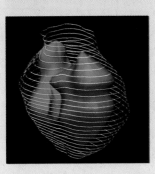
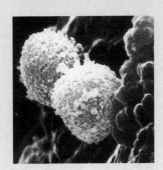

Dima's heart has been reconstructed from 26 X-ray "slices" by computer tomography. White lines show the outer surfaces. Inside, the right auricle and ventricle are in blue, left auricle and ventricle in red. (Compare the heart, top.)

Dima's blood cells, magnified about 2,000 times by electron microscope, show two white cells (left); two red cells in a blood vessel (above); and a red cell with the characteristic ring shape and a fungal tube growing into it (above left).

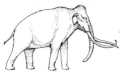

HABITAT AND DIET

The main habitat of the woolly mammoth during the last Ice Age, between about 100,000 and 12,000 years ago, was the vast expanse of grassy vegetation which covered much of Europe, northern Asia and northern North America. This vegetation has no precise modern equivalent. It is known as "mammoth steppe", or "tundra steppe", because it resembled in some ways the grassy steppe of southern Russia today, although the vegetation was more diverse than in this region. Contrary to popular belief, the mammoth did not live in a habitat dominated by ice and snow. The continental land-masses were expanded by lowered sea levels, and the weather is believed to have been dominated by high pressure systems, so little rain or snowfall reached their interiors.

"The stomachs of several frozen mammoths contain the remains of their last meal"

The plants of the dry grassland of the "mammoth steppe" were faster growing and more abundant than today's tundra plants. In addition to various species of grasses, they included dry-ground sedges, small shrubs, such as Arctic sagebrush, and many herbaceous plants including members of the pea, daisy and buttercup families. This was the habitat that supported large numbers of woolly mammoths, as well as other grazers such as bison, horses and woolly rhinoceroses. Large areas of the landscape were treeless, but scattered birch, larch and other trees occurred locally, especially in more southerly regions.

Details of the "mammoth steppe" vegetation have come from plant remains preserved in dated fossil deposits. However, we also have a more direct and dramatic source of evidence about the mammoth's diet. Several of the frozen carcasses found in Siberia include the animal's stomach and intestines containing the remains of its last meal. Most spectacular among these is the Shandrin mammoth, whose entrails contained no less than 640 lb (290 kg) of partially digested food, resembling densely compressed hay. The Yuribei mammoth, a relatively late carcass dated to around 10,000 years ago, still had green grass in its stomach. When the Beresovka mammoth was discovered, it even had food between its teeth and on its tongue, the squashed grasses still bearing the imprint of the animal's molars.

Detailed botanical investigation of these remains have provided important clues to the mammoth's diet. Leaves, seeds, fruits and pollen can be identified to at least the general group of plants (e.g. grasses, buttercups), and sometimes to the exact species.

These analyses show that the woolly mammoth's diet was dominated by grasses and sedges. For example, the food in the stomach of the Beresovka mammoth comprised largely grass, with additional remains of various herbs. The guts of the Shandrin mammoth contained 90 percent grass by volume, with a few twig tips of willow, birch, larch and alder. The animals clearly liked to supplement their food with some herbaceous plants and shrubs, and even the occasional tree-browse when available. Like living elephants, they needed this variety to provide the different nutrients necessary for growth, and the details of these supplements probably varied considerably, depending on the local vegetation.

The Columbian mammoth, inhabiting the southern half of North America, probably covered a greater variety of habitats

Mammoths ranked among the three main species of northern steppes in the late Pleistocene. These charts, based on the numbers of bones of each species recovered, also show that the composition of grazing animals was very similar in the "mammoth steppe" of Siberia and Alaska.

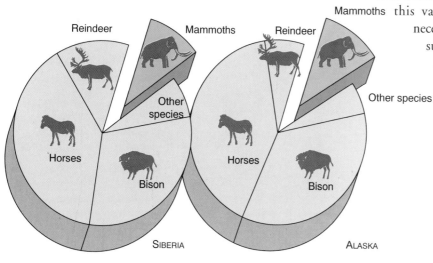

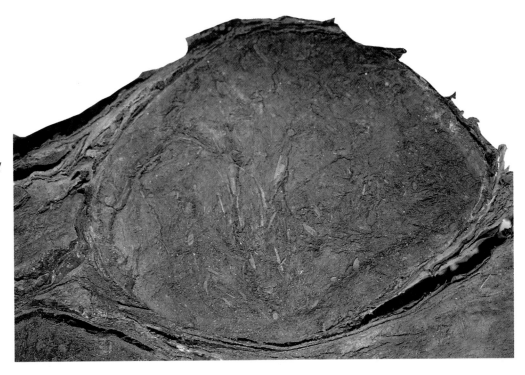

*A slice through the **intestines** of the Shandrin frozen mammoth, unearthed in Siberia in 1972, shows how the animal's gut was completely packed with chewed-up, fibrous vegetable food. Detailed study of the leaves, seeds and pollen has revealed much about the woolly mammoth's diet.*

Grass *(Festuca vivipara)*

Arctic sagebrush *(Artemisia frigida)*

Clubmoss *(centre)*

Dwarf birch *(Betula nana)*

Woolly mammoth food was dominated by grass but included hundreds of plant types identified from frozen stomachs. These photographs of living plants show some of the most common species eaten. The picture at bottom left includes – in addition to clubmoss (Selaginella selaginoides) – *dwarf willow* (Salix repens) *in the foreground, and sedge* (Carex) *to the rear.*

in the last Ice Age than did the woolly mammoth farther north. Many regions are thought to have been clothed by a "mosaic" vegetation of grasses, herbaceous plants, shrubs and trees. In some areas this would have been predominantly grassy and meadowlike, with trees and shrubs concentrated along river courses; in others the trees and shrubs were scattered more evenly, forming a savanna-like or "parkland" landscape. Elsewhere there were coniferous or deciduous woodlands with extensive understorey. Only areas of true forest would not have been favoured by the mammoths, although even here locally open areas could have provided grass and herb graze.

Since no carcasses of Columbian mammoths have been preserved, stomach contents cannot be examined. However, two caves in southern Utah have yielded large quantities of mammoth dung, giving a direct insight into the diet of *Mammuthus columbi*. The dry conditions and the relatively uniform temperature in these caves on the Colorado Plateau have allowed the dung to survive without decay for thousands of years. At Bechan Cave a dung blanket 16 in (41 cm) thick, with a total volume of 8,000 cubic ft (227 m³), has been excavated.

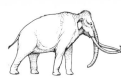

A unique quantity of mammoth dung has been found at Bechan Cave in Utah, including this complete bolus (above), about 8 in (20 cm) across, flanked by two smaller fragments. Dissection of the dung balls gives a direct insight into the Columbian mammoth's diet, while other plant remains, such as oak leaves and acorns (below), provide more information on the mammoth's environment.

Grasses, sagebrush, *Ephedra*

Juniper bush (*Juniperus communis*)

Columbian mammoth food, *like that of woolly mammoths, consisted primarily of grasses and sedges, supplemented by shrubs. Sagebrush (Artemisia), Ephedra and juniper bush were among the common shrubs included in the diet.*

The Bechan deposit includes droppings of various smaller mammals, but the most spectacular are large, spherical boluses about 8 in (20 cm) in diameter. These are very similar to modern elephant dung and so are identified as belonging to the Columbian mammoth, the only possible candidate among the local Pleistocene fauna. The quantity of dung in the cave seems extraordinary, but since an adult African elephant drops an average of 25 lb (11 kg) every 2 hours, and 200–300 lb (90–135 kg) every day, a small group of mammoths could easily have produced the Bechan deposit in a short time, or over a few seasons. The name "Bechan" is derived from a Navajo word meaning "large faeces".

Bechan mammoth dung has been radiocarbon dated to between 13,500 and 11,700 years ago, and comprises 95 percent grass and sedge by weight. Woody plants also occurred, in quantities varying from zero to 25 percent between boluses. These supplements to the grassy diet included saltbush, sagebrush, water birch and blue spruce. Although the dominance of grass and sedge parallels the diet of the woolly mammoth, tree- and shrub-browse probably played a larger role in that of the Columbian mammoth.

The observational powers of cave artists are powerfully demonstrated in this drawing from Rouffignac Cave in France. The end of the mammoth's trunk clearly bears two projections, the outer longer than the inner, as seen in trunks from the frozen carcasses (above right). The artist has also noticed how the foot swells when weight is placed on it, just as it does in living elephants.

The trunk tip of baby mammoth Dima (below left) *shows clearly the "finger and thumb" projections used in feeding. The same structures are seen in the trunk of the Middle Kolyma adult* (below right). *This tip was hacked from the carcass, so the two breathing tubes (nostrils), which ran the length of the trunk, can be seen at the cut surface.*

FEEDING

Like living elephants, an adult woolly mammoth of 6 tons needed about 400 lb (180 kg) of fresh food a day to fuel its great bulk and may have spent 20 hours or more a day feeding. For the larger Columbian mammoth, even more food would have been required. The mammoths were superbly equipped for procuring and dealing with this quantity of food, especially with their specialized trunk and teeth.

The mammoth's main feeding apparatus, as in living elephants, was its trunk. Since all four legs were permanently occupied in support and movement, the trunk was a crucial organ, acting like a free hand for moving, breaking and manipulating all kinds of objects. It was also highly sensitive in touch, both for feeding and in social interaction.

Packed with small muscles, the trunk was capable of movement in any direction and also contraction and extension. The trunk of the Liakhov mammoth was frozen at 6 ft 6 in (2 m) in length. In baby Dima, six months old, the trunk measured about 2 ft 6 in (76 cm).

> *"Mammoths may have spent up to 20 hours a day fuelling their great bulk"*

The most interesting aspect of the mammoth's trunk was its tip. In 1924 the end of a trunk was found frozen in the Middle Kolyma region of Siberia, complete with its two long, fingerlike projections at the tip. The front one is about 4 in (10 cm) long and relatively narrow and pointed. The back one is broader and about 2 in (5 cm) long. Exactly the same structures were seen, smaller of course, when baby Dima was excavated in 1977.

In feeding, the trunk was used in two main ways. First, the whole trunk could be wrapped around large tufts of grass, which would be pulled up or broken off before being stuffed into the animal's mouth. Where trees or shrubs were

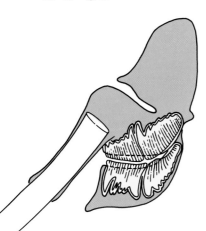

The huge molar teeth at the front of the jaw, just one upper and one lower on each side, ground together to provide the mammoth with considerable chewing power. Behind them, still largely buried in spaces within the jaw bone, the replacements are forming.

available, the trunk would have been used to break off leafy branches. Second, the "finger and thumb" at the end of the trunk could be used for delicate operations. These would have included picking flowers or buds, but perhaps also eating the relatively short grass of the mammoth steppe.

Once inside the animal's mouth, the food was attacked by the mammoth's great molar teeth. Grass is a particularly tough food, and given the quantity that the animal needed to process each day, the teeth had to be wear resistant. This requirement was all the more necessary because the grit that the animal inevitably picked up with its food.

Each molar tooth comprised numerous ridges of hard enamel, separated from each other and held together by dentine and cement. As the teeth ground together, the sharp enamel ridges on the upper and lower molars cut past each other to break up the food. Because the enamel ridges ran from side to side in the jaw, they cut past each other when the animal moved its jaw back and forth. This contrasts with deer or cattle, where the enamel ridges run from back to front and the main chewing movement is sideways.

Like living elephants, a mammoth went through six sets of teeth in its life. At any one time only one tooth was fully in operation in each of the four jaws (upper and lower, left and right). As that tooth wore out, it was replaced from behind in a sort of continuous conveyor belt system, the process being repeated five times. This contrasts with humans, where each tooth is changed only once (in childhood), and the replacement grows from below.

In step with the animal's growth, successive molar teeth were progressively bigger and had more enamel ridges. The first tooth, already erupted at birth, was only ½ in (13 mm) long and lasted about 18 months. However, by six months the second tooth had already started to erupt behind. This

was followed by the third tooth, which lasted until about 10 years of age. The process continued for about 30 years, when the sixth and final molar came into play, the largest of the series and lasting the animal for the rest of its life. These teeth were commonly over 1 ft (30 cm) long and 4 lb (1.8 kg) in weight.

Only 1 in (2.5 cm) or less of each molar actually projected above the gum; below it the crown was up to 9 in (23 cm) deep. As well as moving forward, the tooth was also being pushed up to expose more crown as the chewing surface wore down. These high crowns further enhanced the chewing life of each tooth. When the last molar finally wore down to the root, the animal could no longer chew, and this would have caused the demise of animals that had reached an advanced age.

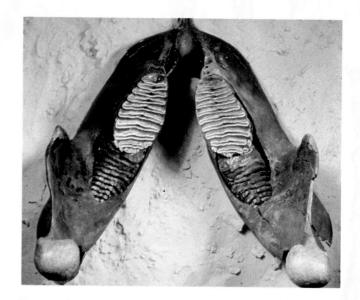

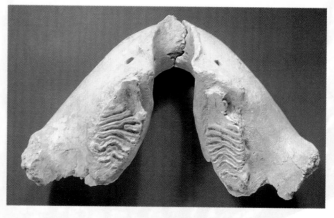

The teeth reveal the age of a mammoth skeleton. In the woolly mammoth jaw from Condover, England (above right), seen from above, the sixth molars are beginning to replace the fifth set from behind, indicating that the animal was about 30 years old at death. The jaw from Polch, Germany, (right) shows the sixth molars almost worn out. The animal, at least 60 years old, may have died through reduced ability to feed.

These upper molars of a woolly mammoth show the great difference in size between baby and adult teeth. *The first molar* (bottom left), *with which the animal was born, is no larger than a human molar, while the third of the series* (below left) *is about 6 in (15 cm) long. The background image shows the actual size of the vast sixth molar* (right).

CHEWING POWER

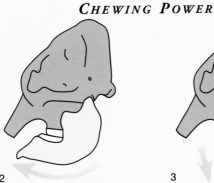

1   2   3   4

POWERFUL MUSCLES OPERATED THE JAW. IN THE FIRST STAGE, food was held between the molars. In the second, the lower jaw slid forward, chewing the food. In the third, the lower jaw opened and was pulled back, while in the fourth stage it closed, ready to move forward again in another chewing stroke. As the lower teeth ground against the upper teeth, which were fixed motionless in the skull, the hard enamel ridges cut across each other, breaking up the plant food.

The tiny milk tusk of a woolly mammoth (below, shown life size) *was shed after about a year. This rare specimen came from a frozen carcass of a baby mammoth found in 1992 near the Indigirka River in northeastern Siberia.*

THE MAMMOTH'S TUSKS

After its woolly coat, the mammoth's tusks were its most conspicuous feature. The world record woolly mammoth tusk, from the Kolyma River, measures 13 ft 7 in (4.2 m) along the curve, and weighs 185 lb (84 kg). Weights of very large tusks in excess of 200 lb (91 kg) have been reported. More typical is a length of 8–9 ft (2.4–2.7 m) and a weight of about 100 lb (45 kg). These figures apply to males; in females, the tusks were considerably smaller and also thinner and less tapering. Typical female tusks were about 5–6 ft (1.5–1.8 m) long and weighed only 20–25 lb (9–11 kg).

> ## "The largest mammoth tusk in the world is more than 16 feet long"

The tusks of the Columbian mammoth were as large as or larger than those of their woolly cousins. Celebrated examples include the skeleton from Jonesboro, Indiana, in the American Museum of Natural History in New York, whose tusks measure 11 ft 6 in (3.5 m), and the Franklin County skull, Nebraska, with tusks of at least 12 ft 6 in (3.8 m). A tusk from Mexico measured 13 ft 9 in (4.12 m), but the world record for any proboscidean tusk is in a skull of a Columbian mammoth from Post, Texas, measuring more than 16 ft (4.9 m). It was presented to the American Museum of Natural History in 1934.

The massive tusks were preceded in baby mammoths by tiny milk tusks. Only a couple of inches long, these erupted at about six months and lasted about a year. They were replaced by the permanent tusks which grew continuously through life, although the rate of growth slowed down in adult animals. Up to a quarter of the tusk length was embedded in the socket in the skull, and it was here that new tusk material was added, at a rate of between 1 and 6 in (2.5 and 15 cm) per year.

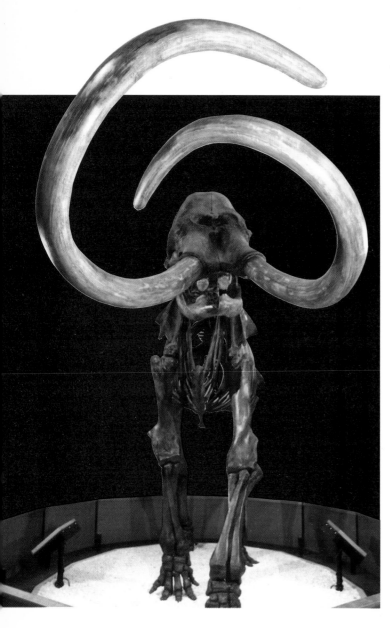

The imposing size and unusual shape of the mammoth's tusks are dramatically shown in this male skeleton of a Columbian mammoth from the tarpits of Rancho La Brea, California (see pp.56–57).

This tusk of an adult female woolly mammoth is about 5 ft (1.5 m) long, and its slender form makes it lighter in weight than a male tusk. The curve is also less developed than in many male tusks.

A spectacular male skull of an early form of woolly mammoth was unearthed at Ilford, near London, England, more than a hundred years ago. Mammoth tusks first grew almost vertically downward from the skull, before curving upward and outward, then inward again.

The shape of mammoth tusks was different from that of living elephants. Mammoth tusks have been described as having a "twist" or a "writhe". They grew in the form of a spiral or corkscrew, in some cases quite tightly, in others very openly. The left and right tusks twisted in opposite directions and occasionally formed almost complete circles, with the tips crossing in the middle.

As in the case of living elephants, the mammoth's tusks were undoubtedly used for a variety of activities. A key use was in intimidating, sparring and fighting with other individuals. Males would have fought for access to females, and both sexes would have had occasional tussles over favoured feeding spots. Such contests would primarily have involved pushing and twisting as a trial of strength. The markedly curved tusks would have been unsuitable for stabbing the rival, the aim of serious fights among elephants today. An alternative may have been to crash the tusks down on the rival's back, as seen also among living elephants, and as suggested by broken mammoth shoulder blades *(see p.91)*. The large curved tusks of adult males may have acted as a sexual attractant to females and would have been a deterrent to predators.

Tusks were also used in feeding. Mammoth tusks very frequently show areas of wear, sometimes forming a flat, polished facet up to 1 ft (30 cm) long, usually on the side of the tusks that would have touched the ground. This type of wear has led to the theory that the tusks were used as a snow plough, the animal moving its head from side to side to clear away snow and expose vegetation beneath. Although this may have been an occasional use, it must be remembered that snowfall was not a serious problem over much of the mammoth's range. Moreover, modern elephants also often show wear and scratching near the tips of their tusks. These result from stripping bark and digging up plants, activities that mammoths would have undertaken, especially when trees or shrubs were available. It has also been suggested that an important function of the tusks was to break up ice to eat in winter, when there was no accessible unfrozen water to drink. If this was so, this practice would certainly have contributed to wear on the tusks.

TUSK WEAR AND TEAR

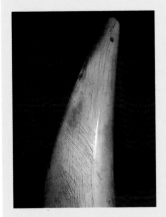 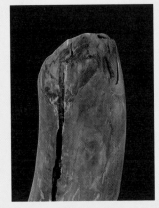 

DESPITE THE HARD, DURABLE NATURE OF IVORY, TUSKS OFTEN SHOW SIGNS OF WEAR AND STRESS. The lower sides of the end of the tusks usually became flattened, polished and scratched *(left)* through abrasion against the ground during feeding. The end could also be snapped off *(centre)*, perhaps during fighting. In this example, the shattered tip has been polished smooth by subsequent wear. A split tusk *(right)* shows the structure of the ivory. Tusks grew by the addition of successive cones of dentine (the base of the tusk is beyond the top of the picture).

FIGHTING AND MATING

Two male mammoths fight for access to a female in this Siberian setting during the last Ice Age about 15,000 years ago. Other mammoths gather excitedly around, while in the background a third male takes advantage of the situation to begin courting the disputed female.

With a gestation period of 22 months, *woolly mammoths may have mated mainly in the summer to ensure birth in the spring nearly two years later. Alternatively, breeding a few months earlier would have allowed the new youngsters to take advantage of spring growth just when they were starting to eat solid food. Only females in breeding condition (oestrus) would be attractive to the males, which themselves may have undergone cycles of aggressive behaviour related to mating.*

Mock or ritualistic sparring, as in living elephants, was probably common among male mammoths and would have involved head butting, pushing and clashes of tusks. Just displaying his tusks would often have been enough for one male to assert his superiority. Occasionally, however, serious fights could develop, especially between evenly matched individuals pursuing a receptive female. These were violent and could sometimes result in the death of one or both combatants.

A unique fossil find was unearthed in Nebraska: two mammoths that had died with their tusks interlocked. Mammoths could turn their curved tusks into deadly weapons, by thrusting them upward, swiping them sideways or crashing them down from above. Interlocked, they provided leverage for a twisting and pushing contest, which could occasionally have resulted in the breakage of a tusk.

MOTHERS AND YOUNG

A family group of woolly mammoths would usually have been composed of up to a dozen adult females and their young, which formed a closely knit social unit. This Ice Age scene is set in northern Siberia during the spring, when a young mammoth has fallen through thin ice and is helped to safety by its mother.

The matriarch, an old and experienced female and leader *of the group, stands to the left, surveying the scene. The other adults are likely to be her sisters, offspring or nieces. If any individual became sick or injured, others would offer constant assistance. If a mother died, her offspring would be adopted by one of the other females.*

A female mammoth suckles her baby while caressing its back with her trunk. Unusually among mammals, mammoths (like living elephants) had their mammary glands toward the front of the body. This was the only time in a mammoth's life when it took food directly with its mouth (right). Some plant food was taken from a few months of age, and the animal was weaned by the age of two or three, by which time the mother would be ready to breed again.

Like other juvenile mammals, mammoth youngsters were constantly at play. One animal clambers over its mother's back, while another tugs at the tail of an older cousin. On reaching maturity at about 10 or 12 years of age, young males gradually spent less time with the group before finally setting off on their own, like the adolescent seen in the background of this scene.

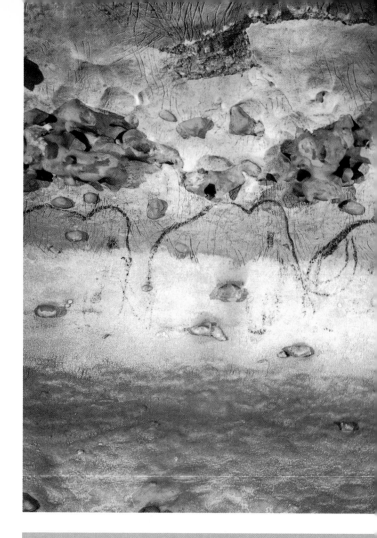

A drawing in the cave at Rouffignac, France, seems to suggest that mammoths shared the close social bonding so evident in elephant families. It shows a meeting between two small groups, similar to the renewal of bonding that occurs when related elephants meet after a period of separation.

LIFE CYCLE AND BEHAVIOUR

All elephants are highly social animals, and mammoths were no exception. It may seem surprising that social behaviour can be deduced for animals known only from bones and carcasses. However, certain fossil finds, together with Ice Age art and our knowledge of modern elephants and the mammoth's environment, allow the broad features of its life cycle and behaviour to be outlined with some confidence.

> *"Evidence suggests that mammoths shared patterns of behaviour with living elephants"*

Elephant society is matriarchal: it is organized into family groups led by adult females, with one experienced female, the matriarch, dominant. A family group may comprise anything from 2 to 20 or so individuals, with the average group size being about 10. Adults within a group are relatives: mothers and daughters, sisters, aunts and nieces. They are accompanied by their offspring of both sexes, up to the age of about 10. Above this age, young females stay within the family group, but males start to move away. Adult males live singly or in small bachelor groups, associating with females mainly for purposes of mating.

Apart from the likelihood that, being close relatives, mammoths shared a similar social structure to living elephants, there is some indirect evidence for it. At the fossil site at Dent in Colorado, for example, the remains of Columbian mammoths seem to comprise entirely females and young. It is debated whether they met their death naturally or at the hands of prehistoric people *(see pp.126–31)*, but in either case a female-led family group is implied. At other sites, the opposite is found. For example, at Hot Springs in South Dakota all except one of the numerous skeletons is male. This site was a sinkhole forming a natural

The close kinship of mammoths to living elephants makes it likely that they shared many aspects of behaviour. Here two male African elephants engage in a ceremony of greeting, recognition and assessment. Their ears are limp, indicating no serious aggression, although such activities may sometimes develop into shoving and butting matches.

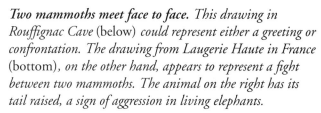

Two mammoths meet face to face. This drawing in Rouffignac Cave (below) *could represent either a greeting or confrontation. The drawing from Laugerie Haute in France* (bottom), *on the other hand, appears to represent a fight between two mammoths. The animal on the right has its tail raised, a sign of aggression in living elephants.*

trap into which animals fell. With modern elephants, it is usually single, roving males that are the more adventurous and more likely to get into difficult situations, while the females, living in groups, are more cautious and help each other out of trouble. The Hot Springs site has been interpreted as an accumulation of individual male deaths over a long period, implying that, as in living elephants, male mammoths roamed alone. Moreover, most of the animals were in their early adult life – the time when male mammoths were probably at their most active and adventurous.

Among elephants, larger herds are sometimes formed as family groups come together. Before the great reduction in elephant numbers in recent decades, gatherings of up to a thousand elephants were occasionally seen, usually for migration to new feeding grounds. It is probable that mammoths also sometimes formed large herds; indeed, there are reasons for thinking that this was more prevalent than in the living

DANGER FROM PREDATION

SPOTTED HYENAS, SEEN HERE scavenging the carcass of an African elephant, lived in Europe during the Pleistocene. At Kent's Cavern in southwestern England, a former hyena den, thousands of hyena fossils have been excavated, mingled with bones of juvenile woolly mammoths, many of them chewed.

At Friesenhahn Cave in Texas, juvenile Columbian mammoth bones were accumulated by the now extinct scimitar-tooth cat, *Homotherium*. Neither hyenas nor big cats could have hunted mammoths in their prime but they may have picked off young animals.

elephants. First, it is generally found that large animals living in open country are more likely to form herds than related species in woodland or forest. Examples are seen in the herds of antelope on the African plains, in contrast to the comparatively solitary existence of their forest-dwelling relatives. Mammoths, especially woolly mammoths, lived in a largely open, treeless habitat, so herding may often have occurred.

Second, it can be argued that mammoths would have needed to make long seasonal migrations in search of food. The northern mammoth steppe provided a rich source of vegetation during the spring and summer when plant growth was at its peak. In the autumn and winter months, however, fresh food would have been scarce, and mammoth herds may have migrated south.

There is no direct evidence for such migrations among mammoths, and some researchers believe that the mammoths tended to stay in one place, relying on fat reserves that they had built up during the growth period. This would parallel the behaviour of the living musk ox, which remains in the Arctic north throughout the winter.

The northern habitat of the woolly mammoth may have had a direct effect on its life cycle. In common with other tropical animals, modern elephants breed at all times of the year. However, on the African savanna many individuals time their breeding so that the young are born in the rainy season when food is most plentiful. Mammoths lived in northern climes during the Ice Age, when the variation between summer and winter was more intense than in the modern tropics. It is therefore quite likely that their breeding was strictly timed so that young were born only at the beginning of the plant growth season in the spring. A similar pattern can be seen, for example, in today's deer from Europe or North America, which give birth in the spring, in contrast to tropical deer from South America and Southeast

A "lunar landscape" was exposed at the site of Murray Springs, Arizona, excavated in the 1960s. Several skeletons of Columbian mammoths were discovered, together with stone implements. In one area, removal of sediment revealed a series of depressions identical to modern elephant footprints in soft ground. The tracks appear to lead up to one of the skeletons.

Rings seen on the outside of tusks mark the edges of growth cones inside (see p.81). They reflect periods of slower and faster tusk growth, between seasons and between good and bad years, but are unlikely to represent precisely one year of growth each. Under optimal conditions, tusks could grow 6 in (15 cm) or more per year.

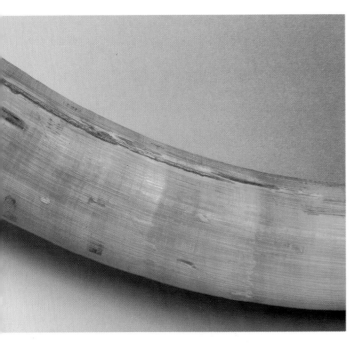

Asia, which breed all year round. Like living elephants, the gestation time of mammoths was probably 22 months, so a mating season in the summer, producing young in the spring nearly two years later, can be calculated.

The total lifespan of different mammoth species can be estimated from their size. Among mammals, there is a close relationship between a species' size and its longevity. On this basis, woolly mammoths, at around 6 tons, probably lived as long as living elephants – about 60 years. Columbian mammoths, which frequently reached 10 tons, presumably lived longer – perhaps up to 80 years or more. Some scientists have attempted to calculate the age of individual mammoths by counting the "growth rings" visible on tusks, believing them equivalent to annual tree rings. On this basis they have suggested ages of 80 years, even for woolly mammoths. However, it is not certain that the rings were strictly annual.

"Like living elephants, mammoths may have remained with their dead, apparently mourning their loss"

At Murray Springs in Arizona an extraordinary piece of "fossilized behaviour" was discovered. A trail of buried footprints was uncovered which can only have been produced by an elephant, and the only possible local candidate is the Columbian mammoth. Moreover, the footprints were found to lead up to a fossilized skeleton of that species. Two explanations are possible. Either the footprints belonged to the preserved individual and represent its last moments alive; or they may belong to another individual which came to help the dying animal, or mourn its death. Modern elephants spend days guarding the corpse of a dead relative, even "burying" it with leaves or soil. It is not certain that mammoths showed the same traits, but their close relationship to living elephants makes it a distinct possibility.

Because of a "log jam" in the forward progression of teeth, this molar, belonging to an ancestral mammoth, was pushed into a curve. The molar of a woolly mammoth (below right) has a large root cancer and abscess in the left-hand side.

The shoulder blade of a woolly mammoth from Condover, England, had suffered a severe fracture earlier in life but healed over. Normal scapulas are flat in the region indicated.

HEALTH AND DISEASE

Mammoths were not immune to health problems, as can be seen from various traces of disease preserved in bones, teeth and tusks. A survey of nearly 2,000 mammoth fossils showed that about 4 percent had some signs of illness. These diseases can be identified by comparison with veterinary studies of present-day species.

> ## *"Fossils show that some mammoths suffered from severe tooth decay"*

One of the most common abnormalities seen in mammoth fossils is distortion of the molar teeth, due mostly to disruption of the process of tooth replacement. If the normal forward progression of the teeth was interrupted, the teeth coming from behind could get squashed into unusual shapes during their growth. Several such teeth have been recovered as fossils; the fact that many subsequently came into use indicates that normal tooth replacement had begun again and the animal had survived, at least for a while.

A few teeth show evidence of periodontal disease or dental decay. Periodontal disease results from build-up of bacteria between tooth and gum, dissolving away part of the surface mineral of the tooth. A cavity (caries) may develop, which in advanced cases leads to further infection and an abscess at the base of the tooth. Among a sample of mammoth teeth from Ice Age Britain, about 2 percent showed periodontal disease, of which about half had proceeded to a caries. The relatively low sugar content of the mammoth's diet (grass rather than fruits or berries) may have helped to reduce the prevalence of these diseases.

Occasionally cancerous growths are seen in teeth, resulting in abnormal outgrowths of dental tissue. These are more often found in the fossil state than bone cancers because the latter so weaken the bone that preservation is unlikely.

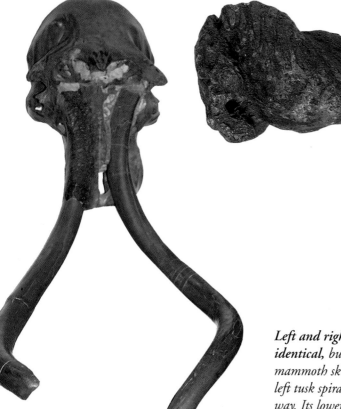

Left and right tusks were seldom precisely identical, but in this 14,000-year-old woolly mammoth skull, from Bzianka in Poland, its left tusk spirals downward in a most abnormal way. Its lower end has been flattened and polished through rubbing against the ground.

Being organs that continue to grow through life, the tusks were susceptible to growth defects of various kinds. The two tusks of an individual were rarely perfectly symmetrical, and it is a matter of judgment at what point a difference between left and right is regarded as abnormal. For example, a skull found in Bzianka in Poland has a normal right tusk (though broken during life), but the left tusk curls downward in a most unusual fashion.

The most common bone disease, found in about 2 percent of mammoth bones, is osteoarthritis. This results from the wearing away of the cartilage between joints, followed by abnormal growth of the bone ends and their possible fusion. A striking example is seen in the woolly mammoth skeleton from Praz Rodet, Switzerland, where several vertebrae in the lower back are completely fused together.

A few bones show evidence of bacterial infection such as osteomyelitis, in which bacteria gain entry to the bone tissue, resulting in abnormal outgrowths of bone. This condition could have become fatal if the infection had spread throughout the body.

Finally, there are examples of mammoths having broken a bone, but surviving with the fracture healed. One bone which may have been particularly prone to fracture was the shoulder blade, a relatively thin, flat structure. In one specimen from Siberia, the whole back part of the right shoulder

blade had been snapped off and had healed in roughly the natural position. A similar fracture is seen in the left shoulder blade of the mammoth from Condover, England, which had been broken along the top edge and knitted together with extensive growth of new bone. As a result, the healed blade in the region of the fracture is many times thicker than normal. There are numerous possible explanations for such fractures, among which are falling down a hole or being tusked by another mammoth. A possible example of the former scenario is provided by the Beresovka carcass *(see pp.44–45)*, which may have broken its right shoulder blade on falling to its death.

Among large mammals living in the wild today, most limb bone fractures in adult animals lead to the death of the individual. It is therefore likely that the healed fractures seen in fossil mammoth bones were the result of an injury while the animal was young, at an age when the bone was still capable of healing.

THE SOLLAS "EGG"

ABNORMAL GROWTHS ON TUSKS OCCASIONALLY RESULTED from damage to the tissues that lay down tusk mineral in the socket. A famous example of this came from excavations at Paviland Cave in Wales *(see p.96)*. In about 1820 Dean William Buckland discovered, among a quantity of mammoth ivory, a fragment of tusk with an unusual, hollow cavity. He perceptively guessed that this was an abnormality – similar to that seen among modern elephants where the growth organ inside the tusk socket has been damaged.

Nearly a century later, during renewed excavations in the cave, W. Sollas unearthed an egg-shaped lump of ivory which fitted into the hollow of Buckland's specimen. This ivory "egg" had formed as part of the abnormal growth of the mammoth's tusk. Moreover, it had been discovered by prehistoric people, who had pierced a hole in it to make it into a pendant.

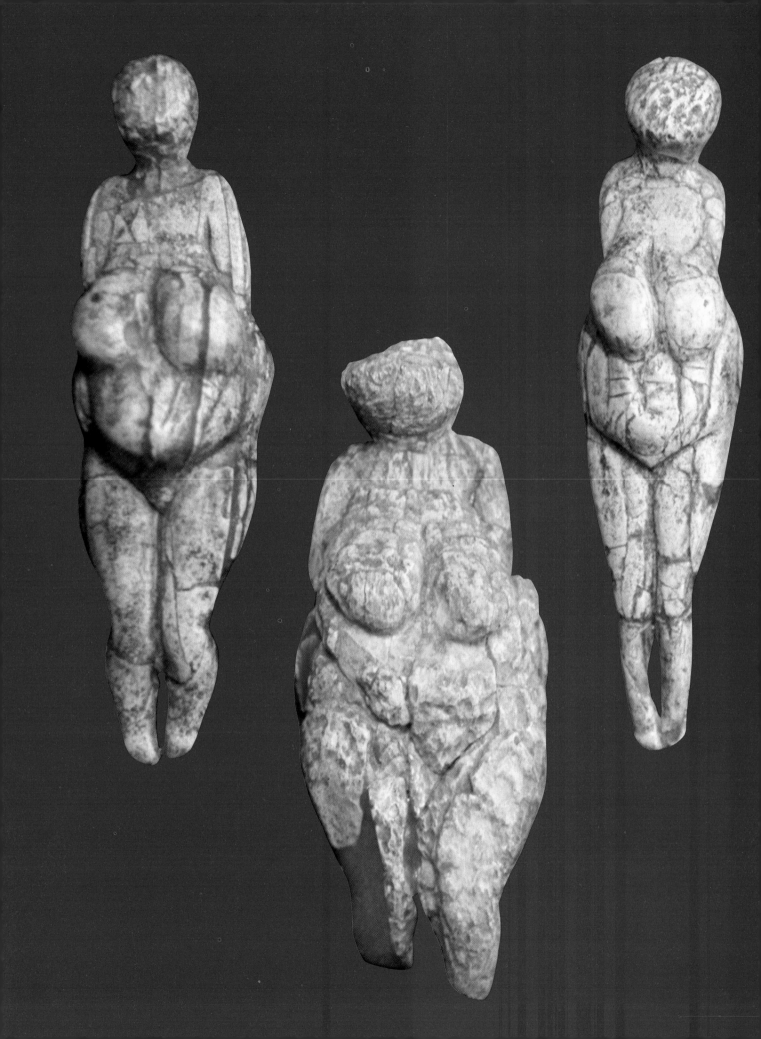

MAMMOTHS AND HUMAN CULTURE

O*F THE MANY EXTINCT ANIMALS THAT ONCE roamed the Earth, mammoths are among those which lived at the same time as humans, often even alongside them. The vivid, lifelike depictions of mammoths in cave paintings, and the ever-growing archive of evidence of the way humans made use of mammoth bones and ivory, not only prove that mammoths and humans coexisted but also help underline the importance of mammoths in the daily lives of our ancestors.*

From a plentiful supply of mammoth bones and tusks – probably scavenged more than acquired by hunting – humans made anvils, tools and even hut-style dwellings. Prehistoric sculptors also recognized the beauty of ivory and fashioned it into highly original and sophisticated carvings, which are among the first of their kind created by human hand. And today, thousands of years later, fossil mammoth ivory is still being crafted to make jewellery and ornaments.

A series of remarkable figurines carved in mammoth ivory has been found at Avdeevo in Russia. They are about 4 in (10 cm) high and at least 12,000 years old.

94 MAMMOTHS IN THE ARTIST'S EYE

Artists work in the glow of naked flames to decorate a cave in southern France, about 15,000 years ago. The large number of paintings that have survived indicate that cave decoration was a widespread activity in certain regions. Mammoths feature regularly among the animals depicted.

Cave painters used a variety of naturally occurring pigments to create their colours. Iron oxide (hematite or ochre) produced red; manganese dioxide and charcoal produced black. Various colours, from yellow to purple, can be produced by heating ochre. It is not known which binding medium was used: experiments suggest that calcium-rich cave water was best for fixing pigments on the damp rock faces, but recent analyses of paint from several caves suggest the use of animal and plant oils.

Many of the caves were completely dark inside. To illuminate their work, the cave painters may have used stone lamps filled with animal oil. An engraved sandstone lamp (right) was found at Lascaux, France's most famous decorated cave. Wood fires and brush torches would also have provided plenty of light.

Most cave walls were within easy reach of the artists, but in a few cases high panels or ceilings were decorated with the aid of ladders or scaffolding. One gallery at Lascaux has about 20 sockets cut into the rock on both sides, 6 ft (1.8 m) above the floor, which probably held platform joists.

Paint was applied to the rock with the fingers or, more often, with some kind of tool. None has survived, but experiments suggest that brushes of animal hair or of crushed and chewed plant fibres would have produced the best results. Pads covered with dampened powder were used in some caves. On rough surfaces, or to make hand stencils, artists would spray liquid paint through a tube or directly from the mouth.

In the early 19th century many paleontologists and geologists were beginning to ask questions about the antiquity of the human race, and whether it was conceivable that in the remote past people had lived alongside animals that were now extinct. Some finds had already suggested such a coexistence, but their significance had not been recognized. For example, in about 1690 a piece of pointed black flint was found close to some elephant bones in a gravel pit in Grays Inn Lane, in London, by John Conyers, a pharmacist and antiquary. It was, in fact, an early Stone Age handaxe, but at the time it was assumed to be a weapon used by a Briton to kill an elephant brought over by the Romans in the first century A.D.

> ### "In the early 19th century it was generally believed that humans could not have lived at the same time as extinct animals"

In 1823 the Reverend William Buckland, an Anglican priest and the first professor of mineralogy and geology at Oxford University, published details of his discovery of an Old Stone Age male skeleton, stained with red ochre, in the Goat's Hole Cave at Paviland in Wales. Also in the cave were rhino and bear bones, together with fragments of slender ivory bracelets, rings and rods and lengths of tusk *(see p.91)* and the skull from an "elephant". It has since been established that the ivory and skull were mammoth, but Buckland did not believe that humans and fossil animals could have lived at the same time, and so suggested that the "Red Lady of Paviland", as the human skeleton was mistakenly labelled, was Romano-British.

Other people digging in western Europe, however, were being led to different conclusions, since they repeatedly found tools of stone and bone

sealed beneath stalagmite floors in caves or rock shelters. These tools had been made by humans and were clearly associated with the remains of extinct animals. In some finds from southern France the animal bones even bore cut-marks that could only have been made by humans.

The mounting evidence was becoming overwhelming, and international recognition of the intermeshing of human history with that of extinct animals was finally won by the work of amateur archaeologist Jacques Boucher de Perthes in the Somme gravels of northern France. By 1859, the year which saw the publication of Darwin's *On the Origin of Species*, the great antiquity of the human race was accepted by all but a few diehards.

In May 1864 the French paleontologist Edouard Lartet made a find remarkable enough to convince the remaining sceptics in the scientific community. Digging in the rock shelter of La Madeleine in the Dordogne, he came upon a lifelike engraving of a mammoth on a large piece of mammoth ivory. This was not the first piece of Ice Age art to be found, but it was among the first whose true age could be proved from its careful excavation and its context.

PORTABLE MAMMOTHS
Humans were producing art in the form of cave paintings and sculpture throughout the latter part of the last Ice Age, from about 30,000 to 10,000 years ago. Although this art is dominated by apparently abstract motifs and by images of horses and bison, the mammoth was also a frequent subject. More than 360 depictions of it are known, spanning a wide range of mediums, from paintings and engravings on cave walls in Spain, France and Russia to engravings and

A mammoth carved from antler 14,000 years ago formed the decorative end for a spear-thrower found at Bruniquel in central southern France. The broken tail would have provided the hook onto which a spear could be mounted to provide extra leverage for throwing. The tusks are carved in low relief along the antler shaft, while the head itself is lowered and the trunk descends to the feet.

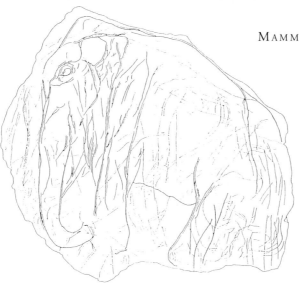

A mammoth engraved on mammoth ivory, found at La Madeleine in France, proved that humans once coexisted with mammoths.

An Ice Age artist exploited the shape of a stone plaque for an engraving found at the French rock shelter of La Marche.

three-dimensional carvings in bone, stone, antler and ivory ("portable art").

The discoveries of Ice Age portable art in the 1860s led to a headlong treasure hunt in caves and rock shelters in Europe. Depictions of extinct animals, or of animals that are no longer found in southern Europe, such as reindeer, were particularly prized. As a result of this wave of enthusiasm, scores of portable engravings and carvings of mammoths were unearthed, and many more have since been discovered.

Unlike depictions on cave walls or rocks, most of these portable images can be confidently dated to the Ice Age because they have been found in the same archaeological layers as tools and other remnants of occupation from that

period. By far the biggest collection was found in the 1960s during the excavation of an open-air camp dating to about 12,700 to 12,400 years ago at Gönnersdorf in northwestern Germany. It contained hundreds of small stone plaques, many of them engraved with animals or stylized women. There are at least 62 mammoths, drawn on a total of 47 plaques. About half of the figures were found intact.

Like sketches from an artist's notebook, the Gönnersdorf engravings have the freshness of a rapid impression. This engraving, 6¾ in (17 cm) long, is probably a fairly accurate rendering of observations from real life. Since the images, carved in stone more than 12,000 years ago, are hard to pick out against their stone background, drawings of them provide a clearer indication of their content.

In common with all Ice Age examples of mammoths, the Gönnersdorf mammoths are depicted in profile and are rather static, although the features provide clear evidence of how mammoths must have looked. It appears that both adults and young are shown, identified by the line of the back: in the adults this descends steeply to the tail, which is level with the mouth. The young have a domed back that is highest in the middle, while the lower part of the body is so shaggy that the stomach cannot be seen.

In the adults and young alike, the head generally has a small protuberance in front of the eyes, the ear is small and mostly hidden by hair, and the eye is bean- or walnut-shaped, with curved wrinkles around it. The outer line of the trunk is

EARLY HUMANS

THE OLD STONE AGE OR PALEOLITHIC PERIOD IS THE earliest and longest phase of human prehistory in the Old World. It began with the first recognizable stone tools (about 2.5 million years ago) and lasted until the end of the Ice Age, about 10,000 years ago. It is divided into three parts: the Lower Paleolithic corresponds to the period of the early human forms, up to and including *Homo erectus*. The Middle Paleolithic is broadly equivalent to the period of the Neanderthals, 200,000 to 35,000 years ago. Debate still rages as to whether Neanderthals were in any way ancestral to modern humans, or whether they were an evolutionary dead end. They display some sophistication in technology, and their burial sites betray signs of religious belief. They had no figurative art, as far as we know, although many simply decorated objects have been found.

Modern humans, *Homo sapiens sapiens*, seem to have originated in Africa more than 100,000 years ago, and spread through Europe between 40,000 and 30,000 years ago, where they coincided with the Upper Paleolithic and the last of the Neanderthals. They were people exactly the same as ourselves in build and appearance, and presumably with the same intelligence. It was they who were responsible for Ice Age art – everything from beads and sculpted figurines to multicoloured paintings – and, apart from an occasional mention of Neanderthals, it is the Upper Paleolithic people who are the focus of this chapter.

always drawn with a single continuous line, while the inner edge is often hatched to indicate hair. Tusks are often missing altogether *(see box opposite)*.

Although often depicted as a simple semicircle at the end of the legs, the feet sometimes have a more realistic flared shape; some even show a protuberance just above the foot, which living elephants have. The short tail curves downward and is sometimes concealed in hair; there is often a tuft of hair, like a brush, hanging down from its end.

"Ice Age sculptures and engravings of mammoths have been found in abundance"

In Ice Age art as a whole, there is usually no correlation between what was depicted and what was hunted or eaten. Gönnersdorf is no exception: the mammoth is the second most frequently depicted animal (after the horse), but mammoth bones rarely feature among the site's animal remains. Reindeer, by contrast, were one of the most hunted species and a major food source, and while reindeer bones abound, reindeer themselves are completely absent from the art. At Gönnersdorf most of the mammoth engravings were found inside a habitation, near the hearth, with another concentration a few yards away. Depictions of birds in this site were concentrated precisely in those zones devoid of mammoths, while depictions of horses and humans were distributed all over the excavated area. Since the mammoth engravings came from a winter habitation (according to the animal remains) and the birds from a summer one, it is possible that there is a significant link between season and depicted species at this site.

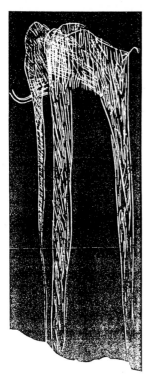

The only piece of Ice Age art found north of the Arctic Circle is the extraordinary, elongated mammoth engraved on the tip of a mammoth tusk from Berelekh (drawing, left), which is about 10,700 years old. The ivory carving of a mammoth (above), from Předmostí in the Czech Republic, is probably more than twice this age. A mammoth was selected for the decorative end of a spear-thrower from Canecaude in France (top). The tusks encircle the eye, rather like musk-ox horns.

A delicate engraving of a shaggy mammoth can be deciphered on this piece of ivory, 3½ in (9 cm) long, found at Obere Klause in southern Germany. It dates to the end of the Ice Age, about 12,000 years ago.

Another major collection of portable mammoths – a set of stone plaques which date to 14,300 years ago – has been found at the French rock shelter of La Marche *(see p.97)*. Engravings on ivory, similar to that of La Madeleine, have been discovered at Obere Klause in southern Germany, and Mal'ta in south-central Siberia.

The biggest collection of three-dimensional figures comes from Paleolithic sites on the Russian Plain. Among the 40 found so far are 10 tiny sculptures from Kostenki. Carved in the soft stone marl, they measure just 1 in by ½ in (2.5 cm by 1.3 cm). Larger three-dimensional sculptures of mammoths have also come to light, including one in limestone, 4 in (10.6 cm) long, from Avdeevo in Russia. Ivory statuettes of mammoths were found in the caves of Vogelherd and Geissenklösterle in southwestern Germany; they date to at least 30,000 years ago and are among the oldest known figurative images in the world.

CAVE ART: MAMMOTHS AS DECORATION

It was first suggested in the 1870s that the walls of caves and rock shelters in Europe were decorated with Ice Age art, but the reality of this was not accepted by the archaeological establishment until 1902; this was largely by virtue of the discoveries of cave art in France. The debate inspired another wave of enthusiasm that led people to re-examine the walls of known caves, and to explore new ones, in the hope of finding examples of this hitherto unimagined artistic heritage. Decorated caves are still being found, at the rate of about one a year, mainly in southern France and Spain. Most are dated to the Paleolithic period on the basis of the style of their figures, which can be compared with dated specimens of portable art. New advances in pigment analysis and in radiocarbon dating have also been applied to the materials used and have confirmed the Paleolithic date of five caves.

A tiny depiction of a mammoth, as well as the head of an ibex, was spotted on a smooth pebble just 3 in (8 cm) long, found in the Petite Grotte de Bize in the Aude region of France. The site dates to around 17,000 years ago.

TUSKLESS MAMMOTHS

MANY DETAILS IN ICE AGE DEPICTIONS OF MAMMOTHS, such as the small ears and hairy tails in the engravings *(above)* at Gönnersdorf in Germany, are extremely realistic and coincide with observations on frozen mammoths in Siberia. It is curious, therefore, that although a few of the engravings of the adult mammoths from Gönnersdorf have small, short tusks, most have none at all. Similarly, there are no tusks on the far older mammoth figures from Vogelherd and Geissenklösterle in Germany, nor on an engraving from Kostenki in southern Russia, nor on a number of paintings and drawings on cave walls in France and Spain.

It has, therefore, been suggested that some mammoths had no tusks. An absence of tusks might have been associated with small body size, perhaps through a depletion in natural resources: a mammoth femur found in Gönnersdorf was only 35¼ in (90 cm) long, which indicates that the animal stood less than 8 ft (2.5 m) at the shoulder (at the low end of the range for woolly mammoths). But it is not certain that this one bone is representative of the Gönnersdorf mammoth population as a whole. Two pieces of ivory found at the site were of average size, indicating mammoths with large tusks. Although it is possible that these tusks were already in fossil form when they were introduced into the site by its occupants, two skeletons of similar age to the Gönnersdorf mammoths – found at Condover in England and Praz Rodet in Switzerland – also have average-sized tusks, suggesting that tusks were indeed the norm.

Conceivably, the Gönnersdorf engravings point to a physical difference between the sexes, with the females in some regions perhaps lacking tusks altogether, as in many populations of Asian elephants today. Since, however, there is no fossil evidence for this, most specialists would prefer to attribute the lack of tusks in paintings and sculpture simply to artistic licence. At La Marche, for example, some mammoths are depicted with long tusks, some have short tusks, and others have none at all.

In the Grotte du Mammouth – the "mammoth cave" – at Domme in France, a mammoth was sculpted in bas-relief 13 ft (4 m) above the present cave floor. Although it is 4 ft (1.2 m) high, it went unnoticed until 1978, when it was caught in the glare of artificial light.

Ice Age wall art encompassed an impressive variety and mastery of techniques. Engraving was by far the most common method used, and the natural formations of walls often directly inspired, or were incorporated in, the representation of figures. In areas of France where the soft limestone could be easily carved, bas-relief sculpture has also been found, always in parts of rock shelters or caves where natural light could reveal the contours of the image. The mammoth of Domme in the Dordogne is an outstanding example of this technique.

> *"A single cave in France contains almost half the world's Ice Age depictions of mammoths"*

Of the cave sites where mammoths have been depicted, a few stand out from the others. First and foremost is the huge cave of Rouffignac, also in the Dordogne, with its miles of decorated galleries. It contains almost half of the 360 or so depictions of mammoths known in the world – a unique concentration of engravings and black drawings. Some on one low ceiling are so big – more than 6 ft (2 m) in length – that it would have been impossible for the artists to see the whole image at once.

Other notable groups of figures in France include the 37 engravings in Les Combarelles (many of them quite cursory, limited to a partial, sketched outline) and those of Pech-Merle, Font de Gaume, Bernifal, Jovelle, Chabot and Arcy-sur-Cure. There are also examples in Spain, as well as in Russia, where paintings have been discovered at Kapova and Ignatiev in the Urals.

Most of the mammoths portrayed show few signs of movement, except for little touches of animation such as a raised tail or curled trunk. Nor are the mammoths generally presented in scenes; however, one notable exception is the

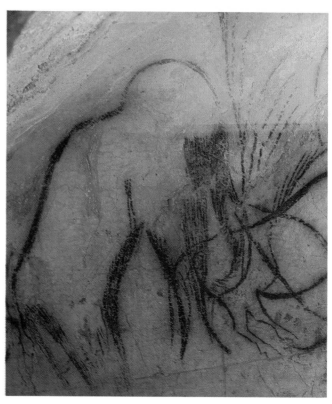

Mammoths appear among horses, bison and wild cattle in the Black Frieze at Pech-Merle, in the Lot region of France. Experiments with materials similar to those used 15,000 years ago have shown that the entire frieze, consisting of 25 animals and stretching for 23 ft (7 m), may have taken the artist only an hour to complete.

A dramatic engraving of a woolly mammoth, from the cave of Rouffignac in France, not only deftly captures the distinctive physical shape of the animal but also suggests something of its imposing character. Its real size is 2 ft 7 in (80 cm) high by 4 ft (1.2 m) long. The lumps protruding from the rock face are nodules of flint.

This highly stylized beast drawn with fingers dipped in red clay is one of the most unusual depictions of a mammoth produced in the Ice Age. It was discovered in 1940 in the French cave of La Baume Latrone. The body, 4 ft (1.2 m) long, is in profile, but the short tusks are both depicted as if seen from the front. In contrast to the boldness of the rest of the mammoth, the mouth and trunk tip seem to have been painted with particular attention to detail.

An outline sketch of a mammoth was engraved into the ceiling of the Grotte du Cheval at Arcy-sur-Cure in France. Most cave art figures are fairly modest in scale: at 1 ft 7 in (50 cm) long, this one is of typical size.

The rare depictions of mammoths or mastodons in the southwest of the United States are all petroglyphs, hammered into rock faces. This petroglyph is on the bank of the Colorado River near Moab in Utah.

A mammoth found in the cave at Bernifal, in the Dordogne in France, was painted in yellow on the ceiling of a high natural chimney. Although this has long been a well-known cave, the painting was not spotted until the 1970s.

apparent depiction of a whole group of mammoths in the cave at Rouffignac, drawn as two lines facing each other *(see pp.86–87)*. Pairs of mammoths are sometimes found head to head, perhaps greeting one another.

Outside western Europe and the Urals, no depictions of mammoths have ever been found in caves or rock shelters. However, a small number of what appear to be mammoth figures have been discovered in the open air on the Colorado Plateau in the southwestern United States. These petroglyphs (figures hammered into the rock) may be the only authentic contemporary representations of mammoths in North America. Whereas all European depictions are of the woolly mammoth, *Mammuthus primigenius*, the Colorado Plateau petroglyphs must be based on the American species, the Columbian mammoth, or conceivably the mastodon.

HUTS MADE OF MAMMOTH BONES

Some 15,000 years ago the natural accumulations of mammoth bones in eastern Europe provided a convenient source of building materials. Skulls and other large bones were used for the foundations, while roofs probably consisted of hides slung over a structure of wood or bones and tusks.

All the bone huts so far discovered are variations on the same architectural theme. The arrangement of the huts, however, varies from site to site: in some cases they may be only a few feet apart, whereas in others they are scattered over a large area.

Many of these camps were primarily occupied in the winter and were the scene of a wide variety of activities – cooking, toolmaking, hide preparation and the production of art objects. How long they were inhabited is difficult to estimate, although the thousands of artefacts at some sites suggest a prolonged stay by a large group.

Various tools made of mammoth bone have been found at the Upper Paleolithic site of Avdeevo in Russia. These include elegant spatulas (see p.109) and two spoons (right).

Pairs of tusks may have been used to create imposing hut entrances, or may have been incorporated into the structure of the hut as roof supports. In cold weather, entrances would probably have been kept as small as possible to keep the heat in, as is the case with igloos.

Scores of mammoth carcasses were required to produce the number of bones present at each site. Some huts contain bones from a number of mammoths which had clearly died over a span of several thousand years.

MAMMOTH-BONE HUTS

During the last Ice Age quantities of mammoth bones lay strewn across various parts of central and eastern Europe – enough for humans to consider using them to build dwellings in sites where caves and rock shelters were not available. A total of more than 70 mammoth-bone dwellings is now known from about 15 sites on the central Russian Plain, particularly in the Ukraine along the River Dnieper and its tributaries, with single examples also in southern Poland (Kraków, Spadzista Street) and Moravia (Milovice) in the Czech Republic.

As long as 40,000 years ago, Neanderthals had used mammoth bones for the construction of shelters. At the Ukrainian site of Molodova, a large oval area of mammoth bones containing 15 hearths is thought to have been a structure in which the bones held down skins stretched over a wooden framework. But the most spectacular structures of this type were produced by fully modern people between 30,000 and 14,000 years ago.

At first sight the remains look like disorderly heaps of bones – in fact mammoth-bone dwellings were not recognized as such by archaeologists for many years. Since medieval times, the villagers of Kostenki in Russia had been finding large bones (the name comes from *kost'*, the Russian word for bone); a legend claimed that they were the bones of antediluvian giants. In the 18th century Tsar Peter the Great took an interest in the finds, but attributed them to war elephants from a wandering army of ancient Greeks.

A century later Kostenki was recognized as a prehistoric occupation site, but the existence of mammoth-bone structures was not suspected until excavations during the 1920s: until then the bone heaps were thought to be food refuse.

The huts were round or oval, between 13 and 22 ft (4 and 7 m) across at the base, enclosing from 86 to 258 sq ft (8 to 24 m²) of living space. At some sites they are set out in rows, at others in a rough circle or rectangle, depending on the terrain. Mammoth skulls, jaws, shoulder blades and other large bones formed the foundations, and tusks may have been used to create a framework for a porch or entrance; in some cases they were joined together with a bone sleeve, while in others they were simply left in their sockets in the skull. The roof is likely to have been a wooden frame covered with animal skins or turf held in place by more bones and tusks. In some, the floor was 16 in (40 cm) below surface level, making the huts semi-subterranean.

> ### *"The remains of more than 70 Ice Age huts built out of mammoth bones have been found across the Russian Plain"*

Many of the dwellings include the site of a fireplace in which the occupants burned bone as fuel, no doubt because timber was so scarce in these regions. Bone burns well as long as it retains its collagen and fat content; indeed, some Eskimo groups today still use bone as a fuel source. The first few minutes are smoky and smelly, until the fat has been scorched off, but after this bone provides a long burn, with a steady flame and a high heat yield. Suitably fresh or "green" bone was probably stored in pits in the permafrost or simply scavenged from carcasses preserved by the extreme cold.

The best-known bone-hut site is probably Mezhirich in the Ukraine, where at least five dwellings have been found dating to about 15,000 years ago. The construction of dwelling No. 1 is typical; in this, a total of 25 skulls was placed in a semicircle to form the interior base wall, their frontal bones facing inward and their tusk sockets buried in the ground. These were supplemented by 20 mammoth

Even after 15,000 years of disuse, mammoth-bone hut No. 4 at Mezhirich, in the Ukraine, gives a powerful impression of its original scale. The structure has collapsed inward, producing the jumbled mass of bones in the living area. By sectioning off the site with ropes and carefully numbering the bones, archaeologists were able to reassemble the site like a jigsaw puzzle.

pelvises and 10 limb bones, also fixed into the ground. On top of this foundation were 12 more skulls, 30 shoulder blades, 20 femurs, 15 pelvises and segments of 7 vertebral columns. Higher still, and probably used to hold down the roof-hides, were 35 tusks.

Some 95 lower jaws, placed chin-down, one on top of the other in a herringbone design, formed an outer wall, which has various interpretations. It may have acted as a retaining wall or held down the hides that covered the shelter; alternatively, it may have provided a layer of heat insulation between the hides and the snow that drifted against the jaw bones – or may simply have been a supply of raw material and fuel. Mammoth leg bones were placed upright at the small entrance. Inside was a mammoth skull decorated with zigzags and dots of red ochre, which one Soviet archaeologist interpreted as representing flames and sparks.

Other dwellings at Mezhirich are variations on this basic theme, with jaws placed chin-upward, for instance, or with a range of different bone types used in the base wall. Some bones have holes drilled into them and may have been held in position by bone or wood inserted into them as pegs; alternatively, they could have been used for suspending garments to dry, or for hanging up meat and other necessities, or even as peepholes in the outer layer of the walls or roof.

The amount of labour and materials involved in these structures varied. Dwelling No. 1 at Mezhirich, for example, is reckoned to contain some 385 bones weighing a total of 46,300 lb (21,000 kg); other huts at the site contained between 33,000 and 42,000 lb (15,000 and 19,000 kg) of bone. At other sites no more than 2,200 lb (1,000 kg) were used for each dwelling. Archaeologists have estimated that it would have taken 10 people at least five or six days to build dwelling No. 1, and four or five days for each of the others. The smaller dwellings at other sites may have required no more than half a day each. To this must be added the labour involved in collecting the bones in the first instance: some idea of what this entailed can be gauged from the fact that a

NORTHERN PEOPLES TODAY, SUCH AS the Eskimo and Samoyed, always have a dance hut in their villages. This is the same size as a dwelling, but is set aside for song and dance, entertainment and ritual, and is used especially in the festivals of autumn and winter, at the start of the winter hunt. The site of Mezin in the Ukraine, dating to about 20,000 years ago, contains a mammoth-bone hut which may have been devoted to a similar use. Although the interior space was probably too constricted by roof supports to allow for dancing, the floor appears to have been kept clear of domestic refuse – a sign that it was perhaps used for ritual purposes.

A set of mammoth bones painted with red ochre and a reindeer-antler hammer were found in a group on the floor of the hut. Originally they were thought to be art or cult objects. However, subsequent analysis revealed areas of surface damage on all of them, as well as signs of smoothing, thinning, polishing or rubbing. The conclusion must be that they formed a set with some common function that involved concentrated blows, as well as rubbing and polishing through prolonged contact with hands. The reindeer antler has the polish of long use on its handle, while its working surface is very worn and its spongy pores have reddish ochre in them, picked up from the decorated surfaces on the mammoth bones.

A controversial interpretation of this evidence is that these bones were used as musical instruments, in a kind of Ice Age orchestra. The bones were presumably percussion instruments, struck with hammers. The mammoth shoulder blade *(above)*, decorated with linear and zigzag stripes in red ochre, bears traces of polish on the neck, corresponding to the positions of the palm and thumb, suggesting that this was where it was held with the left hand, while the right hand struck the body of the instrument with a hammer. Other areas of wear possibly indicate that the bone was hit in different places to vary the tone of the note produced.

A femur had had the soft, spongy material extracted from inside, perhaps to increase its resonance. It may have been played horizontally, like a xylophone, perhaps on a support. A half-pelvis and two jaw bones, likewise painted with red parallel stripes, appear to have been used in a similar way. A piece of bone from a skull, decorated with spots of red colour, was probably used as a drum: the cranium's cellular structure creates an unusual resonance, as experiments with modern elephant skulls have shown.

Finally, among this set of bones was a "bracelet" made of five very springy rings of ivory, perforated so that they could be tied together, and all incised with a herringbone design. This too may have been a kind of musical instrument, producing a sound similar to castanets.

The hut also contained 4½–6½ lb (2–3 kg) of red and yellow ochre as well as bone pendants, needles and awls. Some archaeologists have speculated that these may have been used to prepare for ritual performances.

In 1976, after restoration and conservation at the Hermitage Museum in St. Petersburg, the original Mezin instruments were played by a group of percussionists using bone hammers under the direction of V.I. Kolokolnikov of the Kiev State Orchestra. The musicians were able to produce a variety of resonant sounds: using their knowledge of the music of northern peoples today, they were able to give a rendering of what Ice Age music might have sounded like.

The interpretation of the bones at Mezin as musical instruments has led to a re-examination of earlier finds from other sites bearing similar traces of decoration and wear. Several bones found at Gorodok and Mezhirich in the Ukraine and Předmostí in the Czech Republic, for example, may also have been musical instruments.

defleshed and dried mammoth skull with relatively small tusks weighs a minimum of 220 lb (100 kg) and often far more, while the other large bones are by no means light. However, since the huts were no doubt very sturdy and robust and would last from one season's visit to the next, it was probably worth investing a considerable amount of time and effort in them.

It is obvious that a huge number of mammoth skeletons was available in these areas. Some of the bones used in the dwellings might conceivably have come from kills or even mass-drives by the occupants, but it is more probable that the building materials came from carcasses, the product of natural deaths or of the predation of mammoths by other animals. Rivers and streams would also have created natural accumulations of bones, and these would have remained unburied and relatively fresh under periglacial conditions. (The question of whether mammoths were hunted, or whether their remains were simply scavenged, is discussed more fully in chapter 5; *see pp.126–131.*)

"The age of the mammoth bones used in individual huts spans 8,000 years"

The inconsistent state of preservation of the bones suggests that some were recovered from long-dead skeletons: radiocarbon dating has revealed that bones used within a single structure at Mezin, in the Ukraine, range in antiquity from 22,000 to 14,000 years. Many bones had been gnawed by carnivores: studies of modern elephant carcasses left in exposed sites show how scavengers soon scatter the bones as they pull carcasses apart.

The Mezhirich site contains the remains of at least 149 individual mammoths, and other Ukrainian sites also have about 100 each. Some of the bones might have been accumulated gradually, over the years, but in the case of Mezhirich dwelling No. 1 the 25 skulls used to build its foundation had to be collected before construction could begin. If the greater part of the material came from natural mammoth "cemeteries" or accumulations of bones, then it must be assumed that these lay close to the bone-hut sites.

The number of people occupying these hut groups is impossible to estimate, since it is not clear whether all the structures were dwellings, and whether they were all built and used simultaneously or in sequence. Archaeologists working at Mezin have assumed that the five huts formed a settlement for a number of families (about 50 people). Modern populations in the frozen north, whose members still construct huts of similar shape (though no longer of bones), use them for 15 to 20 years, as long as the wooden frame is sound; then they build a new settlement elsewhere. This may also have been the pattern with the Ice Age huts, although the useful life of a mammoth-bone hut may have been considerably longer, since bone is far more resistant than wood to frost, humidity and insects.

Most of the mammoth-bone hut groups have large storage pits, 6–26 ft (2–8 m) long, which were dug up to 5 ft (1.5 m) deep into the permafrost and then filled with hundreds of mammoth and other bones, presumably as a supply of food, fuel and construction material. Most also have distinct "activity" areas, where various stone or bone tools were manufactured.

MAMMOTH-BONE TOOLS

A wide range of tools and even furniture was also made out of mammoth bones. At Kostenki the shoulder blade of an adult mammoth seems to have been set vertically in the ground, inside a hut; its upper surface, 13–16 in (33–40 cm) above the ground, would have reached the chest of a seated person,

A number of mammoth-bone spatulas have been found at Avdeevo in Russia, a site dating to 22,000–12,000 years ago. The handles of many of them have been decorated with catlike heads. It is not clear what function such spatulas performed.

Two cleavers made from mammoth shoulder blades were found at a site in South Dakota where mammoths had been butchered. They were sharpened by flaking away pieces of bone. The areas of flaking have been marked on the cleaver to the left.

and the dents and notches in it suggest that it may have been used as some kind of work surface or anvil. Mammoth foot bones bearing percussion marks may also have been used as anvils, even by Neanderthals – as, for example, in caves in the Crimea such as Kiik Koba. These compact, cuboid bones, about 8 in (20 cm) across, would have been ideal for this purpose. Paddle-shaped shovels, 10 in (26 cm) long with blades 2½ in (6 cm) wide, cut from femurs, have been found at Předmostí and Kostenki, as have ribs sharpened at one end by chopping – possibly to make digging sticks. A rib found at Kostenki appears to have been used as a palette for mixing pigments. Předmostí has also produced what appears to be a fishing hook of mammoth bone, possibly about 25,000 years old.

"Cleavers, spatulas, wrenches and shovels were fashioned out of mammoth bone"

In the United States, at the Lange-Ferguson site in South Dakota, an adult and a juvenile mammoth were butchered 10,670 years ago using two heavy cleaver-choppers made from the flat part of a mammoth shoulder blade. At Murray Springs, Arizona, an intriguing tool was discovered in 1967. It was a perforated baton, 10 in (26 cm) long, made of a mammoth femur and dating to about 11,230 years ago. It is thought to be a shaft-wrench – a tool for straightening wood or bone to make the shafts of spears. Shaft-straighteners have also been found at Mezin and Molodova, and a square-headed specimen was found in the Sungir graves *(see p.112)*.

Mammoth bones played a part in burials and have been found covering a number of Upper Paleolithic graves in Europe, such as a grave in a deep pit at Kostenki. Shoulder blades are wide enough to span most of a human body,

protecting it like a coffin lid from the earth heaped over it. This practice appears to have been common in Moravia: a scapula was used to cover the grave site at Brno II, while the grave of a woman at Dolní Věstonice had a scapula as well as a piece of a mammoth pelvis over it.

By far the most impressive Moravian example was the collective burial excavated at Předmostí in 1894, where 8 adults and 12 youngsters lay in an area 13 by 8 ft (4 by 2.5 m), covered by numerous large bones including two mammoth shoulder blades. Were these large, flat bones simply convenient covers, or do they denote some belief in the protective powers of the mighty mammoth? A similar question is raised by mammoth bones found at some Russian sites, where tail vertebrae and some foot bones, still in anatomical order, were carefully placed (or purposely hidden) in small pits near the hut walls.

FROM TUSKS TO ART OBJECTS

Consider the daunting task facing an Ice Age sculptor, armed with nothing more than the simplest stone tools, attempting to transform an enormous mammoth tusk into delicate figurines, bracelets and beads. Tusks could be up to 10–13 ft (3–4 m) long and weigh 185 lb (84 kg); and ivory itself is hard and unyielding.

There were several ways of cutting through a tusk. The most direct was, quite simply, to chop through it with stone axes. Alternatively, since it is easier to chisel ivory than to chop it, a deep, circular groove might be chiselled around the

The oldest known "art object" made from mammoth, this segment of a molar was polished – and one of its faces covered in red ochre – by Neanderthal hands 100,000 years ago. It was found at Tata, near Budapest.

cylinder. When only a narrow neck of ivory remained, it could be broken by a sharp blow, perhaps simply by striking the tusk against a rock. A tusk could also be split along its length. The crudest method was to strike off irregularly shaped flakes by hitting the tusk with a pointed stone tool. Where more regular shapes were desired, longitudinal grooves could be cut with a sharp-edged flint tool called a burin before the flake was struck off.

"Workable pieces of ivory had to be cut from the huge, tough tusks with Stone Age tools"

Obtaining long, thin pieces of ivory was more difficult. Craftsmen in Europe could apply techniques learnt through antler-working, which was widely practised in the last Ice Age, but the process was more complicated for ivory. It was relatively easy to cut grooves down an antler and then prise strips out, away from the soft, spongy centre, but since ivory does not have a soft centre, similar strips had to be chiselled out. After making the longitudinal grooves, the craftsman had to split off the strip, probably by using a bone chisel in the same way that modern Eskimos work walrus ivory. One remarkable unfinished specimen from the Russian site of Eliseevich has preliminary shallow grooves cut down the whole length of a tusk.

Having broken down the raw material into pieces or strips of ivory, the Ice Age artists then set about fashioning it into an impressive range of tools, figurines and ornaments. They used a variety of techniques, involving whittling, cutting and engraving.

Mattocks – chisel-like tools – were produced at Mezhirich from sections of tusk and bevelled at one end to make a massive kind of spatula that may have been used to dig pits in the hard ground. Narrow ivory chippings were also sharpened into stabbing or thrusting weapons.

At Eliseevich a 10-in (26-cm) dagger was made from the end of a tusk, its natural point sharpened by whittling. The handles of such tools were often engraved with cross-hatched cuts to provide a firm grip.

The Moravian sites contained numerous ivory tools, including a spoon from Dolní Věstonice that was decorated with an engraved geometric motif. The German site of Kniegrotte contained a kind of large comb as well as a fragment of a unique ivory harpoon, with barbs on both sides and with engraved decoration along its length. Eyed needles made of ivory have been found at Mezin.

Ice Age craftsmen were also able to bend or, alternatively, straighten ivory. A child's grave at Mal'ta in central Siberia contained a diadem made with a thin hoop of ivory. Conversely, the Ice Age children's graves at Sungir in Russia, dating to around 25,000 years ago, contained two heavy spears of straightened ivory 8 ft and 5 ft (2.4 m and 1.6 m) long. How these were made remains a puzzle, considering the marked natural curvature of mammoth tusks. Steaming is the most likely solution: the ivory was probably soaked in water for a long time before being held over a fire and heated to 250°F (120°C) or more in damp conditions to prevent it from cracking when its shape was altered. In an interesting experiment carried out some 50 years ago, the Russian scientist Mikhail Gerassimov thoroughly soaked a piece of ivory for five days, then wrapped it in a pre-soaked fresh animal skin and placed it in the hot ashes of a

An intricate and apparently abstract design has been engraved into the tip of a tusk dating to about 27,000 years ago, found at the open-air site of Pavlov in Moravia. Some archaeologists have interpreted the engraving as a mountain landscape, or as a chart or map.

The body of a child in a 25,000-year-old grave at Sungir in Russia lies surrounded by carved ivory objects. These include numerous beads, a spoked disc and a spear of straightened ivory, which lies alongside the skeleton.

camp fire. After 1¾ hours the skin had charred and fallen to pieces and the ivory was extremely hot. On cooling, it could easily be whittled with a flint knife, and thin strips were flexible enough to bend. Siberian and Alaskan Eskimos have an alternative method of softening bone and ivory for carving: they soak them in urine.

Similar techniques may have been used to make the boomerang found in the Polish cave of Oblazowa. With a total span of 2 ft 3 in (70 cm), it is up to 2½ in (6 cm) wide and ½ in (1.5 cm) thick. One side preserves the external, convex tusk surface, whereas the other has been polished almost flat, forming an elegant aerofoil section with thin, tapering edges.

Experiments with a cast suggest that this boomerang was of the type used by modern Australian Aborigines to stun or kill prey animals. It was not designed to come back to the thrower – indeed, those that do so are often toys rather than weapons. The very existence of this unique ivory object is vital to our knowledge of Ice Age hunting skills, since killing sticks can be accurate up to about 660 ft (200 m), much farther than a man can throw a spear or stone.

"The bodies of children buried at Sungir were each adorned with about 3,500 beads made of mammoth ivory"

The Sungir burials included numerous ivory objects besides the remarkable ivory spears. There were three bodies: a 60-year-old man in one grave, two children aged 8 and 13 placed head to head in the other. They were surrounded by ivory staves, daggers, long bodkins, small carvings (including a flat, perforated ivory horse) and two pierced ivory discs. Around the man's upper arms were ivory bracelets, with holes for lacing them together (like the bracelet of Mezin, *see p.115*). Each body was adorned with about 3,500 beads

of mammoth ivory, arranged in rows across the forehead, across the body, down the arms and legs and around the ankles. It is probable that these beads were strung on lengths of sinew, which were then attached to items of clothing that have since disintegrated.

It has been estimated that it would have taken about 45 minutes to make each Sungir bead, if the whole process of cutting the tusk, shaping the bead and drilling the hole is included. This means that each body had 2,625 hours of beadwork buried with it. The standardized and uniform appearance of these objects suggests that they were produced by a limited number of people.

In western Europe, far more ivory beads have been found in places where people lived than at burial sites. A series of round and basket-shaped beads in various stages of manufacture has been unearthed in the southern French rock shelter of Blanchard, dating to about 30,000 years ago. These demonstrate clearly the sequence of production. Small rods of ivory, up to 4 in (10 cm) long, were circum-incised and then snapped into sections, separated into pairs, then worked in a dumbbell form before being perforated and separated for the final shaping and polishing.

The oldest boomerang in the world was made of mammoth ivory 20,000 years ago. It was found in the cave of Oblazowa in Poland in 1987. Contrary to popular belief, such curved killing sticks are not restricted to Australia. Wooden boomerangs have been found in prehistoric sites in the Netherlands and Jutland and in Egyptian tombs. This is, however, the only known ivory example.

Given the crude nature of most Stone Age tools, the production of ivory tools, weapons and beads is impressive enough. But it is the statuettes and figurines – and notably the "Venus" figurines – produced by prehistoric carvers that show that they were capable not simply of remarkable feats of craftsmanship, but of startling artistry as well.

"Many of the most striking carvings of prehistory were made from mammoth ivory"

Ivory is easy enough to engrave along the grain, but not across it. Nevertheless, by scraping away the surface ivory it was possible to make a design stand out from a background, rather like a cameo, and images of figures were produced in this way. Fully three-dimensional figurines were also carved from ivory at an early date: indeed, some of the earliest known pieces of Ice Age art are the ivory statuettes which come from a series of sites in southwestern Germany. These include animal and human figurines from Vogelherd and the fragments of two mammoths from Geissenklösterle. The

"VENUS" FIGURINES

WITH THE RARE EXCEPTION OF a few clearly identifiable males, most Ice Age carvings of humans are female. Several of these are highly distinctive images of obese women, with enormous breasts and buttocks. A typical example *(left)* from the Russian site of Avdeevo stands 4 in (10 cm) high, and is one of a series that dates to about 22,000 years ago. In the 1860s the first carving of this kind to be found was labelled the *"Vénus impudique"* (the shameless Venus) and this anachronistic name is now applied to all such figures. Not all of them, however, show such exaggerated proportions: many depict normal females – and at every stage of adult life.

Only a handful of west European Venus figurines are carved from ivory – stone was the usual material – but in central, and especially eastern, Europe and Siberia, mammoth ivory was widely used. These ivory carvings were found over a range of some 2,000 miles (3,000 km), from southwestern France to Russia; then there is a 3,000-mile (5,000-km) gap to the nearest Siberian specimens.

In Ice Age depictions of humans, details such as eyebrows, nostrils, fingers, navels and nipples are generally rare. The arms on Venus figurines are usually held close to the body, resting on the breasts or stomach. Few statuettes, apart from those from Siberia, have any facial detail. A number of eastern statuettes – from Avdeevo and Kostenki, for example – seem to be wearing bracelets; clothing, however, is rarely clear, although belts are occasionally depicted.

While most of the examples in western Europe came from caves and rock shelters, those of the east came from open-air settlements and seem to have had a special role in the home. Intact female figurines have often been found in special pits in hut floors. For example, one found in Kostenki in 1983, and dating to about 23,000 years ago, was standing upright in a small pit and facing the centre of the living area and the hearths; the pit was filled with soil mixed with red ochre and was capped by a mammoth shoulder blade. Such statuettes are often interpreted by Russian archaeologists as mother- or ancestor-figures, or as mistresses of the house.

Russia and Siberia include many female statuettes and stylized birds, several of which are decorated with elaborate geometrical markings.

Some idea of how the Russian figurines were made is provided by the finds at Kostenki and other sites. These are so numerous that there are examples of every stage of creation, from crude rough-outs to highly polished finished items. To make a figure, a piece of tusk was probably first prised out by cutting two deep grooves into the ivory; this was rubbed into rough shape with sandstone, and a burin or other form of sharp blade was used to carve the legs and other details. The finished piece may then have been polished with leather straps – although long handling would also have smoothed away some of the inevitable marks of the arduous and time-consuming labour that ivory carving demanded.

MAMMOTH IVORY IN THE MODERN WORLD

The importance of the mammoth to prehistoric people in some parts of central and eastern Europe can hardly be overestimated: in fact, human occupation of some areas seems to have depended almost entirely on the existence and the presence of the animal. Its bones were used for construction and as fuel, as well as for tools and even musical instruments, while its tusks were fashioned into ivory tools, jewellery, art and ritual objects.

Mammoth ivory continued to be exploited even after the mammoths' extinction and, thousands of years later, it is still being used. Even today it remains a vital resource to some communities of craftsmen.

effortless grace of the horse from Vogelherd (*below, 2*), which has been dated to around 30,000 years ago, suggests that it was preceded by a long tradition in ivory carving.

The rich collection from France includes a delicate, tiny human head from Brassempouy; the Venus figurine from Lespugue, with her arms resting on her large breasts; a superb horse statuette from Lourdes; and two reindeer from Bruniquel. Moravia in the Czech Republic yielded the well-known head from Dolní Věstonice, and the mammoth from Předmostí *(see p.98)*. The numerous specimens from

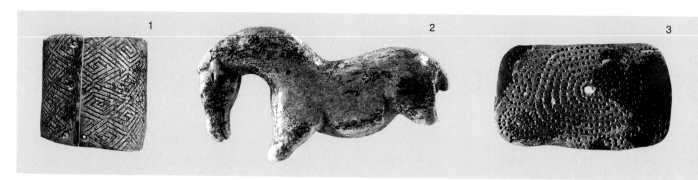

A grave at Brno in Moravia, dating to around 25,000 years ago, contained a unique ivory doll. Like those of a marionette, its head, arms and legs were clearly once fastened to the body. The doll is 5 in (13 cm) tall.

Fossil ivory is mentioned in Chinese writings of the fourth century B.C., and it was probably already being imported to China at that time. There are records of it being exported from Russia to central Asia and Europe in the 10th century A.D.: the throne of the Mongol Khan Kuyuk (1206–48), grandson of Genghis Khan, was allegedly made of it.

The first fossil ivory known to reach western Europe was a tusk purchased from Samoyeds in Siberia and brought to London in 1611. After Russia conquered Siberia in 1582 it became a regular commodity, and the tsars tried to monopolize this trade. From the mid-18th century onward, the Siberian ivory industry expanded greatly, and the statistics are impressive. For instance, a single collector returned from the New Siberian Islands in 1821 with 18,000 lb (8,165 kg) of ivory, equivalent to 50 animals. During the first half of the 19th century, 36,000 lb (16,330 kg) were sold at Yakutsk every year – in addition to the smaller amounts sold at other towns. Some authors speak of large boats on the Lena River laden with mammoth ivory, and it has been estimated that during the first 250 years after the Russian occupation tusks from at least 46,750 animals must have been excavated – and that in later years an average of 250 animals needed to be found annually to meet the demand. In the 19th century mammoth ivory became a significant source of raw materials for billiard balls, piano keys and numerous ornamental objects, such as jewellery boxes, combs and figurines.

Siberia was once considered to hold an inexhaustible supply of this "white gold"; but it is a non-renewable resource which needs to be protected. Locals, however, claim that they have industrial quantities to offer – some estimates suggest that there are 10 million mammoths still lying in the Siberian deep freeze.

MAMMOTHS TO THE RESCUE?

In the past few years mammoth ivory has come to further prominence, as a result of the ban on elephant ivory. If there is so much mammoth ivory in the world, could it be used to help save its modern counterpart from extermination? Certainly it has proved its worth to many contemporary ivory carvers.

"There may be 10 million mammoth carcasses lying in the deep freeze of the Siberian permafrost"

For example, the little town of Erbach im Odenwald in Hessen, Germany, has specialized in ivory carving since 1783, when the "Ivory Count", Franz I, introduced the art to the community and opened a workshop for that purpose in his palace for the bone carvers and wood turners of the area to improve their economic lot. Ever since, Erbach has been the centre of ivory carving in Germany, winning renown for its carved trinkets, bracelets, boxes and seals.

4

Many prehistoric objects carved from mammoth ivory show great craftsmanship and a remarkably sophisticated sense of design. A herringbone pattern has been used in the broad bracelet from Mezin (1), which is about 15,000 years old, while the ivory plate (3) from Mal'ta in Siberia is decorated with spiralling dots, which may represent a kind of calendar. The ivory horse from Vogelherd (2) measures under 2 in (5 cm) in length; dating back some 30,000 years, it is one of the world's oldest sculptures. The tiny pendant from Dolní Věstonice (4) dates to about 22,400 years ago and is only 1 in (2.5 cm) high. One of a series of eight, it may represent stylized breasts or testicles.

A mammoth tusk can make a valuable prize for anyone who discovers one in the rivers and thawing permafrost of Siberia. A single tusk today can fetch $1,000 or more.

The legislation of June 1989 following the Lausanne Conference prohibited the purchase of all new elephant tusks and threatened to put an end to the community's livelihood: the 30 remaining Erbach carvers, who once numbered 1,500, still used 1.5 tons of elephant ivory – between 200 and 300 tusks – every year. Unlike Steinway, manufacturing pianos in Hamburg, they could not switch from ivory to plastic. Then the town's mayor remembered the stocks of mammoth ivory in Siberia: being extinct, mammoths are not an endangered species. The first consignment of more than a ton, from Yakutia, arrived by truck in 1990.

"Mammoth ivory has saved the threatened livelihood of traditional ivory carvers"

Meanwhile, a considerable output of mammoth-ivory carving, both for the local tourist market and for export, continues to flow out of Yakutia. A similar craft industry has developed in Alaska.

There is a slight difference in colour between mammoth and elephant ivory. Mammoth ivory is usually not pure white but creamy or brown, with a slightly coarser texture. Some of the Japanese ivory craftsmen, who in 1988 imported 106 tons of African elephant tusks for piano keys and personal seals, have expressed disappointment in mammoth ivory, complaining of poor quality and cracks. On the other hand, exquisite and intricately carved objects have been made from mammoth tusk throughout the centuries in Russia, and are a match for anything made out of elephant ivory. The switch in materials has been a success in Erbach and has even increased interest and sales. With the growing global interest in mammoth ivory, the price has gone up; inevitably carcasses are plundered for their tusks alone while the rest is simply abandoned. The precious remains of an extinct animal, which could provide invaluable information for scientists, are being lost at a greater rate than ever before.

A further problem is posed by the substitution of mammoth ivory for elephant ivory. Several thousand ivory objects were seized at American ports of entry in 1990: about 95 percent of those examined turned out to be made of

A cross-section of a mammoth tusk reveals the characteristic criss-cross patterning of the ivory. In contrast to modern elephant ivory, mammoth ivory is often honey-coloured, although pure white tusks are also found.

A continuous tradition of mammoth-ivory carving links the prehistoric with the modern. This 19th-century casket is typical of the vast range of ivory products made in Yakutia, where the craft survives to this day.

mammoth ivory. It is relatively simple to distinguish ivory from bone or walrus tusk, since it alone has a cross-hatched grain. It can, however, be difficult to tell pale mammoth ivory from that of modern elephants, especially once carved. Proper analysis (for example, by microscopic observation and radiocarbon dating) is expensive and time-consuming, but if shipments are allowed to pass untested, what purports to be mammoth ivory, but is actually poached from elephants, may slip through the net. Customs officials cannot be expected to identify which is which: only an expert can tell them apart.

Thus, far from saving its modern cousin, the mammoth may unwittingly provide a means for its continued persecution by prolonging the ivory trade and masking an illicit trade in elephant ivory.

MODERN MAMMOTH-IVORY OBJECTS

THE ART OF MAMMOTH-IVORY CARVING HAS A LONG tradition in Russia – both Peter the Great and Catherine the Great pursued it as a hobby. It is witnessing a renaissance in modern Russia, where figurines and jewellery make popular tourist souvenirs.

EXTINCTION

T̲WENTY-FIVE THOUSAND YEARS AGO MAMMOTHS thrived across a vast territory, encompassing Europe, Asia and North America and covering millions of square miles. By ten thousand years ago, they had completely disappeared from the planet, except for a small population on a remote Siberian island, which itself died out a few thousand years later. What caused the demise of the once widespread mammoths? Various theories have been proposed, based on the apparent influence of humans and on crucial changes in the environment. Only by analysing and weighing the evidence is it possible to propose a convincing explanation of why, after four million years of evolution, the mammoths finally died out.

Several magnificent shaggy mammoths form part of the Black Frieze in the cave of Pech-Merle in southern France. Within a few thousand years, this common inhabitant of the Ice Age world had disappeared for ever.

The last woolly mammoths cling to the remaining areas of grassland in this scene set in southern England 12,000 years ago. As the climate became warmer and wetter, the advancing birch forests progressively reduced the extent of the mammoths' habitat and, according to one theory, led to their extinction.

Modern African elephants *help to maintain their savanna habitat by destroying trees, so preventing the spread of forest. Mammoths, in favourable circumstances, could similarly have helped maintain their steppe and parkland habitats. But they were unable to halt the inexorable advance of forest caused by climatic warming at the end of the last Ice Age.*

9,000 years ago

*As **the ice retreated** (white), forests (dark green) advanced over Europe from the south and east, replacing the mammoth steppe (light green). Although 12,000 years ago areas of steppe habitat still remained, they were fragmented and deteriorating, and could have been insufficient to support viable mammoth populations.*

***There is some evidence that as feeding conditions changed** for the worse, mammoths became smaller. Examples are seen in the Berelekh remains from eastern Siberia and the Sevsk population from European Russia (see pp.50–51), both less than 14,000 years old and no more than 8 ft (2.4 m) in height. But this effect is not seen everywhere – the later skeletons from Condover, England, and Praz Rodet, Switzerland, are of normal size.*

A mammoth is caught in a pit trap in southern North America, about 11,000 years ago. Historical elephant hunting in Africa and India has shown that pit traps are an effective means of immobilizing a large animal. However, the archaeological evidence for mammoth hunting by prehistoric people is not extensive.

Pitfall traps may have been dug on paths used by mammoths and camouflaged with branches and brushwood. If the sides were smooth and sloping, converging at the bottom, the animal's legs would be pinned together, leaving it helplessly exposed to the hunters' weapons.

Clovis points, finely carved spearheads of stone, were hafted onto long shafts with pitch and sinew. They were efficient weapons which could penetrate thick hide even when thrown from 70 ft (20 m) away. Modern replicas of Clovis points, attached to 7-ft (2-m) wooden shafts, can penetrate deeply into the back and rib cage of (already mortally wounded) elephants in Africa, as experiments have shown. The points are undamaged by repeated use unless they hit a rib.

One of the mammoths painted in the
Russian cave of Ignatiev (right), in
the southern Urals, has a curious motif
beneath it that might be interpreted as
a missile aimed at the animal; a second
such motif occurs about 2 ft (60 cm)
below the first. The mammoth itself is
about 9 in (23 cm) in length.

A rock painting from Ndedema Gorge in South Africa (left) depicts
a Zulu hunter about to hamstring an elephant. His iron axe indicates
that the image can be no more than 2,000 years old. Elephants in
Africa and Asia were not hunted in large quantities until the expansion
of the ivory trade in the 19th century.

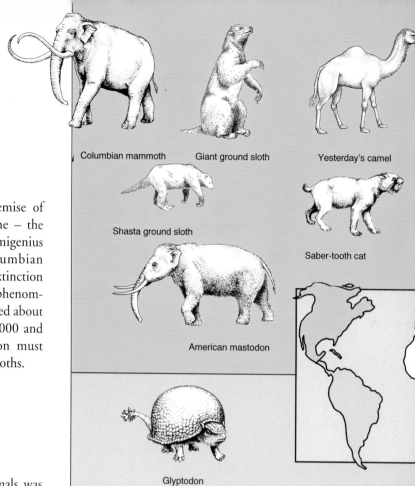

Columbian mammoth   Giant ground sloth   Yesterday's camel

Shasta ground sloth   Saber-tooth cat

American mastodon

Glyptodon

Litoptern   Notoungulate

Mammoth extinction involved the demise of two species at roughly the same time – the woolly mammoth Mammuthus primigenius acrossthe northern hemisphere, and the Columbian mammoth M. columbi in North America. But the extinction of the mammoths was also part of a much wider phenomenon of disappearance of large mammals, which started about 40,000 years ago and reached its peak between 12,000 and 10,000 years ago. A full explanation of extinction must account for all of these losses, not just that of mammoths.

"Numerous other large mammals became extinct at about the same time as mammoths"

The Late Pleistocene extinction of large mammals was the most recent in a series of periodic mass extinctions made apparent through the fossil record. The most celebrated is the demise of the dinosaurs, sea reptiles and other creatures around 65 million years ago. There are many theories for the cause of the dinosaurs' extinction, ranging from an asteroid impact to intense drought. These theories, hotly contested, relate to events in the very distant past. The extinction of the mammoths and other Pleistocene creatures is much closer to us in time, so there is a greater wealth of detailed information available, and a better chance of unravelling the factors that might have been responsible.

To understand the cause of mammoth extinction, it is essential first of all to establish as accurately as possible when it occurred, and to look at what was happening in the world at that time. The chief technique for determining the timing of extinction is radiocarbon dating, which gives, within a certain range of error, the date at which a particular specimen was alive. Radiocarbon dating of the most recent mammoth fossils from around the world indicates that mammoths did not die out everywhere at exactly the same time. In Eurasia

THE GLOBAL EXTINCTION OF LARGE MAMMALS

BETWEEN 40,000 AND 10,000 YEARS AGO MANY OF THE WORLD'S larger mammals died out. North America lost some 40 species, or 70 percent of the total. In addition to the mammoths, losses included various species of ground sloths, camels, deer and cats. South America lost 80 percent of its large mammals, including horses, armadillos and giant rodents. In Australia, more than 40 species, or 90 percent of the total, died out, including giant kangaroos, wombats and marsupials resembling rhinos and big cats. In Europe and northern Asia there were fewer large mammals to begin with but, in addition to the woolly mammoth, the woolly rhinoceros, cave bear and giant deer all became extinct.

Almost all of the species that vanished at this time were mammals weighing 90 lb (40 kg) or more; in general the larger the species, the more vulnerable it was to extinction. Thus, in northern Eurasia and North America, all species above a ton in weight were lost. In the middle size range – deer, antelopes and the like – some species died out while others survived. The smallest species – mice, shrews and so on – almost all survived.

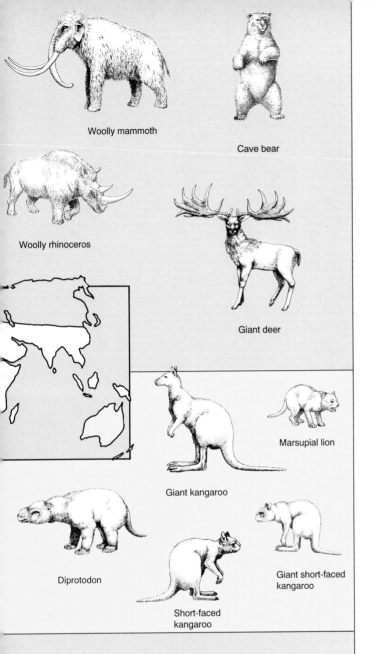

Woolly mammoth

Cave bear

Woolly rhinoceros

Giant deer

Marsupial lion

Giant kangaroo

Diprotodon

Short-faced kangaroo

Giant short-faced kangaroo

the southernmost populations, such as those in China, may have died out as early as 20,000 years ago. In Europe, and probably across much of the range eastward across Siberia, the mammoths had gone by about 12,000 years ago, although pockets survived up to a thousand years later.

Among the latest remains from Europe are skeletons from Condover in England and Praz Rodet in Switzerland, each around 12,000 years old, while the Berelekh mammoth "cemetery" in eastern Siberia stopped accumulating at a similar date, close to the time of disappearance in that area. The last continental populations lived in the northernmost parts of Siberia, the Taimyr Peninsula and surrounding areas, where they survived until about 10,000 years ago. Thus, in Eurasia, there seems to have been a general shrinking of the range northward before final extinction.

In North America, the latest woolly mammoth dates indicate survival until around 11,000 years ago. Data available for *M. columbi* suggest that its range was already shrinking by 12,000 years ago, but that it persisted in some areas, the latest date being 10,600 years ago at both Dent in Colorado and Big Bone Lick in Kentucky.

Various theories have been advanced to account for the extinction of the mammoths and other Late Pleistocene mammals. The only two in serious current contention are climatic and vegetational changes, and the impact of humans. The timing of mammoth extinction shows that its cause lies in events immediately preceding, and during, the interval 12,000 to 10,000 years ago. It happens that two major global revolutions were occurring at that time. First, there were dramatic changes in climate and vegetation as the last Ice Age drew to a close. Second, human populations were rapidly expanding and developing various new technologies, including those associated with hunting. The fact that these two potential causes coincided complicates the issue and makes the mystery of extinction more difficult to solve. But on the other hand, it renders the problem all the more intriguing and may even hold the key to the solution.

There are two main reasons for this imbalance. First, larger mammals tend to have smaller populations and are therefore more vulnerable to extinction. For example, a given area of habitat might have supported, say, 10 mammoths and 10,000 mice. A reduction in population size of both species by 90 percent would leave only one mammoth but 1,000 mice. The mammoth population would die out, while the mice would survive.

Second, large mammals have a much slower rate of reproduction and so find it more difficult to recover from any decimation of their numbers. A single pair of mice can, in a few years, give rise to several generations comprising thousands of individuals. Mammoths, on the other hand, were unlikely to reproduce before the age of about 15, had a gestation period of nearly two years, produced only a single calf per litter, and a female would be unlikely to give birth again for three or four years. Their rate of population growth was therefore slow, and a series of local die-offs – due either to hunting or to climatic change – could lead ultimately to extinction.

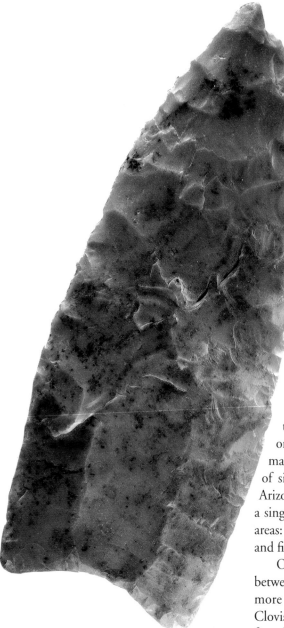

THE HUNTING THEORY

The theory that human hunters were responsible for the demise of mammoths and the rest of the vanished megafauna is termed "overkill". It is based on the relatively sudden extinctions in North America that happened within about 500 years (11,500–11,000 years ago) of the appearance of the "Clovis hunters", who are thought to have entered the continent across Beringia and then swept south. These big-game hunters, with their characteristic hafted, fluted stone spearpoints, take their name from the site of Clovis in New Mexico.

To decide whether overkill could have been responsible for the extinction of the mammoth, two questions have to be addressed. Did people hunt mammoths; and did they do so to a degree that could have caused extinction?

There are just over a dozen sites in the United States where sharpened stone spearpoints of the Clovis type have been found with remains of mammoths, but only one that seems to show truly direct evidence of mammoth hunting. At Naco, one of an important group of sites on a stretch of the San Pedro River in southern Arizona, no fewer than eight Clovis points were found with a single adult mammoth, virtually all of them in vital target areas: one at the base of the skull, one near a shoulder blade and five among the ribs and vertebrae.

Other sites show a greater or lesser degree of "association" between mammoth bones and Clovis points, and so provide more circumstantial evidence of mammoth hunting. At Clovis itself the remains of at least 15 mammoths were found, as well as those of horses, bison and other animals. Stone points were discovered with the remains of more than six mammoths. The skeletons were nearly complete, with the bones still in anatomical position, indicating only partial butchering. At the site of Lehner Ranch, 10 miles (16 km) away from Naco, 13 Clovis points were found, together with

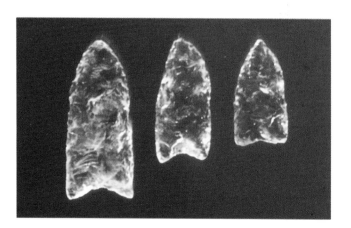

The Clovis point was a formidable weapon. Made of stone flaked to a razor-sharp tip and edge, it was bound to a wooden shaft up to 7 ft (2 m) in length. Jewel-like quartz points (left) were found with mammoth bones at the Lehner Ranch site in Arizona.

Excavation at Dent, Colorado, in 1932 produced the first clear evidence for the association of projectile points with mammoth remains in North America.

charcoal from two fires, and the remains of 13 *M. columbi* calves or young adults, dating to about 11,200 years ago.

A number of other such sites are known – for instance, Lange-Ferguson in South Dakota, Colby in Wyoming, Escapule in Arizona and Miami, Texas. The Dent site, in Colorado, contained the remains of 11 juveniles and young adult females, plus one adult male, together with three Clovis points and a number of boulders clearly brought there by people. The small number of stone points in sites such as this might indicate that most of the precious and reusable artefacts were simply collected and removed by the hunters. Alternatively it may be linked to the method of killing, since some archaeologists think that at Dent the herd was stampeded over the edge of a bluff. If this were the case, some animals may have been killed by the fall, while others were finished off with spears and boulders.

"Spearpoints have been found between mammoth bones"

It has been suggested that sites such as Dent could perhaps represent the killing of a matriarchal group of females and young. But the advantages of mass kills are debatable, and the accumulation of bones at such sites may, rather, represent a series of deaths over a decade or more, perhaps a mixture of natural mortality and kills. Even if

At Naco in Arizona
Clovis points were found wedged between mammoth bones. This is one of the few apparently clear indications of mammoth hunting.

animals were hunted, this may represent the "finishing off" of individuals already dying or in distress.

Another possible source of accumulated mammoth fossils is carcasses from groups of animals that died due to environmental stress. In Africa today, droughts can produce concentrations of elephant bones at water sources; these are dominated by vulnerable youngsters, a fact that could easily lead archaeologists to the erroneous conclusion that a whole family group had been slaughtered there. Humans may still have utilized such carcasses, leaving behind their stone tools, but without hunting the animals or contributing to their demise.

In some cases the association of artefacts and skeletons may be accidental and far from contemporaneous. Artefacts can accumulate near animal bones through being transported and redeposited by water, or through humans leaving objects at a waterhole or under a shady tree next to animal bones deposited long before or after. For example, at the Lamb Spring site in Colorado a bone bed contains about 40 mammoths as well as many other species, together with a battered stone cobble and a quartzite tool. Was human predation responsible, or natural mortality, or both? The different stages of weathering present, the evidence of gnawing on some bones, and the fact that the bone breakage could easily have been caused by the trampling of other animals have led some specialists to see this as a predominantly – or totally – natural accumulation.

In short, although regular mammoth hunting in

America cannot be ruled out, clear evidence is limited. In Eurasia the possible contribution of hunting to the demise of mammoths and other large mammals is even more uncertain.

One apparently clear indication of prehistoric elephant hunting is the site of Lehringen in Germany, dating to 125,000 years ago, where a wooden spear more than 7 ft (2 m) long was found in fragments between the ribs of a straight-tusked elephant, *Palaeoloxodon antiquus*, suggesting an early capacity to kill, or at least finish off, a proboscidean. Other sites, although they have been labelled "kill sites", in fact provide evidence of no more than carcass processing. Near Tomsk, in western Siberia, the broken and splintered bones of a young mammoth were found close to a fireplace together with hundreds of stone blades and flakes. At Kraków, Spadzista Street, in Poland the remains of at least 60 mammoths have been found, dating to about 21,000 years ago. The presence of 19 hyoids (tongue bones), all of which bear cutmarks, suggests that the occupants of this site had feasted on roast mammoth tongues.

The existence of mammoth-bone huts *(see pp.106–9)* has led many archaeologists to assume that mammoth meat was the staple diet of their occupants, who hunted and killed every animal represented by the bones. The first major accumulation of bone stockpiles to be found was that of Předmostí in Moravia, known since the 16th century, but excavated in the late 19th century. The remains of 1,000 mammoths of all ages were found, with a high proportion of 10–12 year olds. These vulnerable youngsters, just venturing away from the protection of the herd, could have been attractive to human hunters, but equally so to predators such as hyenas, whose kills people might have scavenged.

The presence of gnawed bones in the huts and bone accumulations of central and eastern Europe, and of bones of different dates and degrees of weathering within the same structure, points to the conclusion that they were probably collected and scavenged from natural accumulations in nearby localities and brought in as building materials, raw materials for tools, and as fuel. This, in turn, suggests that mammoths were less significant as a food source than might be thought from the quantity and prominence of their remains in these sites, where reindeer or horse were generally the staples. The occasional mammoth may well have been hunted and killed nonetheless.

Whether mammoths were killed or scavenged, they were probably not difficult to butcher. In an experiment designed to investigate finds at Olduvai Gorge in Tanzania, where an array of simple tools had been found with early elephant skeletons, it was shown that lava and flint flakes could easily slice through the hide of a dead elephant. The Efe pygmies of Zaire occasionally kill elephants: they can butcher the carcasses without chopping, cutting or marking the bones. In other words, the presence of cutmarks on prehistoric bones may well indicate that butchery took place, but their absence – as is the case in the majority of fossils – does not rule out the possibility that the carcass was processed by humans.

A variety of barbed "harpoons", finely carved in antler, demonstrate the sophistication of hunting technology at the end of the Ice Age in Europe. They were probably designed primarily for fishing, but there is evidence for their use on larger prey such as elks.

LA COTTE: MAMMOTH HUNTING ON JERSEY

AT LEAST ONE POSSIBLE EPISODE OF MAMMOTH HUNTING, dating to more than 128,000 years ago, can be seen in a ravine at La Cotte de St. Brelade, on the English Channel island of Jersey. The bones of about 20 mammoths (adults and young) and 5 rhinos were found here in two apparently deliberate heaps, some set up vertically, and some shoulder blades stacked neatly. All the mammoth skulls (shown in dark blue; tusks in white) were smashed open at the back and top, perhaps for access to the brains.

Since the ravine is near the end of a headland, the excavators believe that the animals may have been funnelled and stampeded along it and over the edge of the steep fissure, where some fell more than 100 ft (30 m) to their death. The presence of the

skulls certainly suggests that, if hunted, they died at this ready-made trap, since there would be no point in transporting the heavy skulls which have little food value. However, it has also been suggested that the mammoths may have fallen in by accident, though subsequently butchered by people.

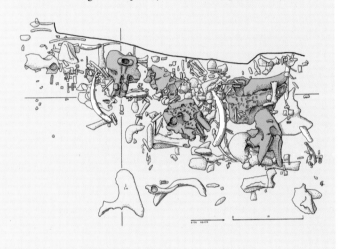

Thus, although there are some cases in which projectile points have been found closely associated with mammoth remains, archaeologists can only speculate about whether these animals were hunted. As in so much of prehistory, it is likely that all possible scenarios reflect some truth, and that circumstances – the number of people available, the weaponry at their disposal, the number of mammoths in range, the amount of meat needed and the luck of the enterprise – will have produced every possible outcome over the millennia.

Nonetheless, it is clear that there is no convincing

Font de Gaume is one of several caves in France that contain mammoth figures together with "tectiform" (hut-shaped) figures, interpreted by some as gravity traps or pitfalls.

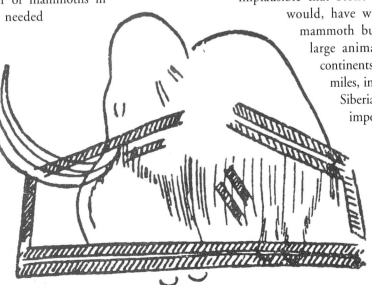

evidence – even in America – for kills on a scale that could have caused the extinction of the species. To save the overkill theory from this problem, the idea of a "Blitzkrieg" has been put forward: the mammoths were killed off so quickly that little evidence was preserved. This idea is ingenious but is difficult to prove one way or the other. In any case it seems implausible that Stone Age hunters could, or would, have wiped out not only the mammoth but also dozens of other large animal species, across three continents and millions of square miles, in less than 2,000 years. In Siberia, for example, a vast and important area of mammoth

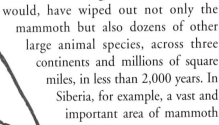

Late Ice Age stone tools in Eurasia took a wide variety of forms. Some were little more than simple flakes, which probably acted as multi-purpose blades or gouges.

distribution, there is evidence of only sparse human occupation before 10,000 years ago.

There are also questions over the timing of overkill. In Australia, for instance, the extinctions occurred toward the end of the Pleistocene, but people had arrived in that continent at least 40,000 years previously, and perhaps much earlier. Europe had been inhabited for hundreds of thousands of years before the mammoths became extinct. Even in America, it is becoming increasingly clear that the Clovis people were not the "First Americans"; there is growing evidence, especially from South America, of earlier immigrations.

The overkill theory might still be tenable if the Clovis people in North America, and their contemporaries on other continents, were the first to have hunted mammoths and other big game extensively. In fact it is becoming clear that they had a broader subsistence base than hunting the largest herbivores. Both in America and in Eurasia, the peoples of the late Ice Age relied on medium-sized animals – such as deer and bison – as their staple resources, as well as on small game and plant foods. Nor is there any clear indication of a technological advance that would suddenly have made the hunting of mammoths more likely or more feasible.

In addition, many herbivores have been exploited since the Ice Age by much higher human population densities, yet they were not driven to extinction. Native Americans, for example, hunted bison, pronghorns, deer and wild sheep for millennia without causing their disappearance. In fact,

POSSIBLE HUNTING METHODS

CLUES TO THE WAYS IN which people may have hunted mammoths may be found in the methods used by native peoples who hunted elephants in recent times. Killing individual animals would presumably have been the most frequent practice, since not many mammoths would have been required for food at any one time: a female elephant weighs around 6,610 lb (3,000 kg) and provides 4,000 lb (1,800 kg) of meat.

includes camouflaged pit-traps; dropping heavily weighted spears on a passing elephant from a tree; and setting foot- or trunk-snares to hold an animal so the hunter can approach and hamstring or disembowel it. Cameroon pygmies cover themselves with elephant dung to mask their scent and crawl from downwind toward their prey until they are close enough to their prey to thrust in a poisoned spear or cut a foot tendon.

There are a number of ways to kill a single elephant. The only way to drop one in its tracks is to reach the brain, which would have been difficult for Stone Age hunters. The heart is fairly inaccessible to a thrust or thrown spear, but the lungs make a good target, since even a miss here will hit the intestines. Such wounds may be fatal, especially with poisoned arrows, but only some hours or even days later. A variety of low-risk methods, historically preferred by Africans and Asians for felling these massive, powerful, agile, intelligent and dangerous animals,

In theory, there are advantages in the culling whole herds because injured individuals would otherwise be protected by the rest of the herd. If mammoth herds were ever hunted, the most efficient method would no doubt have been a cooperative hunt involving a large group of people, perhaps driving the animals into pits or toward a precipice, by means of noise and fire, in the same way that North American Indians are known to have exploited herds of bison. Surrounding elephants with a prairie fire would have made it possible to spear them as they tried to escape.

except in special cases of human arrivals on islands, it is rare in the archaeological record to find people wiping out their prey – when a resource becomes scarce, hunters will generally switch to another and the species will recover. Human hunters, in general, live in symbiosis with their prey, like any other predator.

But if hunting cannot account for the mammoth's demise, can the blame be laid at climate's door?

Two contrasting pictures depict historical elephant hunting in Africa: a rock art scene from South Africa (above), *and an illustration from a book by the British explorer David Livingstone about his travels in Africa in the mid-19th century* (left).

It is unlikely that hunters would have driven elephants into marshy ground to trap them, since healthy or adult animals would not get bogged down easily, and it would be very difficult to butcher and extract edible meat from the mud.

A storage pit at the Russian bone-hut site of Kostenki contains a hoard of mammoth bones. They were probably collected from natural accumulations and served as raw materials and fuel.

CLIMATE AND EXTINCTION

According to the climatic theory of extinction, it was dramatic changes in global climate and vegetation that led to the demise of the mammoths and other large mammals. The last major glaciation, between about 25,000 and 15,000 years ago, saw the expansion of ice caps down to mid-latitudes of Europe and North America. The ice excluded mammoths from a large terrain, and severe conditions may have reduced their numbers even in unglaciated areas. However, this was not the time when the mammoths and other species became extinct. Areas of the woolly mammoth's steppe habitat remained in the more southern part of the Eurasian range, while suitable vegetation for Columbian mammoths persisted south of the North American ice sheet. The mammoths survived the onslaught of the glaciation, only to succumb to later pressures.

Around 15,000 years ago global climate began to warm up and the ice sheets started to melt. As dated by the radio-carbon method, warming reached a peak at about 13,000 years ago and then started to decline again, leading to a short period of renewed cold and dry climate between about 11,000 and 10,000 years ago. The end of this phase marked the true finish of the last Ice Age and the beginning of the modern era, when a prolonged period of relatively mild climate began. Recent research indicates that these changes of climate occurred very rapidly. Around 13,000 years ago, for example, global temperature may have soared by 11°F (6°C) within 10 or 20 years – a far greater jolt than the current increases attributed to greenhouse warming.

This series of dramatic climatic changes occurred at the appropriate time to be a strong candidate for the reduction and eventual disappearance of mammoths from the Earth between 12,000 and 10,000 years ago. However, supporters of the climatic theory do not generally believe that it was the direct effects of the weather that caused the animals to die out. Woolly mammoths, though adapted to life in a cold climate, could survive through milder episodes, as shown by

their persistence through earlier warm phases within and before the last Ice Age. Nor was the Columbian mammoth, with a range extending as far south as Mexico, dependent on cold conditions and unable to cope with the heat. Rather, the changes in climate caused major shifts in the pattern of vegetation around the world, and these changes in turn led to the demise of many herbivorous mammals, such as the mammoth, which depended on particular plant foods. Carnivorous mammals also died out because their prey species had disappeared.

"Changes in climate caused major shifts in the pattern of vegetation"

There is much evidence, from fossil plant remains, that vegetational changes at the end of the last Ice Age were profound. Across the northern parts of Eurasia and North America, the vast expanse of steppelike vegetation, which had supported the woolly mammoth and many other species, was gradually squeezed out. This occurred because the cool, dry climate which had favoured it changed to one of greater warmth and moisture. The increased warmth also melted ice caps, and as sea levels rose, the size of the continents was reduced, raising precipitation in their interiors. The milder, wetter climate encouraged the spread of forests. In the far north, thawing of ice led to waterlogging, which, together with increased snow cover and cloudier skies, reduced plant growth to a tundra condition.

In this way, the mammoth steppe was replaced by landscapes of boggy tundra in the north and coniferous forest in the south, which still exist today. Today's tundra is slow growing and poor in nutrients, and is capable of supporting only limited numbers of specialized mammals feeding on lichen and moss, such as reindeer and musk oxen. The forests, on the other hand, support tree-browsers such as the moose. Neither of these habitats was suitable for mammoths

South of the tundra stretches a vast coniferous forest known as taiga, seen here in its autumn colours near Vladivostok. Such forests gradually took over the southern part of the mammoth steppe, but were unsuitable habitats for mammoths.

The treeless tundra of the Aleutian Islands, off the coast of Alaska, shows the kind of landscape that replaced the northern part of the mammoth steppe. According to the climatic theory, this tranformation of the mammoth steppe – which had a richer and more varied vegetation – spelt the end of the mammoth and other large herbivores.

and other grazing beasts, which were adapted to a diet of grasses and other herbaceous plants.

In North America, south of the ice sheets, the Columbian mammoth also suffered the loss of its natural habitat. The "parkland vegetation" of the Pleistocene, a rich mosaic of grasses, herbs, shrubs and trees which had provided the Columbian mammoth's mixed diet, largely disappeared. It was replaced in many areas by dense forest; on the open plains by uninterrupted grassland; and in the southwest by semi-desert. Specialist feeders, such as browsing deer in the forests or grazing bison on the prairies, took over.

The reduced diversity of plants in postglacial landscapes may have accounted for the demise of other species as well as the mammoth. Numerous herbivores had existed side by side in the rich mosaic vegetation of the Pleistocene, each species taking its own combination of plant foods. There was a longer period of good feeding each year, since some plants produced growth earlier in the season, some later. There had thus developed a complex web of animals and plants similar to those of the African savanna today. In the forest, tundra and grassland zones of the postglacial, by contrast, lower plant diversity and a shorter growing season reduced the diversity and abundance of large mammals which could be supported.

Whatever the precise nature of the changes, it seems clear that the mammoth's habitat was progressively eroded by the new vegetation belts. In Eurasia, the process seems to have started in the south, which would explain why the mammoth's range gradually contracted from south to north and the last enclaves finally died out in northernmost Siberia. In some areas mammoth populations may already have been vulnerable to these changes. In Europe, finds of mammoths in the period after 15,000 years ago are much rarer than in earlier times, perhaps because their populations never recovered from the effects of the glaciation 25,000 to 15,000 years ago. The subsequent vegetational changes may thus have been the "last straw".

One problem with the climatic theory of extinction is that the mammoths and other large mammals died out only at the end of the last Ice Age. There have been at least 22 major climatic cycles in the Pleistocene, and thousands of minor ones, but these did not result in such severe levels of extinction. We know that mammoths survived previous interglacial periods of warm climate; why then could they not survive into the present interglacial? This is a powerful objection to the climatic theory, but counterarguments have been raised.

Some claim that although previous interglacials were as warm as today their vegetation was not zoned into forests and tundra. Instead it retained a "mosaic" character, supporting a great variety of plants – the type of habitat that mammoths and other herbivores needed to survive. Others, however, believe that pollen found in deposits from these interglacial periods, indicates that separate zones of forest and tundra did exist as they do today.

It may also be that while earlier mammoths could tolerate interglacial conditions, the last populations had become too restricted to cold steppe habitats as a result of evolutionary specialization, and so could not survive into the postglacial. Yet, while this is conceivable for the mammoth, it can hardly account for the extinction of all the species that died out worldwide at the same time.

Another objection to the climatic theory suggests that favourable habitats for mammoths *did* remain in the postglacial period. So, if that was the case, what prevented them from surviving there? As far as the modern tundra is concerned, it is clear that this is not at all like the mammoth steppe that occupied the same area in the Pleistocene. Its vegetation is slower growing and less nutritious, and has a

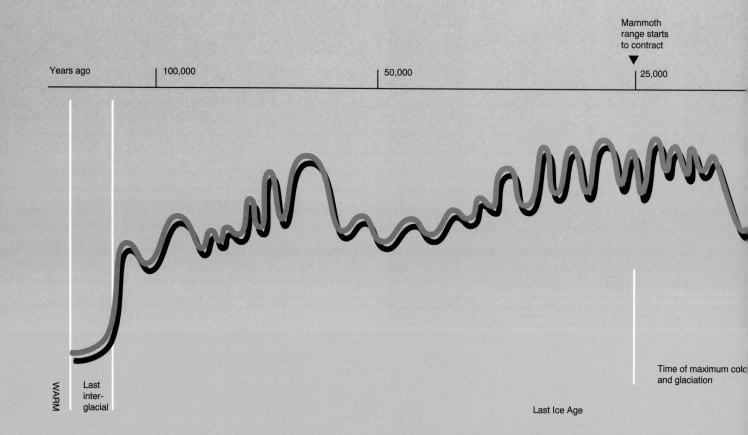

Mammoth range starts to contract ▼

Years ago   100,000   50,000   25,000

WARM

Last inter-glacial

Time of maximum cold and glaciation

Last Ice Age

EXTINCTION 135

much shorter season of availability. It could not, therefore, have formed a suitable habitat for the mammoth.

would have lost out in competition with grazing specialists like bison. Finally, there seem to be at least some places today where mosaic vegetation has survived naturally. Were these areas simply too small to support mammoth populations?

"Why did mammoths die out only at the end of the last Ice Age?"

Better candidates are the productive grasslands that did survive into the modern era – the American prairies and Russian steppes. On the face of it, these might have supported mammoths. However, some researchers have countered that modern grasslands are monotonous and dominated by only a few grass species. Mammoths, whose metabolism required a varied diet, with supplements to pure grass, would have found such habitats less favourable and

That climate alone can cause extensive animal extinctions is abundantly evident from the rest of the fossil record; for example, the dinosaurs died out long before humans had appeared on the scene. Crucial to the climatic theory of late Pleistocene mammal extinctions is the demonstration that the changes at the end of the last Ice Age were different from those of previous glacial cycles. But while the last transition is understood in great detail, knowledge of previous ones is much less complete. Researchers will need to demonstrate in greater detail how vegetation changed then, and in earlier times, to make a watertight case for the climatic theory of mammoth extinction.

TIMES OF EXTINCTION IN DIFFERENT AREAS

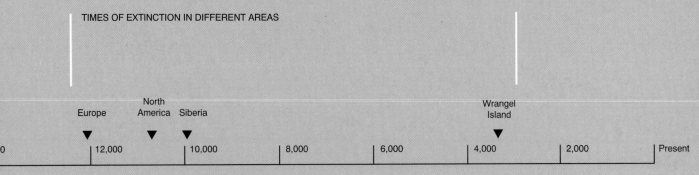

Europe | North America | Siberia | Wrangel Island

000 | 12,000 | 10,000 | 8,000 | 6,000 | 4,000 | 2,000 | Present

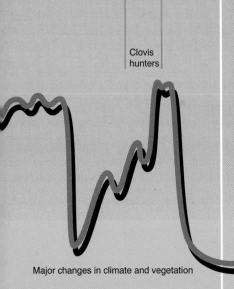

Clovis hunters

Changes in climate beginning with the last warm interglacial 120,000 years ago, through the generally cold but fluctuating last Ice Age, into the present warm postglacial are shown on this curve, based on polar ice-core studies. Radiocarbon dating is used for the timing of events from 25,000 years onward. Following the major glaciation 25,000 to 15,000 years ago, there was a sudden warming, which was interrupted by a cold snap around 11,000 years ago.

A thousand years later, the postglacial began. The greater warmth of this period encouraged the spread of forests and tundra and may have led to the demise of the mammoth steppe fauna. The very stability of the postglacial climate may also have contributed to the formation of monotonous landscape zones, in contrast to the almost constant variations through the last Ice Age, which perhaps helped to maintain a "mosaic" vegetation by shifting and mixing plant distributions.

Major changes in climate and vegetation

Postglacial

WHAT (OR WHO) KILLED THE MAMMOTHS?

This question is not as simple as it might seem, and the answers are complex. Two different species of mammoth were involved, extinction happened at different times in different areas, and the environmental and human pressures varied from place to place across the mammoths' vast range. Various factors may, therefore, have combined to produce the total global extinction of the lineage.

Disease is an unlikely cause, as no known bacterium or virus could wipe out such a range of mammal species. Nor is there evidence for a cometary or asteroid impact at that time.

Although it appears certain that humans did hunt mammoths, there is no evidence that this was more than an occasional activity. The arguments that climatic and vegetational change would have stressed mammoth populations and squeezed them into ever-smaller areas of habitat ("refugia") seem convincing. However, the idea that there was nowhere at all that these or any of the other extinct species could have survived leaves a lingering doubt about whether they died out entirely by "natural causes".

Several researchers have suggested that climatic and human factors may have combined to force the extinction of

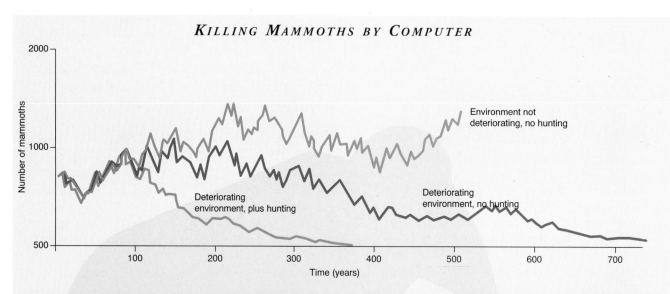

KILLING MAMMOTHS BY COMPUTER

MATHEMATICAL MODELLING HAS BEEN USED BY RESEARCHERS to examine the effects of predation and climate on mammoth populations. The most recent computer simulations suggest that an isolated population of mammoths could become extinct in just a few hundred years due either to environmental deterioration or to a relatively low level of hunting. The impact on the mammoths reaches a maximum when environmental and hunting pressures are combined.

Although earlier modelling had pictured a huge, thriving mammoth population being rapidly exterminated, the real-life situation was inevitably more complex. For example, mammoths would move between areas, and groups could be kept going by immigrants from elsewhere. Also, hunters themselves would have moved to a fresh locality, or switched to other prey, if mammoths had started to become scarce.

The key to the mammoths' last days was their progressive shrinking into small, isolated groups. The climatic theory

suggests that as their habitat gradually disappeared, patchy mammoth populations clung to remaining areas of mammoth steppe or parkland vegetation. Local factors may have contributed: for example, the western United States may have been affected by drought around 11,000 years ago, perhaps resulting in mass deaths of animals.

Whether by loss of vegetation or by loss of water, small groups of mammoths would have experienced increased competition among themselves and with other herbivores, and may even have "eaten out" their remaining food supply. The populations may have become too small to sustain themselves reproductively. Finally, they died out. Striking parallels are seen in modern Asian elephant populations reduced and isolated by destruction of their habitat.

Many such terminal mammoth populations simply expired; others may have been finished off by humans. The pattern undoubtedly varied from region to region.

THE LAST MAMMOTHS ON EARTH

THE BELIEF THAT MAMMOTHS HAD BECOME EXTINCT BY 10,000 years ago was shattered in March 1993 when three Russian researchers announced the discovery of woolly mammoth remains between 7,000 and only 3,700 years old. The fossils, from Wrangel Island in the Arctic Ocean, show that the mammoths were dwarfs *(see pp.34–35)* that had survived the extinction of other mammoths by more than 6,000 years.

At first, colleagues were sceptical about the radiocarbon dates: were they reliable? Now more than 50 dates have been obtained by laboratories in Russia and the United States. All agree in placing the dwarf mammoths well into the postglacial period. While the pyramids and Stonehenge were being built, mammoths roamed the Arctic island of Wrangel.

The reason for their survival may lie in the exceptional vegetation of the island *(above)*, which even today hosts a much greater variety of plant species than are found on the mainland. Because of its unusual climate and geology, Wrangel has preserved a relict of the mammoth steppe.

The cause of the Wrangel mammoths' ultimate demise may have been related, as elsewhere, to either climatic change or human hunting. Clearly they were hanging on under marginal conditions and, given the small size of their population, any changes in habitat could have spelt disaster. On the other hand, there is some evidence that humans may have been involved. The earliest evidence of human occupation on Wrangel dates to around 3,400 years ago. Thus, it is quite possible that the mammoths and people overlapped in time. The early hunters would have found the dwarf mammoths easy prey, and the animals could neither escape nor replenish their numbers from elsewhere.

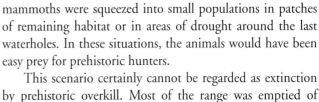

the mammoths and other large mammals. Their numbers drastically reduced by changes in climate and vegetation, mammoths were squeezed into small populations in patches of remaining habitat or in areas of drought around the last waterholes. In these situations, the animals would have been easy prey for prehistoric hunters.

This scenario certainly cannot be regarded as extinction by prehistoric overkill. Most of the range was emptied of mammoths by the direct effect of the changing landscape, not by hunting. The proportion of mammoths killed by humans would have been relatively small, but it could just have tipped the balance between survival and extinction.

BRINGING MAMMOTHS BACK TO LIFE

The finds on Wrangel Island off the northeastern Siberian coast, show that mammoths survived far longer than had been supposed, at least in one part of the world. An Egyptian tomb painting dated to about 3,500 years ago shows a very small, apparently hairy, tusked elephant which some have suggested could be a dwarf mammoth. The picture is much more likely to represent a stylized African elephant; nonetheless, the Wrangel mammoths have taught the lesson of keeping an open mind.

Man meets mammoth: this fanciful reconstruction (above) of an encounter with a mammoth in the frozen north was inspired by the discovery of the Adams mammoth in 1799.

A robotic mammoth was built in 1988 at Le Thot in France, using a jointed metal framework. Its lifelike movement is powered by bursts of air pressure controlled by computer.

Is it possible that mammoths existed in even more recent times? Various legends told by peoples of northern latitudes preserved the idea of a living animal. For example, the Inuit of the Bering Strait believed in a huge animal that burrowed underground. Some Alaskans said that "Kilukpuk" had lived in the sea with the other big cetaceans until it quarrelled with Aglu, another sea monster, and was kicked out and forced to live on land. Kilukpuk therefore "swam" under the ground, and had teeth like a walrus, but straight. Such tales have also been found in South America: in the 19th century, Charles Darwin's guides showed him a mastodon skeleton on the Paraná River in Argentina, and claimed it to be a burrower of enormous size. Some old Yakuts still believe that the mammoth is a living animal that burrows beneath the ground. They will cover up any exposed remains to avoid illness and bad fortune.

Many North American Indian tribes also had tales that seem to concern the animal: the Northeast Algonkians told of a "great moose" with a kind of limb growing between its shoulders, a fifth leg used to prepare its bed; while the Naskapi of northeastern Labrador knew of a monster with a long nose which it used to hit people.

More intriguing perhaps are the apparent sightings of mammoths in Siberia in recent times. At the end of the 16th century, beyond the Ural Mountains, a traveller reported meeting a "large hairy elephant", which the natives described as a valued source of food. In 1920 an illiterate hunter, returning to Vladivostok after spending four years alone in the taiga, stated that two years previously he had come upon fresh animal tracks in mud. They were huge, egg-shaped prints, about 2 ft (60 cm) long and 1 ft 7 in (50 cm) wide. He also claimed to have encountered a huge heap of dung containing vegetation, and tree branches broken at a height of 10 ft (3 m). He followed the tracks for days; they were eventually joined by a second set. Finally, at a distance of 900 ft (275 m) in the forest, he saw "an enormous elephant, with white, very curved tusks". The animal was dark brown and had long hair.

Even in these instances, other explanations seem more likely. Siberian and Alaskan natives have been digging up mammoth carcasses for centuries, and this could be the source of their knowledge of the animal's appearance and legends about seeing the animal alive. While one cannot totally rule out the possibility of more recent survival (Siberia covers millions of square miles and is only sparsely populated), present evidence indicates that mammoths died out thousands of years ago. But have they gone for ever, or can we hope to restore them to life?

The excellent condition of mammoth tissue preserved frozen in Siberia has led to speculation that it might be possible to produce a living mammoth. In the 1960s and 1970s, Russian scientists devised an experiment to test this theory. Genetic material would be extracted from a mammoth cell and transplanted into the egg of a female elephant which had had its own genetic material removed. The egg would be re-implanted into the elephant, where it might grow into a mammoth, or into a mammoth-elephant hybrid if the female mated with a male elephant. All such experiments failed, but speculation remained, partly as a result of spoof press reports of the birth of a "mammontelephase".

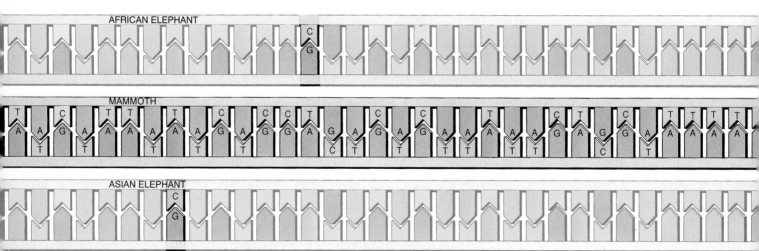

AFRICAN ELEPHANT

MAMMOTH

ASIAN ELEPHANT

The completed model at Le Thot moves its ears, eyes, tail and front legs. It breathes air through its trunk, lifts its head and trumpets at onlookers.

139

More recent research explains why all such attempts are doomed to failure, but demonstrates what really can be done with mammoth genes. Techniques developed in the 1980s allow the extraction and purification, from fossil remains, of minute quantities of DNA (deoxyribonucleic acid), the molecule that codes genetic information.

"DNA has been recovered from the carcasses of frozen Siberian mammoths"

Several laboratories around the world have succeeded in extracting DNA from Siberian frozen mammoth tissue. The bulk of the DNA extracted is not from mammoth genes at all, but from bacteria which infested the carcass after death. Some mammoth DNA is, however, still present, although it is damaged and broken up into small pieces. This results both from the inherent instability of the DNA molecule and from such factors as the mammoth's own enzymes, soil chemicals, heat and bacterial decay, in particular during the period immediately after death but also more slowly over the succeeding millennia. These processes are less marked in bone than in muscle tissue, so bone provides the best source of mammoth DNA. Even so, each of the remaining pieces of DNA represents only a fraction of the mammoth's total genetic code, and they are no longer organized in the complex way necessary for the growth of a baby mammoth. That is why there is no foreseeable prospect of creating a living mammoth. In any event, the ethics of resurrecting a species whose natural habitat has disappeared are questionable, and resources are probably better employed conserving the elephants that are still alive but themselves in danger of extinction.

Although insufficient to produce a whole animal, the preserved pieces of mammoth DNA can provide evidence of the relationships of mammoths to other species. To date, fragments of DNA containing 200 to 300 units of the genetic code have been extracted. These can be compared with the equivalent stretches of DNA extracted from modern Asian and African elephants and other mammals, to help calculate the rate of genetic change over time and to reveal the likely correlations between the species. The more similar the DNA sequences, the more closely related the species. The results of this work, currently in progress, will mark a new chapter in our understanding of the mammoth.

The individual bands on this plate, *visible under ultraviolet light, represent fragments of the genetic material, DNA. From these data, estimates of the genetic differences between species can be obtained. The diagram illustrates a small part of the DNA sequence of a mammoth, determined for the first time in 1994. Most of the mammoth sequence is identical to that of living elephants, but some differences are highlighted.*

GLOSSARY

Words in SMALL CAPITALS indicate cross-references to other definitions.

Absolute dating Any method of dating that gives an estimated age in years (compare RELATIVE DATING).

Accelerator mass spectronomy (AMS) A form of RADIOCARBON DATING in which the proportion of different ISOTOPES in the sample is determined by direct measurement of the weight of carbon atoms.

Adaptation Any aspect of an organism's anatomy, physiology or behaviour that arose in EVOLUTION because it performed a certain function. The principal force bringing about adaptations is believed to be NATURAL SELECTION.

Alluvium Sediment deposited by rivers at points along the FLOODPLAIN.

Amebelodon A genus of MASTODONT belonging to the family Gomphotheriidae, native to North America in the late MIOCENE. It had small upper tusks and large, flattened lower tusks probably used to dig up roots.

Anal flap A flap of skin lying beneath the tail and covering the anus.

Ancestral mammoth A term used here to describe *MAMMUTHUS MERIDIONALIS*.

Archaeology The study of the human past through the systematic recovery and analysis of its remains.

Artefact A product of human workmanship.

Artesian spring Water rising to the surface from an underground reservoir formed from permeable (water-containing) sediments enclosed by impermeable strata.

Barytheres A group of early PROBOSCIDEA of elephantine size and build, with two pairs of short tusks in upper and lower jaws. Their remains have been found in the Sahara region.

Base The part of a DNA NUCLEOTIDE that provides the genetic code. There are four varieties of base, forming a four-letter alphabet whose sequence in a given gene specifies the structure of a protein. The complementary pairing of the bases on the two chains of the DNA molecule provides the basis for DNA replication. Thus, adenine (A) always pairs with thymine (T), and cytosine (C) always pairs with guanine (G).

Bas-relief A sculptured figure in art which stands out from its background because material has been removed from around it.

Behemoth Name for a primeval creature mentioned in the Old Testament, from the Hebrew *behemoth*; a possible derivation of the word "mammoth".

Beringia The area of land comprising northeastern Siberia, Alaska and the Yukon, plus areas of the adjacent continental shelf including the Bering Strait which today divides the continents. These areas became joined at various times during episodes of low sea level in the PLEISTOCENE.

Blitzkrieg Literally "lightning war", a term borrowed from the German advances of World War II to denote the supposedly rapid killing off of MAMMOTHS and other animals.

Browser A HERBIVORE that eats predominantly the leaves of trees and shrubs.

Caries Tooth decay caused by the dissolution of hard tissue, leading to a cavity.

Carnivore An animal that eats predominantly animal matter. Written "carnivore", it can refer to any carnivorous animal. Written "Carnivore", it usually refers to the group of placental MAMMALS that includes the cats, dogs, hyenas and bears, some of which (e.g. the giant panda) are HERBIVOROUS.

Cave bear Large, mostly vegetarian, extinct species of European PLEISTOCENE bear, *Ursus spelaeus*. It coexisted with the WOOLLY MAMMOTH and hibernated in caves, where most of its remains have been found.

Cement A dental tissue, not as hard as DENTINE or ENAMEL, which forms the outer surface of the root and fixes the tooth in the jaw. In ELEPHANTS and MAMMOTHS, a layer of cement holds the TUSKS and MOLARS in their sockets. It also fills the spaces between the enamel and dentine ridges of the MOLAR CROWNS.

Cemetery A term used informally to refer to large accumulations of bones of living ELEPHANTS or fossil MAMMOTHS. It originated from the erroneous belief that elephants "choose" to die in certain places, whereas these sites are usually just the last waterholes where animals gather in times of drought. In the case of mammoths, the "cemeteries" result from natural processes which cause bones to accumulate, such as river flow or soil movement. The term "elephant (or mammoth) graveyard" is also used.

Champlevé Technique whereby material around a figure (e.g. on bone or antler) is scraped away to create a cameo effect.

Chitin The tough flexible substance forming the cuticle of insects and other arthropods.

Cleaver A tool with FLAKES removed from both sides, which has a broad cutting edge.

Clovis The earliest type of fluted POINT made by PALEO-INDIANS, characterized by its symmetry, careful flaking and the removal of a small "flute" (FLAKE) from its face. Clovis points are between 11,000 and 11,500 years old.

Clubmoss A group of primitive non-flowering plants (Lycopsida) similar in appearance to mosses but related to the horsetails.

Collagen A fibrous protein extracted from fossil bone for RADIOCARBON DATING.

Columbian mammoth The common name for *MAMMUTHUS COLUMBI*.

Computer simulation An attempt to imitate, by computer, the course of a given process (e.g. mammoth extinction) to assess the likely outcome from various starting conditions.

Computer tomography X-ray analysis whereby an image of an internal slice of an object (a section) can be obtained without cutting the object open. The sections can then be integrated by computer to produce a three-dimensional reconstruction.

Crown The part of any tooth above the root, usually covered by ENAMEL. In mammoths, much of the crown was buried within the jaw until the late stages of wear.

Deinotherium An extinct PROBOSCIDEAN which extended from Africa through southern Europe to India. Although not a true ELEPHANT, it was of elephantine form with a TRUNK and downcurved lower TUSKS.

Dentine A dental tissue, not as hard as ENAMEL, which forms the core of most mammalian teeth. ELEPHANT and MAMMOTH TUSK (IVORY) is largely made up of dentine. In the MOLARS, dentine fills the alternate spaces between the enamel ridges, the others being filled with CEMENT. In life, dentine contains living cells and nerve fibres.

Dire wolf A common species of CARNIVORE (*Canis dirus*) in the late PLEISTOCENE of North America. Equalling the living grey wolf in size, it was of heavier build with a very large head and powerful dentition.

DNA Deoxyribonucleic acid, the self-replicating molecule that stores genetic information. An identical full set of an animal's genes is contained within the DNA of each cell, stored within the chromosomes. A DNA molecule comprises two chains twisted into a helix, each chain formed from NUCLEOTIDE units linked together.

Dugong A species of SIRENIA (*Dugong dugon*) up to 12 ft (3.7 m) long, inhabiting coastal shallows in the southwestern Pacific, Indian Ocean and Red Sea.

Dwarf A well-proportioned but very small organism beyond the normal range of size variation in the species. The term pygmy is sometimes used in a similar vein.

Electron spin resonance dating (ESR) A method of ABSOLUTE DATING which measures the electrons trapped in a crystal lattice as a result of environmental radiation received over time. It has been successfully applied to MAMMOTH MOLARS.

Electrophoresis A laboratory process whereby an electric field is applied to a solution of molecules to be analysed. Their rate of movement across the field is proportional to the weight of the molecules, whose relative sizes can therefore be deduced.

Elephant A member of the family ELEPHANTIDAE. Technically, it includes the MAMMOTH, although informally it is often restricted to the two living species. The first known usage of the word was by Homer (and Hesiod), who used it to mean "ivory". The word's origin is unknown, although it may be linked to the Hebrew *eleph* (ox).

Elephantidae The family within the PROBOSCIDEA that includes the MAMMOTHS and living ELEPHANTS. In contrast to the MASTODONTS they have ridged MOLARS and no tusk ENAMEL.

Elephas The genus of ELEPHANT to which the living Asian elephant (*E. maximus*) belongs. Various species evolved in Africa and southern Asia, of which only one remains. The name was once used to describe almost all fossil elephants (the mammoth was first named *Elephas primigenius*) although many of these are now recognized as pertaining to different lineages.

Enamel The hardest mammalian tissue, forming the outer layer of most teeth and the cutting ridges of MAMMOTH MOLARS.

Evolution The process of change by which different forms of life have arisen over long periods of time. The two main processes are, first, the geographical splitting of a lineage to produce two species where one existed before; and second, the change of form within a lineage that results in new structures and ADAPTATIONS. The combination of the two processes explains how a species resembling an ancestral form can continue to live alongside its altered descendant.

Extinction The permanent global disappearance of a species of animal or plant. It may sometimes describe a disappearance from a particular region.

Fauna A community of animals comprising all the species occupying a given area; sometimes erroneously applied to a fossil assemblage derived from a living fauna.

Flake A sliver of stone or bone removed by striking a core with some kind of hammer.

Floodplain The part of a river valley subject to flooding. As floodwaters recede, their sediment load is deposited as ALLUVIUM.

Foraminifera Single-celled aquatic animals which secrete a tiny shell that survives in (and contributes to) sea-floor SEDIMENTS. There are many different species, recognizable by their shell form.

Fossil The buried remains of an animal or plant usually preserved within SEDIMENT. The term is sometimes restricted to remains that have become MINERALIZED.

Gastrointestinal tract The main digestive canal, comprising oesophagus, stomach and intestines.

Giant deer Informal name for an extinct group of Eurasian PLEISTOCENE deer which included the so-called Irish Elk *Megaloceros giganteus*. This species coexisted with the WOOLLY MAMMOTH in Europe and bore enormous, flattened, outspread antlers.

Glaciation A period of time, within an ICE AGE, when the polar ICE CAPS extended far beyond their present limits.

Gomphotherium A common MASTODONT of the HOLOCENE, spreading from Africa through Europe to Pakistan. As large as an Asian ELEPHANT, it bore both upper and lower TUSKS.

Grazer A HERBIVORE whose diet consists predominantly of grass.

Ground sloth An informal term for a number of New World mammalian species belonging to different families within the Order Edentata. At least four species are known from the North American PLEISTOCENE, all extinct by 10,500 years ago. All bore claws and had simple, peglike teeth; they ranged in size up to 18 ft (5.5 m).

Guard hair One of the long, coarse hairs forming the outer, protective layer of the fur.

Herbaceous plant (herb) A plant whose stem is not woody, which usually dies down after the year's growth and may be edible. Includes many grasses and small flowering plants.

Herbivore An animal that eats predominantly or exclusively plant matter.

Holocene The INTERGLACIAL that began 10,000 years ago, and in which we are still living.

Horizon A layer of SEDIMENT representing a particular interval of past time.

Hyoid bones A series of small bones at the base of the tongue which provide attachment for the tongue muscles.

Hyrax A group of MAMMALS (Order Hyracoidea) believed to be distantly related to ELEPHANTS and MAMMOTHS and now restricted to Africa. They range from 1 to 2 ft (30 to 60 cm) in length and are HERBIVOROUS.

Ice age A period of time within which extensive GLACIATION occurred. Sometimes "the Ice Age" refers to the whole of the PLEISTOCENE, including both glacial and non-glacial episodes. At other times it refers to a particular period within the PLEISTOCENE, as in "the last Ice Age". Even such periods, however, incorporate both times of genuine glaciation and cool but unglaciated intervals. There were other ice ages much earlier in the geological record.

Ice cap Thick mass of glacial ice and snow that permanently covers an area.

Ilium The largest bone of the PELVIS, forming the upper and side parts of the pelvic girdle surrounding the birth canal.

Incisors The front teeth, used for biting in most MAMMALS. Primitive placental mammals (e.g. shrews) have three pairs, upper and lower; humans have two pairs; and ELEPHANTS and MAMMOTHS one pair, the TUSKS.

Interglacial An extended period during the PLEISTOCENE when the climate was as warm, or slightly warmer, than today, and when forests generally extended into northern latitudes. Interglacials do not account for all the time between GLACIATIONS, nor are they used for very short warm phases. Interglacials are generally 10,000–20,000 years long.

Isotopes Varieties of a single chemical element that are the same in their chemical properties but that vary in mass due to differing numbers of neutrons in their atoms.

Ivory The TUSKS of certain mammals used as a resource, especially those of ELEPHANTS and MAMMOTHS, but also those of walruses and narwhals (tusked whales).

Lamut A major group of people within the TUNGUS complex, who live in SIBERIA along the Sea of Okhotsk and rely on hunting and reindeer breeding.

Loxodonta The genus of ELEPHANT to which the living African elephant belongs. The earliest species, *L. adaurora*, is found in African deposits 4–5 million years old. The modern species, *L. africana*, is divided into a SAVANNA form (*L. a. africana*, the largest living land mammal) and a smaller forest form (*L. a. cyclotis*). The name derives from the lozenge-shaped ENAMEL ridges on the MOLAR teeth.

Mammal A group of vertebrate animals (Class Mammalia) divided into the monotremes (egg-laying mammals), MARSUPIALS (pouched mammals) and placentals (all the others, including the PROBOSCIDEA). Characterized by features such as hair, lactation and the presence of three middle-ear bones.

Mammoth An extinct ELEPHANT of the genus *MAMMUTHUS*. The word is often used to refer implicitly to the woolly mammoth *M. PRIMIGENIUS*. Some believe that the name comes from the Hebrew *behemoth* via the Arabic *Mehemot*. No obvious source word exists in any Siberian tongue. The TUNGUS call the animal *cheli*, and the YAKUTS call it *uukyla*, but a possible origin is from the western TUNGUS term *namendi* (bear). The likeliest candidate, however, is the Estonian for earth (*maa*) and mole (*mutt*), linking the name to the widespread early belief that the animal burrowed beneath the ground.

Mammoth steppe A term, coined by U.S. paleoecologist D. Guthrie, to refer to the landscape of northern Eurasia and North America during various phases of the PLEISTOCENE, especially the last ICE AGE. The vegetation comprised a rich mixture of STEPPE and TUNDRA plants unlike any community today, and supported abundant mammalian FAUNA. It had a greater steppe component in the south and more tundra in the north.

Mammut A genus of forest-dwelling MASTODONT, belonging to the family Mammutidae, which included the American mastodon *Mammut americanum*. It was not closely related to the MAMMOTH, but like it survived until the end of the PLEISTOCENE.

Mammuthus The genus within the ELEPHANTIDAE that comprises the mammoths, characterized by twisted TUSKS and other features. The name, first applied scientifically by the Englishman J. Brookes in 1828, is simply a Latinization of "mammoth". The various species of the genus are listed with the abbreviation "*M.*" for *Mammuthus*.

M. africanavus An early species of MAMMOTH found in North Africa, dating from around 3 million years ago. Named by the Frenchman C. Arambourg in 1952.

M. columbi The COLUMBIAN MAMMOTH, principal MAMMOTH species of southern North America, first named by the Englishman H. Falconer in 1857. Derived ultimately from American *M. MERIDIONALIS*, it ranged from the northern United States to central Mexico, and survived until around 10,500 years ago.

M. exilis The DWARF MAMMOTH of the California Channel Islands. The name, given by Americans C. Stock and E. Furlong in 1928, refers to the supposedly "exiled" status of the island mammoths. However, the Channel Island fossils may represent more than one event of isolation and dwarfing and hence, technically, more than one species.

M. imperator Name given to many MAMMOTH fossils from North America and first applied to a tooth from Nebraska by the American J. Leidy in 1858. Colloquially called "Imperial mammoth", its status is unclear. Some of the material may represent an intermediate stage between *M. MERIDIONALIS* and *M. COLUMBI*. Other fossils labelled *M. imperator*, however, are best regarded as *M. COLUMBI* itself.

M. jeffersonii Name sometimes given to large MAMMOTH fossils, mainly from southern North America, which may represent an evolutionary stage beyond *M. COLUMBI*. The name, in honour of Thomas Jefferson, was coined by the American H.F. Osborn in 1922.

M. meridionalis The earliest species of MAMMOTH found outside Africa. Its remains occur in Eurasia, dating to between about 3 million and 750,000 years ago, and in North America from about 1.5 million years ago. It was probably ancestral to all later species of mammoths on both continents. Called here the ANCESTRAL MAMMOTH, it has also been termed "southern elephant" because its remains were first recognized in Italy. The name *meridionalis* is Latin for "southern" and was first coined by the Italian F. Nesti in 1825. Some specialists have placed the ancestral mammoth in a separate genus, *Archidiskodon*, while others divide this into an early species *A. gromovi* and a later one *A. meridionalis*.

M. primigenius The WOOLLY MAMMOTH, a species that evolved in Eurasia some time between 500,000 and 300,000 years ago and spread widely across the northern hemisphere until its disappearance from the continents 10,000 years ago. The original name, *Elephas primigenius*, derives from the Latin meaning "first elephant", and was coined by the German J.F. Blumenbach in 1799.

M. subplanifrons The earliest species of MAMMOTH, known from fragmentary fossils 3–4 million years old found in southern and eastern Africa. Named by the American H.F. Osborn in 1928.

M. trogontherii A species of MAMMOTH intermediate in time and anatomy between *M. MERIDIONALIS* and *M. PRIMIGENIUS*. Known as the STEPPE MAMMOTH, it was exclusive to Eurasia and lived between about 1 and 0.5 million years ago. Coined by the German H. Pohlig in 1885, the name derives from the fact that the species was first recognized in deposits that also contained the extinct beaver *Trogontherium. M. trogontherii* is sometimes given another name, *M. armeniacus*.

Manatee Four species of SIRENIA (genus *Trichechus*), 7 to 14 ft (2.1 to 4.2 m) long, that inhabit shallow coastal waters, estuaries and rivers of the tropical Atlantic.

Marsupial A group of MAMMALS, now restricted to Australia and the southern Americas, in which the young are born at an early stage of development and complete their growth in the mother's pouch (marsupium).

Mastodont (mastodon) An informal term for various lineages of extinct PROBOSCIDEA. The word, meaning "breast-tooth", is derived from the hemispherical cusps of the MOLARS. An alternative spelling, mastodon, is sometimes used, especially for the American mastodon *MAMMUT americanum*.

Matriarch In ELEPHANT society, the dominant female of a family group, leading the group in its activities. She is usually an elder relative of many of her subordinates.

Megafauna The larger animal species within a FAUNA. In the context of PLEISTOCENE MAMMALS, species over 40 kg (90 lb) in body weight, about the size of a wolf.

Mineralization The process by which FOSSILS, while buried in the ground, gradually accumulate inorganic minerals which infill and/or replace the original bone, tooth or shell, making them very hard and dense.

Miocene The period of time, between 24 and 5 million years ago, which saw the greatest global spread and species diversity of the PROBOSCIDEA.

Moeritherium The earliest recognized member of the PROBOSCIDEA, known from 40 to 50 million year old FOSSILS from North Africa. Like a small hippo in build, it was amphibious and bore incipient TUSKS.

Molars The cheek teeth of MAMMOTHS and other MAMMALS. Technically restricted to the back three teeth in each jaw, numbered molars 1 to 3, which are not preceded in life by milk teeth; those in front are the premolars, which are the vertical replacements of juvenile milk teeth. In ELEPHANTS and mammoths, the six horizontally-replacing cheek teeth comprise the three milk teeth followed by three molars, the true premolars having been lost during evolution. For simplicity, however, all six teeth in mammoths and elephants are commonly described as "molars" and numbered 1 to 6.

Mosaic vegetation A vegetation comprising a wide range of plant species, often an amalgam of different ecological types. Plant diversity is enhanced by small-scale local variations in species composition.

Mummy The popular name for a body that has been treated artificially to preserve a life-like appearance, as in ancient Egypt, where bitumen was used in mummification (the word derives from *moumia*, the Persian for pitch). The term is also often extended to human and animal bodies preserved by nature.

Musk ox A species of bovid (*Ovibos moschatus*) adapted to the high Arctic and today surviving only in northern Canada and Greenland. Probably related to sheep and goats, it is 4–5 ft (1.2–1.5 m) in height, with large flattened horns and a dense coat.

Natural selection The principal process by which EVOLUTION produces ADAPTATIONS. The natural variation between individuals within a species leads to the differential survival and reproductive success of those individuals better able to feed, attract mates, avoid disease and so on. If these features are to some degree inherited, they will become more prevalent among individuals of successive generations.

Neanderthal An archaic form of human – named after the Neanderthal site near Düsseldorf, Germany – which lived from about 150,000 to 33,000 years ago. Neanderthals had a large brain, massive brow ridges, a receding chin and a heavy muscular build. Debate still rages about whether Neanderthals were an evolutionary dead end or at least partly ancestral to modern humans.

Nucleotide One of the units of the DNA chain. It is built from three molecules: a sugar, a phosphate and a BASE.

Ochre (red or yellow) Soft varieties of iron oxide minerals such as hematite used as pigment for painting and decoration.

Osteoarthritis A degenerative joint disease caused by wear and tear of bone and cartilage.

Ostracods Tiny marine and freshwater crustaceans with a two-valved ovoid or kidney-shaped shell and jointed feeding appendages. Some 200 living species are known, but 2,000 fossil species have been described, many of them only ¹⁄₂₅ in (1 mm) or so long.

Overkill Denotes the theory that human hunters were responsible for the demise of MAMMOTHS and the rest of the vanished MEGAFAUNA.

Oxbow lake A curved lake found on the FLOODPLAIN of a river. It is formed when a loop of the river's meanders is cut off and the river adopts a shorter, straighter course. The American equivalent is bayou.

Ozocerite Term from the Greek, meaning "odoriferous wax", for a yellow to brown native wax (also known as earth wax or mineral wax) made mostly of solid paraffinic hydrocarbons and associated with sources of petroleum.

Pachyderm An informal term for a thick-skinned quadruped such as an ELEPHANT, rhinoceros or hippopotamus, from the Greek *pakhudermos*, meaning "thick skin".

Palaeoloxodon antiquus An extinct species of elephant restricted to Eurasia. Probably derived from a branch of the African *ELEPHAS* stock, it appeared in Europe about 500,000 years ago and became extinct approximately 450,000 years later. This large elephant species, adapted to warm, forested habitats, occasionally coexisted with the WOOLLY MAMMOTH.

Paleo-Indians Hunter-gatherers in the New World, dating from the late PLEISTOCENE to about 7,000 years ago.

Paleolithic The "Old Stone Age", the first period of prehistory covering the time from the first appearance of tool-using humans (about 2.5 million years ago) to the end of the last ICE AGE around 10,000 years ago. Paleolithic people lived as hunter-gatherers. The period is divided into three major phases. The Lower Paleolithic is the time of the early humans with their simple stone tools. The Middle Paleolithic is more technologically advanced and coincides roughly with the NEANDERTHALS. The Upper Paleolithic is the period of fully modern humans and is associated with fine stone and bone tools and the production of imagery and body adornment.

Paleontology The study of the FOSSILIZED remains of living organisms.

Parallel evolution A process of EVOLUTION in two separate species or populations which, from the same starting point, produces similar trends or ADAPTATIONS.

Parietal art Literally meaning "art on the walls", the term covers prehistoric works of art on any non-movable surface, including blocks, ceilings and floors.

Parkland A landscape superficially resembling a modern ornamental or recreational park, with areas of grass and scattered groves of trees and shrubs.

Pelvis A large bone attached to the rear part of the vertebral column. It supports the internal organs, provides the point of articulation with the hind limbs, and includes the birth canal. Also termed the "pelvic girdle", it is fused from three bones: the ILIUM, ischium and pubis.

Periglacial An environment characterized by severe frost action and dominated by processes and features influenced by cold climates, such as ground ice, production of large amounts of weathered debris and strong winds resulting in much deposition of silt and sand. It is often associated with the area fringing modern and PLEISTOCENE glaciers and areas of PERMAFROST.

Periodontal disease Disease of the tissues which support a tooth in the jaw, including the CEMENT and jaw bone.

Permafrost An area of land in Arctic or Antarctic regions where the ground is permanently frozen. In many areas, the surface layer thaws in summer.

Phiomia One of the paleomastodonts, a group of early PROBOSCIDEA found in North African deposits of 40–30 million years ago. They were the short-trunked precursors of MASTODONTS.

Pitfall trap A camouflaged pit, sometimes with a pointed stake at the bottom, dug on paths much used by prey, or near water sources, in the hope that the animal would fall in, so that it could be killed or left to die.

Pleistocene The period from approximately 1.7 million to 10,000 years ago, which included the ICE AGES. Generally divided into Early Pleistocene from 1.7 million to 780,000 years ago, Middle Pleistocene from 780,000 to 127,000, and Late Pleistocene from 127,000 to 10,000 years ago. The term is sometimes extended to include the last 10,000 years, a period now usually termed the HOLOCENE.

Point Category of stone tools, including pointed tools FLAKED on one or both sides.

Polymerase chain reaction (PCR) A laboratory process whereby small amounts of DNA are replicated into numerous identical copies suitable for further analysis.

Portable art Artworks small or light enough to be carried, such as carved or engraved ivory.

Postglacial Another name for the HOLOCENE.

Primelephas An early genus of true ELEPHANT (ELEPHANTIDAE) known from African deposits around 5–6 million years old. It is regarded as close to the common ancestor of the modern elephants and the MAMMOTHS.

Proboscidea The order of MAMMALS that includes the MAMMOTH and the living ELEPHANTS. Characterized, except in the earliest forms, by the possession of a TRUNK (PROBOSCIS) and TUSKS.

Proboscis Technical term for the TRUNK. The word comes from the Greek *proboskis*, literally "means of providing food".

Projectile point The tip of a projectile, made of stone, bone, metal or any suitable material.

Protozoa Single-celled animals, both free-living and parasites.

Quartzite A dense, hard rock that can produce FLAKED tools; small rounded quartzite cobbles also made ideal hammerstones for stoneworking.

Radioactivity The property of unstable ISOTOPES to decay to another type of atom, emitting subatomic particles in the process. The rate of decay is constant for a given isotope, forming a basis for ABSOLUTE DATING.

Radiocarbon dating A means of dating organic matter, including bone and wood. Based on counting the regular decay of isotopic carbon (C-14) to nitrogen, it is accurate back to about 30,000 years ago.

Red cells The most common cell type in the blood, technically called erythrocytes, containing the red pigment hemoglobin. They carry oxygen to the muscles and organs, and remove carbon dioxide.

Relative dating Any method of determining the relative age of FOSSILS or SEDIMENTS without knowing their ABSOLUTE age. The information is expressed as "A is younger than (or older than, or the same age as) B".

Sabre-tooth cat One of a number of extinct species within the cat family (Felidae) which independently evolved very long, flattened and curved upper canine teeth, probably used for stabbing or slashing prey. The best-known is *Smilodon fatalis* from the late PLEISTOCENE of North America.

Sagebrush Common North American name for species of the genus *Artemisia*, a member of the daisy family (Compositae). Usually of shrubby habit, they are known in Europe as mugwort or wormwood.

Saltbush Common North American name for species of the genus *Atriplex*, known in Europe as orache and belonging to the family Chenopodiaceae. They are annuals, commonly found on bare ground by coasts.

Savanna A present-day tropical or subtropical vegetation comprising a grassy plain with scattered trees. Typical savanna is seen in parts of Africa which support a diverse mammalian FAUNA.

Scapula The large, flattened bone forming the shoulder blade.

Scimitar-tooth cat An extinct genus of large cat (*Homotherium*) with long, powerful forelimbs and enlarged, flattened, serrated upper canines. Belonging to a different group from the true SABRE-TOOTHS, the scimitar-tooth cats lived in the PLEISTOCENE of both Europe and North America.

Sea cow A large species of SIRENIA (*Hydrodamalis gigas*) up to 25 ft (7.6 m) in length, formerly inhabiting the north Pacific but hunted to extinction in the 17th century.

Sedge A large group of plants (Cyperaceae) including the rushes and sedges. They are usually plants of damp conditions, but there are also dry-ground species, some of which were common on the MAMMOTH STEPPE.

Sediment In geology, an ancient deposit made up by the accumulation of small particles of clay, silt, sand, gravel or organic matter. FOSSILS are often deposited within it.

Shaft-wrench Also known as a perforated baton, this tool comprises a cylinder of bone or antler with a hole through its thickest part. It was probably a device for straightening the shafts of spears.

Shrub A woody plant usually less tall than a tree, whose stems divide close to the ground.

Siberia A vast area of land, extending from the Ural Mountains in the west (the boundary with European Russia) to the Pacific Ocean in the east. It currently comprises a number of republics within the Russian Federation.

Sinkhole A craterlike depression due to rock or soil subsidence, which may act as a natural trap for passing animals.

Sirenia A group of HERBIVOROUS marine MAMMALS, the closest living relatives of ELEPHANTS and MAMMOTHS. Divided into the DUGONG, MANATEE and extinct Steller's SEA COW.

Solifluction The process of mass movement of water-laden soil and SEDIMENT as the result of the thawing of frozen ground.

Spore The asexual reproductive cell of non-flowering plants such as mosses and ferns.

Stalagmite A mineral deposit precipitated in air-filled caves from seeping waters rich in carbonate.

Stegodon A genus of MASTODONT belonging to the family Stegodontidae. Within this group were late MIOCENE forms from which the true ELEPHANTS are believed to have evolved. Ranging from Africa to southern Asia, some species survived into the PLEISTOCENE and produced DWARF forms on Indonesian islands.

Stegotetrabelodon The earliest known genus of true ELEPHANT from 5 to 6 million-year-old deposits of northern, central and eastern Africa

Steppe A flat landscape devoid of forest but dominated by grassland. Refers chiefly to areas of southern Russia; similar landscapes are represented by the American prairies.

Steppe mammoth The common name for *Mammuthus trogontherii*.

Steppe-tundra An alternative term for MAMMOTH STEPPE.

Straight-tusked elephant Common name for *Palaeoloxodon antiquus*.

Taphonomy Study of the processes whereby animals, plants and ARTEFACTS are incorporated into fossil or archaeological deposits, especially the factors affecting the composition and completeness of excavated remains.

Tectiform A class of apparently non-figurative signs found engraved or painted in PALEOLITHIC PARIETAL ART, named for their supposed resemblance to a roofed hut.

Tethys Sea A large marine basin which formerly extended from what is now the western Mediterranean to Southeast Asia. Many remains of early PROBOSCIDEA have been found in deposits of its former shores.

Tomography *see* COMPUTER TOMOGRAPHY

Trunk Characteristic feature of PROBOSCIDEA, used in breathing, feeding, drinking, grooming and general manipulation. Formed from a fusion of the nose and upper lip, it carries the two nostrils from the head to its tip.

Tundra The dominant landscape of modern Arctic regions, with frozen subsoil and a vegetation dominated by slow-growing herbaceous plants and shrubs.

Tundra-steppe A term for MAMMOTH STEPPE.

Tungus A complex of peoples living in the taiga (subarctic forest) of eastern SIBERIA.

Tusks The enlarged INCISOR teeth of PROBOSCIDEA. Early PROBOSCIDEA had tusks in upper or lower jaws, or both. In ELEPHANTS and MAMMOTHS, only the upper tusks are present, and are formed from the second (side) incisors, the middle pair having been lost. With the exception of the tips of the milk tusks, ENAMEL is absent, the tusks comprising solid DENTINE.

"Venus" figurine The popular but erroneous name for the small female statuettes of the Upper PALEOLITHIC in Eurasia. They span a period from 25,000 to 12,000 years ago, are made of a variety of materials (but often of MAMMOTH IVORY), and depict females of a wide variety of ages and physical types.

White cells Various types of unpigmented blood cells (leucocytes) which act in the body's defence system against disease organisms.

Wolverine A mammalian CARNIVORE (*Gulo gulo*) of the badger family. Up to 3 ft (90 cm) long and powerfully built, it inhabits Arctic regions of Eurasia and North America, hunting small mammals and birds and scavenging from kills of other CARNIVORES.

Woolly mammoth The common name for *Mammuthus primigenius*.

Woolly rhinoceros An extinct species of Eurasian PLEISTOCENE rhinoceros, *Coelodonta antiquitatis*, which coexisted with the WOOLLY MAMMOTH. A large rhinoceros with a shoulder hump and woolly coat, it subsisted largely on the grasses of the MAMMOTH STEPPE.

Yakuts A major native people of SIBERIA, who have expanded from their origins on the middle Lena River to become a large autonomous republic, Yakutia.

Yedoma Gently sloping, rounded hills of silt in SIBERIA that may be composed of up to 80 percent ice. Also used to refer to the SEDIMENT of which they are composed.

Yesterday's camel Common name for *Camelops hesternus*, the most abundant of the PLEISTOCENE camels of North America. It was extinct by 10,500 years ago.

Recent years have witnessed remarkable advances in geological dating, the reconstruction of past climates and habitats, and the interpretation of fossil remains down to microscopic and molecular levels. As a result, paleontology is fast becoming a high-technology science, and much of the information presented in this book is the result of these techniques, which are briefly described in this section.

WHAT IS A FOSSIL?

Fossils are the preserved remains or imprints of once living creatures. Although they are by no means rare, they represent only a tiny proportion of the millions of organisms that have lived. After death, most animals disappear completely by decay or by being eaten. Only a very small number end up in river or lake sediment, enclosed within peat, or otherwise buried. The special situations in which some spectacular mammoth remains have been found – frozen in permafrost, pickled in salty tar or dried in caves – are even rarer, considering the fossil record as a whole. In almost all other situations, the soft tissues quickly decay so that only the hard parts – the bones and teeth of vertebrates or the shells of invertebrates – remain.

Even bones and teeth incorporated into the deposit can change or indeed disappear after burial, but such changes depend on the surrounding sediment and the timespan. Only in favourable circumstances will anything survive. In the case of bones and teeth, acid conditions will dissolve them away until only the hardest parts, or none at all, remain. By contrast, in sediments whose mineral composition is similar to that of bone itself, such as chalk or limestone, the bones may remain little changed for long periods.

Gradually, however, all bones and teeth are infiltrated by minerals dissolved in groundwater. Mineral salts such as calcium and iron will be deposited in tiny pores within the bone, and eventually the bone substance itself, while retaining its original shape, may be replaced atom for atom by substances such as silica. This process, known as mineralization, increases the weight of the fossil and eventually turns it, literally, to stone. In England's Cromer Forest-bed, for example, fossils of the ancestral mammoth, around 1.5 million years old, are frequently heavy and dense, indicating mineralization, while those of the steppe mammoth, less than half as old, are lighter and less altered from their original state. Although it depends greatly on the geological context, as a rule of thumb, bones begin to appear distinctly mineralized after a million years or so. Few mammoth fossils of later species – woolly and Columbian – have suffered significant mineralization, because they are only a few hundred thousand years old or less.

Excavated bones and teeth display a wide range of colours which reflect the nature of the groundwater but are of little further significance and give no indication of age. For example, bones buried in peat for only a few hundred years may become stained dark brown, while others which have lain in white chalk for a million years can retain their original pale colour.

On the matter of terminology, the use of the word fossil is a subjective one. Some people restrict it to animal or plant remains that have become mineralized, but since this process is a gradual one, it would be difficult to draw the line between what is a fossil and what is not. Here, all excavated remains of mammoths, including mineralized and unmineralized bones and teeth, and even frozen carcasses, are regarded as fossils, whatever their age. Traces left by once living animals, such as footprints and dung, are also regarded as fossil remains.

RE-CREATING THE SCENE
The example of the Berelekh mammoth "cemetery"

When mammoth remains are unearthed, scientists try to gather as much information as possible from the bones themselves, from local geology, and from other remains associated with the mammoths. This information is used to build up a picture of how the deposit originated, and particularly how the mammoth remains came to be there – a study known as taphonomy. The origins of several important mammoth sites have been briefly described in chapter two; here, as an example, a more detailed account is given of one particular site – the Berelekh mammoth cemetery in northeastern Siberia (see pp.50–51).

At the Berelekh site, mammoth bones have been known for centuries; thousands have been exposed by soil movements and river erosion. The bone-bearing horizon has been traced for a distance of 590 ft (180 m) along the bank of the Berelekh River, but how far it extends into the hillslope is anyone's guess. Consequently, it is impossible to know how extensive the site is, but it has been estimated that over the past 100 years up to 50,000 bones from 200 mammoths could have been naturally washed out and redeposited in the riverbed.

The bone deposits, up to 6½ ft (2 m) thick, comprise layers of frozen peat and icy silt. The bones, often entwined with bunches of black hair, form a number of dense concentrations: one, 54 sq ft (5 m2) by 2½ ft (80 cm) deep, contained no less than 954 bones. The bones lack signs of abrasion, indicating that they were not carried downstream in a defleshed state. On the other hand, muscle, cartilage and ligaments are largely absent, and many bones – up to 42 percent for some types – seem to have been gnawed by predators, which means that they were exposed at some stage. A further indication of exposure is the discovery of many hatched puparia of meat flies in tusk sockets and other parts of the skulls.

There are fish scales and water fleas in the bone layer, which together with the fine silty sediments indicate that this was originally a very calm section of a river, perhaps periodically cut off as an oxbow lake. On the other hand, the way in which the peaty and silty sediments are mixed together, and the fact that there are no intact skeletons, or skulls with tusks still in their sockets, show that the remains had subsequently undergone some very active movements and complex disturbances, such as solifluction (soil creep) and landslides. Moreover, because the deposits and bones have been moved around since original deposition, collecting associated animal and plant remains truly contemporary with the bones has to be carried out with great care.

Based on tusk shape, about 75 percent of the mammoths recovered are thought to be female, and in terms of age it was young adults that predominated: about 70 percent are between 10 and 30 years old, while some bones of fetuses and sucklings were also recovered. One question for investigators is: does Berelekh comprise a few occasional mass deaths, or a more sporadic collection of individuals and small groups that died over many years or even millennia? Like modern elephants, female mammoths with calves and youngsters tended to stay in small groups of 5 to 15, and adult males usually lived alone, although occasional mixed herds of 100 or more individuals were possible. Seen from that perspective, the Berelekh accumulation could have formed from a mixture of individuals and groups, representing accidents over many centuries.

The interpretation of Berelekh is therefore as follows: over thousands of years, a succession of individual mammoths, and perhaps occasional groups, became trapped or drowned, probably by getting stuck in fluid mud or falling through thin ice. Their carcasses were carried off by the river and came to rest in a meander or backwater. When the water level in this silty reservoir dropped periodically, the corpses were exposed, and the stench attracted flies which laid thousands of eggs, hatching larvae that ate the rotting flesh, thus accounting for the discovery of hatched puparia in the skulls.

At the same time the smell attracted scavengers such as wolverines and wolves, which left their gnaw marks on the bones. As the waters returned, fish ate their share of the tissues. Gradually the remaining bones were covered with a bed of silt deposited by the overlying water, and when the basin was fully silted up, peat-forming vegetation grew on its surface. Periodically, however, soil movements added further deposits on top, and mixed up the existing ones. After some millennia, the Berelekh River began to cut through this "cemetery" in its bank, and the bones started to emerge.

DATING MAMMOTH REMAINS
Relative dating

Calculating the age of ancient finds is essential for making sense of the fossil record, tracing past changes in the environment and following the evolution and extinction of animals such as the mammoth. All dating techniques are either relative or absolute. If one layer or fossil is higher in the geological sequence than another, then its relative age is later (that is, it is younger). Relative dating can also be applied if fossils from different localities are associated with assemblages of other fossil animals or plants whose relative ages are known. This allows the fossils in question to be placed in relative order.

Absolute dating

In absolute dating, an age in years can be placed on a fossil or deposit. Some techniques allow direct analysis of a mammoth bone or tooth; others date the sediments enclosing it. Sometimes, an age is obtained from deposits above or below a fossil so the latter can be calculated as either younger or older than the dated horizon. If the fossil is sandwiched between two dated levels, its age must fall between the two limits.

Radiocarbon dating

Many absolute dating methods are based on the radioactive decay of one substance into another. The best-known of these is radiocarbon dating. A small amount of the heavy atomic form (isotope) of carbon, C-14, exists in the atmosphere and is incorporated into plants and animals during their life. It is unstable, however, and gradually decays into nitrogen at a constant, known rate. After approximately 5,730 years, half the C-14 in a sample will have disappeared, after another 5,730 years, three-quarters, after a further 5,730 years, seven-eighths, and so on. The older the sample, therefore, the less C-14 that remains, so that by determining the proportion of C-14 left in the material, its age can be estimated.

There are two methods of radiocarbon dating. In the first, conventional, method the sample, which is generally many grams in weight, is placed in an instrument that counts the number of radioactive emissions (electrons) given out each time an atom of C-14 decays into one of nitrogen. In the second, newer, method the amount of C-14 is compared to the commoner, lighter isotope of carbon, C-12, by direct measurement in a mass spectrometer. This method, known as accelerator mass spectrometry (AMS), has the advantage that it requires only a gram or less of bone or other substance, allowing the dating of precious fossils or artefacts without destroying the whole specimen. Even pigments in cave drawings are now being dated by the AMS method.

Radiocarbon dating depends on the assumption that the production of C-14 in the atmosphere has remained constant through time. There is evidence, however, that this has varied somewhat in the past, so that radiocarbon dates differ slightly from the true ages of samples, the discrepancy increasing with age. For example, a "radiocarbon age" of 6,000 years implies a true age of nearly 7,000 years. Further back, the discrepancy is not accurately known, but a fossil or event dated to, say, 13,000 years by radiocarbon may in reality be 1,500 or 2,000 years older. Following the normal convention, all dates for mammoth fossils and climatic events given in this book are in "radiocarbon years" ago.

Other radiometric methods

Because of its relatively fast decay rate, radiocarbon is valid for dating only back to about 30,000 years ago. Beyond that, other radioactive atoms, with slower decay rates, can be measured. These include isotopes of uranium, which decay to lead and cover the past several hundred thousand years; and an isotope of potassium which has an even slower decay rate, to argon, and extends millions of years into the past.

ESR dating

An exciting new dating method, particularly relevant to the remains of mammoths, is electron spin resonance (ESR), which in principle can cover remains from the whole Pleistocene and beyond (i.e. from up to 2 million years ago or more). ESR dating depends on the fact that a buried fossil or other object will receive a steady dose of radiation from surrounding minerals and cosmic rays. The radiation results in the liberation of electrons, some of which become trapped in the crystal structure of the fossil. This liberation occurs cumulatively, so the age of a specimen can be calculated by measuring the radiation input from the surrounding deposit and the trapped electrons in the fossil. The former is measured using a radiation meter at the fossil site, the latter by irradiating the fossil with gamma rays and measuring the resultant ESR signal in the laboratory. Crystalline hard parts of animals are suitable for ESR dating, and mammoth tooth enamel is ideal because it is so thick. Many fossils of mammoths are now being dated by this method.

A mammoth molar sampled for ESR dating. A rectangular block has been cut from the tooth using a diamond-wire saw. From an inner surface, a small piece of dentine and enamel has been removed with a dental wheel. This provides a sample of clean, uncontaminated material for analysis and also allows the tooth to be stuck back together with no external damage.

Limits to dating accuracy

All absolute dating methods are accurate only within certain limits, imposed by two main considerations. First, uncertainties associated with laboratory measurements mean that dates are accurate to within anything from 1 to 10 percent of the "real" value. Second, sample contamination may alter the measured date; for example, a fossil from one horizon which had been affected by soil water running down from a higher horizon may have incorporated some carbon of a later date than itself and will thus give too young a radiocarbon date. For this reason, samples must be collected and chosen with great care, and thoroughly cleaned and tested for contamination before analysis.

CLUES TO PAST CLIMATE

Mammoths evolved, lived and finally became extinct against the backdrop of the dramatic climatic changes of the Pleistocene ice ages. Knowledge of these changes is therefore essential for understanding the origins of the mammoth's adaptations, migrations and ultimate demise.

Deep-sea cores

The broad pattern of warm–cold changes in global climate through the Pleistocene *(see p.26)* has been reconstructed largely using cores of sediment taken through the ocean floor and comprising fine particles which have settled and gradually built up on the seabed over millions of years. Successive slices of core provide information on past changes in global climate.

Climatic information is found in ocean cores because of the existence of two types or isotopes of oxygen in sea water (H_2O), one of which (O-18) is slightly heavier than the other (O-16). During times of cold climate, proportionately more water containing the lighter isotope evaporated from the ocean surface, and some of it became locked up as ice when it fell as rain or snow on the expanded glaciers. The water remaining in the sea therefore accumulated proportionately more of the heavier isotope. During times of warmer climate, this effect was less pronounced, and the ocean retained more of the lighter isotope. The relative "heaviness" of oxygen from the ancient ocean therefore provides a measure of past temperature.

The oxygen signal has been preserved in the shells of microscopic sea creatures called foraminifera, or forams for short. In their growth they take in sea water and incorporate the oxygen atoms into the carbonate shells. Thousands of shells of dead forams are preserved in each slice of the sea-bottom sediment, so, by analysing the proportion of O-18 to O-16 within them, scientists can estimate the global temperature at the time that slice of sediment was being deposited.

Cores are drilled and lifted by specially equipped ocean-going vessels. In the laboratory, the cores are divided into slices representing successive intervals of past time. Under the microscope, foram shells are picked from the sediment and then dissolved in acid to produce carbon dioxide (CO_2) from calcium carbonate in the shell. This carbon dioxide is collected and analysed in a mass spectrometer, an instrument that measures how much CO_2 is made from O-18, how much from O-16. The ratio between these figures gives an estimate of past temperature and, by plotting these estimates from slices along the whole core, a graph of past climate change is produced.

Ice cores

Similar analysis performed on cores taken through ice sheets (glaciers) in Greenland and Antarctica has provided a detailed record of climate over short periods (e.g. the last Ice Age – *see pp.134–35*). The ice sheets have been building up over thousands of years due to snow and rain falling on their surface. As in the ocean cores, it is the proportion of oxygen isotopes that bears the climatic signal. Here, however, it is the lighter isotope (O-16) that indicates colder climate, because the ice is formed from water evaporated from the ocean, comprising relatively more of the lighter form as temperature decreases.

RECONSTRUCTING THE MAMMOTH'S HABITAT

While studies of ocean sediments and ice cores provide invaluable information on broad changes in global climate, other methods are used to give more details of the climate and landscape of particular regions at specific times, including the local habitats of individual mammoth finds. These include the study of other animal and plant remains found in dated horizons, or directly associated with the mammoths themselves.

Plant remains

Direct evidence of past vegetation is obtained by studying plant remains in ancient deposits. Some such deposits, for instance those formed of peat, are composed almost entirely of plant matter, as are the remains of mammoth gut contents and dung balls. Others, such as silts or clays from rivers or lakes, must be washed and sieved to reveal and concentrate fragmentary plant remains. Parts that can be recognized include fruits, seeds and leaves. Under the microscope these can often be identified to the level of family, genus or species, with the aid of complete specimens of modern plants for comparison. Trees can often be identified by their wood, because different species have a characteristic appearance when thin sections are examined under the microscope.

Pollen analysis

A particularly important category of plant remains comprises the individual pollen grains shed by long-dead flowers and the spores produced by ancient ferns and mosses. Although generally only one-fiftieth of a millimetre or so in diameter, these have a tough outer wall which is extremely resistant to decay and erosion and often survives in ancient sediments. They also appear to survive attack by mammalian digestive enzymes, and so are preserved in gut contents and dung. Moreover, under the microscope, the spores and pollen of different species of plant have clearly differing, characteristic shapes, which allows them to be identified.

Samples of peat, silt or clay from fossil deposits may contain millions of spores or pollen grains which blew or were washed in while the sediment was accumulating. For study, however, they must be separated from the sediment and concentrated, involving a series of laboratory procedures including flotation, sieving and dissolving away other plant or mineral matter with various chemicals. Eventually, the pollen and spore concentrate is smeared on a microscope slide and systematically scanned, each identifiable grain being noted. From this, a list of plant species and their proportions is obtained.

Interpreting pollen and spore data requires care. Some plants (e.g. pine and birch) are known to produce much more pollen per flower than others (e.g. beech and holly), so their preponderance in fossil sediments could be artificially inflated. Also, some pollen types, such as pine, can blow farther in the wind than others, so their presence does not necessarily mean that there were pine trees in the immediate area. Finally, certain grains (e.g. those of some moss and fern spores) are more resistant to decay than others (e.g. pollen from poplar trees), so are more likely to survive in ancient sediments.

As long as such biases are borne in mind, however, pollen and spore analysis is an extremely powerful means of reconstructing past vegetation. Combining the data from pollen and other vegetational remains can help overcome any possible bias. For example, the guts of the Shandrin mammoth *(see pp.74–75)* contained abundant moss spores, suggesting that moss was a major part of its last meal. However, the actual plant fragments contained only 1 percent moss by volume, giving a rather more accurate indication of its importance.

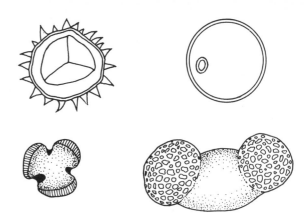

The varying shapes of pollen and spores, magnified 1,000 times. Clockwise from top left: *clubmoss* (Selaginella), *grass (Graminae), pine* (Pinus) and *sagebrush/mugwort* (Artemisia).

Insect remains

Other organic remains are also used to help reconstruct past climate and habitat. These include molluscs, diatoms (microscopic single-celled plants that live in salt and fresh water) and ostracods (tiny freshwater crustaceans). Insects, especially beetles, have been particularly employed in this way, since their hard outer skeleton, made of the tough substance chitin, survives well in ancient sediments. Usually they are not found complete, but isolated parts, such as the head, wing covers or genitalia, have detailed structures which, under the microscope, allow them to be identified to particular species, by comparison with known modern specimens. As with plant remains, the insect parts are recovered from sediments by a combination of sieving, floating and chemical techniques.

Insect remains are particularly valuable for habitat reconstruction because many species survive only within relatively narrow tolerances of climate and vegetation. This is deduced from knowledge of living representatives. For example, some species are restricted to life on a particular plant species, and so their discovery in an ancient sediment indicates the presence of the plant even when remains of the vegetation are absent. Further, many insects have limited temperature tolerances and so their fossils can suggest past climate. Many deposits of the last Ice Age in Britain contain beetle species which today live in northern Scandinavia or Siberia. Conversely, interglacial deposits include beetles now living only in southern Europe. Detailed analysis of beetle species, in comparison with their modern ranges, can allow scientists to calculate past winter and summer temperatures when the deposit was forming.

PUTTING FLESH ON THE BONES
Reconstructing body form

Mammoths are almost unique among extinct prehistoric animals in the detailed information available on their soft parts such as skin and hair, thanks to the preservation of frozen carcasses. Nonetheless, the frozen material is shrivelled, and no carcass except the baby Dima has reached the laboratory wholly intact. Further evidence on the animal's body form is provided by Paleolithic art and the study of skulls and skeletons.

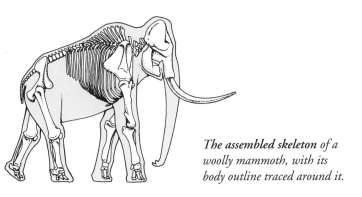

The assembled skeleton of a woolly mammoth, with its body outline traced around it.

Piecing together a mammoth skeleton for museum display is a particularly revealing exercise, for then characteristics such as the size of the animal's rib cage and the relative height of its front and hind quarters become evident. Assembling the spine, it becomes clear that the individual vertebrae fit together in such a way as to produce the sloping back seen in Paleolithic art, with the shoulder hump resulting from long vertebral spines.

The shape of the mammoth's head can be deduced from that of the skull, allowing for flesh using the modern elephant as a guide, in essentially the same way as police reconstructions of faces are made from human skulls. The mammoth's skull shows its eye socket to be relatively far forward, for example. Details such as the shape of the ear are based on frozen material. The top of the skull is rather pointed, but it is clear from Paleolithic art that in life this was padded into a rounded dome, presumably with fatty or other tissue.

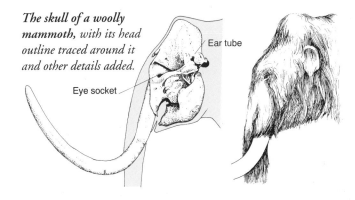

The skull of a woolly mammoth, with its head outline traced around it and other details added.

Ear tube

Eye socket

How to weigh a mammoth

The approximate body weight of a mammoth species can be calculated from its height, by comparison with modern elephants whose body form is broadly comparable. Measurement of elephants has resulted in graphs showing the increase in body weight with shoulder height. For mammoth specimens within the size range of living elephants, body weights can be read directly from these graphs. For example, a mammoth 11 ft (3.4 m) high can be assumed to weigh about 6 tons – about the same as a large bull African elephant of the same height. For smaller individuals, such as dwarf mammoths, juvenile elephants can be used as a guide, with something added for the heavier build and larger tusks of dwarfed adults. Thus, a

6 ft (1.8 m) high adult dwarf mammoth probably weighed around 1.5 tons, slightly above the 1.3 tons of a 10-year-old elephant of comparable height. Conversely, some mammoths, such as *Mammuthus trogontherii* and *M. columbi*, were larger than any living elephant, shoulder heights reaching more than 13 ft (4 m) in large males. In this case, the graph for living elephants can be extended upward, indicating a weight of around 10 tons for these individuals. A check can be made by comparing the girth of the fossil limb bones with those of living elephants, for it is found that these correlate closely to body weight among mammals. By either method, weight is found to increase greatly with relatively small height increments, since a larger animal puts on weight in all dimensions. Weight, in fact, is roughly proportional to the cube of height or length, so that, for example, a doubling in height produces an eightfold increase in weight.

MAMMOTH AGE AND SEX
Age estimation

The age of a juvenile can be roughly estimated from its size, but this is not a very accurate method, and cannot be applied to adults that have stopped growing. Much more precise age estimates can be obtained from the teeth. As explained on p.78, mammoths went through six sets of molars in their life, each successive tooth larger than the previous one. By studying large numbers of teeth, researchers learn to place any fossil molar in its correct position in the sequence, based on its size, crown height and number of enamel ridges. Immediately, therefore, it is possible to get a rough idea of a mammoth's age.

More accurate estimates are made by comparison with modern elephants. Research on African and Asian elephants has shown how the stage of tooth replacement and wear is linked to age. For example, the third molar always replaces the second at about 3–4 years of age, while the sixth replaces the fifth at about 30. These figures can be taken as roughly valid for woolly mammoths too, because the elephants have the same number of tooth replacements as the mammoths, and are of comparable body size indicating a similar total lifespan. Larger species, such as the Columbian mammoth, still had six sets of teeth, but because of their larger size probably lived longer. The age at which each tooth was in use may, therefore, have been spread over more years than in the elephants and woolly mammoths, so a small addition to "elephant tooth ages" must be made.

Male or female?

A few frozen carcasses preserve intact genitalia, so gender can be directly observed. Most usually, however, gender has to be deduced from skeletal remains. Males were generally larger than females, so the sex of very large or very small individuals can usually be guessed. However, in many cases of intermediate size it would be difficult to know from the bones whether they belonged to a large female or a small male. Male skulls are relatively more robust than those of females, especially in the region of the tusk. If tusks themselves are preserved, the much more slender tusks of females compared to the stouter male variety *(see p.80)* may provide a clear clue to gender.

The most reliable method of determining sex is to examine the pelvic girdle. Because this bone contains the birth canal through which baby mammoths were born, its shape differs clearly between males and females. In the female, the birth canal is relatively wider, and the bone surrounding it, the ilium, is proportionately narrow. In males, conversely, the equivalent hole is narrower and the ilium wider. Measurement of a series of skeletons has shown that the ratio of canal width to ilium width is always higher in females than in males.

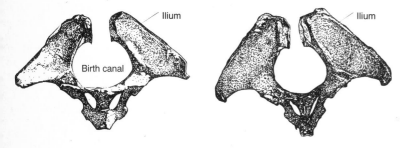

Pelvic girdles extracted from male and female woolly mammoths whose gender is known from preserved genitalia. In the female (left), *the birth canal is wider, and the surrounding bone narrower, than in the male* (right).

CHARTING THE MAMMOTH'S EVOLUTION

The evolution of the mammoth has been traced from African progenitors, via the ancestral mammoth *M. meridionalis*, to *M. primigenius* in Eurasia and *M. columbi* in America. This has been achieved by detailed comparison of fossil skulls, teeth and bones from successive time horizons. In such studies, it is essential that fossils should be accurately dated so that they can be placed in the correct position in the sequence. It is also important that as many specimens as possible be examined from each

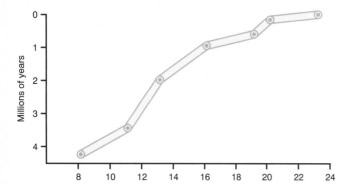

The increase in the average number of enamel ridges on Old World mammoth molars through time. Each point represents the average number of ridges in a sample of back (sixth) upper molars. The earliest two samples, between 5 and 3 million years old, are early and late Mammuthus subplanifrons *from Africa. The next two, at 2 and 1 million years old, are early and late samples of* M. meridionalis. *The point at approximately 750,000 years ago is* M. trogontherii, *and the last two are early and late* M. primigenius.

horizon, so that normal variation between individual animals is not mistaken for evolutionary change. Finally, if possible, fossils should be examined from across the geographical range of the species, because new forms sometimes evolve in one area before spreading to another.

Fossil molars provide the most abundant remains and show pronounced changes in accordance with the animals' diet. The number of enamel ridges on the back molar is one index of this change, as explained on p.25. Quantities of such molars have been measured from each of several dated time horizons, and the average number of ridges in each sample calculated. This information has been plotted against the age of the samples to show the evolutionary trend. The graph suggests a gradual transition, but one which speeded up after about one million years ago. It also indicates that the division of this continuous lineage into distinct species is to some extent arbitrary.

EXTRACTING MAMMOTH DNA

Genetic material, or DNA, is preserved in ancient tissues only in special circumstances where decay is minimized, as in very dry conditions or in quickly frozen carcasses. Surprisingly, bones and teeth may preserve DNA better than soft tissues. The DNA originates in living cells that produce their surrounding hard tissue, and the mineral nature of their environment protects the DNA from decay.

Samples are chosen that show the least contamination (for example, from soil chemicals or handling during excavation), and their surfaces are cleaned and washed. The sample is finely ground, and the resulting suspension treated with solvents that remove non-DNA substances and relax the compressed DNA. In the case of bone, the mineral matter is removed by spinning at high speed in a centrifuge. Even under ideal conditions, ancient tissues preserve only minute amounts of DNA, so the DNA must be multiplied into sufficient quantities for analysis.

This process, known as amplification, is achieved by the inherent potential of DNA to replicate itself, using the polymerase chain reaction (PCR). A DNA molecule consists of two long strands, each formed from a chain of smaller molecules called nucleotides. The nucleotides contain a part known as the base, of which there are four varieties, abbreviated as A, T, C and G. These bases form a sort of genetic alphabet whose order along the DNA molecule specifies the mammoth's genetic code. Moreover, the two DNA strands are linked in such a way that C on one strand always pairs with G on the other, while A always pairs with T. In life, this provides the key to DNA replication, because if the two strands are separated, each provides a template for the growth of a new partner strand.

In the laboratory the double-stranded DNA is separated into single strands by heating. Two "primers" (short pieces of synthetic DNA) are added to this DNA sample, and link up with that part of the animal's DNA which it is intended to replicate. Also present are quantities of the four single nucleotides, which link up to the primer DNA one by one, using the sequence of the mammoth DNA as a template. This process repeats 20–40 times, doubling the amount of DNA with each cycle, producing millions of copies of the original mammoth DNA.

The next stage is to work out the sequence of nucleotides in the mammoth DNA. This is achieved by a complex and ingenious process which can only be outlined here. The sample is split into four parts, to each of which is added a special solution. Molecules present in this solution can identify all the positions along the DNA at which one of the four bases occurs. Between them, the four solutions identify the positions of each of the four bases A, T, C and G in the strand.

The results are observed by electrophoresis *(see p.139)*, in which the final products are placed on a flat gel and subjected to an electric field. DNA fragments in the sample move along the gel forming a series of visible bands that represent successive nucleotide positions along the chain. The positions of bands derived from one of the four solutions give the positions in the DNA chain where that nucleotide occurs. Electrophoresis with each of the four solutions, and combination of the results, yields the complete genetic sequence of the original DNA.

LEGENDS ABOUT EATING MAMMOTH FLESH

Many legends surround the excavation of frozen carcasses, and of these some of the more lurid relate to claims of feasting on mammoth steak. The flesh of modern elephants is something like beef, with excellent flavour, although it is much coarser and tougher. The delicacies are the heart, tongue and trunk, while the feet contain a large, springy pad which is very sweet and

makes good soup. The flesh of the Beresovka mammoth *(see pp.44–45)*, streaked and marbled with thick layers of fat, looked quite fresh and healthy as long as it was frozen, and was dark red like frozen beef or horse meat. Herz, the expedition leader, remarked, "It looked so appetizing that we wondered for some time whether we should not taste it, but no one would venture to take it into his mouth... the dogs cleaned up whatever mammoth meat was thrown to them." They were probably wise to abstain since, on thawing, the flesh turned grey.

One tale recounted that a scientist did in fact take a bite of the Beresovka mammoth, but could not keep the meat down. There are even accounts of mammoth banquets held in St. Petersburg. Another episode concerns an English lord, Talbot Clifton, who undertook a hunting expedition to Siberia in 1901. On the train to Yakutsk, he chanced on Herz and Pfizenmayer. As his wife, Violet Clifton, later recorded, "Herz counselled Talbot to cast his lot with him and join him in search of a mammoth. Talbot was a little tempted to join the man of science, but he did not assent, for he had the instinct to be alone on his travels, not answerable to anyone." Pfizenmayer, however, had a different recollection: "We had got to know an Englishman, who told us he was travelling... to hunt the local wild sheep. When he heard that we were going there too, only much farther east, he was very anxious to join us. His lordship did not seem to see that we were not at all keen on this."

So Talbot and the expedition went their separate ways, but on Christmas day 1901, Lord Clifton was back in Yakutsk. "As a gift Professor Herz had sent some of the flesh of the mammoth that he had found. They ate it thoughtfully, for was it not about eight thousand years old?" However, the reliability of Clifton's accounts is clearly open to question.

In China traders recommended mammoth meat as cooling and wholesome to eat, and a remedy for fever. One Chinese text of 1712 states, "The northern plain near the sea in Russia is the coldest place. There is a kind of beast, which is like a mouse as big as an elephant, crawls in tunnels, and dies as it meets the sun or the moonlight. Its teeth are like an elephant's, white, soft and smooth with no crackles. The native people often find it near the river bank. Its bones are used for making bowls, dishes, combs and fine double-edged tooth combs. Its meat is chilly and cold.... Taking it as food, uneasiness and fever can be ridded off and its Russian name is Momentuowa."

In the 1920s there were several reported cases of travellers being offered, and eating, mammoth flesh. The Chukchi of northeastern Siberia apparently considered mammoths to be evil spirits and had to utter incantations and beat drums whenever tusks were noticed protruding from the earth; but there is a legend that once, when a whole carcass appeared, two Chukchi ate the meat, found it very nutritious and lived on it all winter. Some modern Siberian hunters claim to have eaten cooked mammoth meat and describe it as very fibrous and as tough as rubber.

Extravagant tales surrounding the discovery of frozen Siberian mammoths were the source of legends about eating mammoth flesh, and likewise fuelled the imagination of 19th-century illustrators.

Mammoth Sites in Europe

MAMMOTHS

- Ancestral
- Steppe
- Woolly - Skeleton
- Woolly - Pickled
- Dwarf
- Straight-tusked elephant

SITES

- ◼ Cave depictions of mammoths
- ● Portable depictions of mammoths
- ◆ Ivory and bone craft objects
- ▲ Mammoth-bone huts

ATLANTIC OCEAN

NORTHERN IRELAND
Aghnadarragh ● Belfast

North Sea

Balderton Tattershall Thorpe
Condover West Runton
WALES Cromer Forest-bed
Stanton Norwich Crag AMSTERDAM NETHER-LANDS
Paviland Harcourt Red Crag Brown Bank
Swansea Aveley Deep Water Channel
Ilford Eastern Scheldt
Kent's Cavern Thames Aa BELGIUM Tegelen

English Channel Bergharen GERMANY
Lehringen
La Cotte de St. Brelade Gönnersdorf Ahlen
Bonn Edersleben Leipzig
Polch Voigtstedt
Mosbach Süss
Seine Kniegrott

PARIS Steinheim
Seine Stuttgart Obere Klaus
Mayenne-Sciences Arcy-sur-Cure Geissenklösterle Vogelherd
FRANCE Siegsdorf

La Marche BERN SWITZ. AU
Praz Rodet

● Périgueux

Garonne Señèze Oulen
Chilhac Le Figuier Chabot
El Pindal Brassempouy Durfort La Baume Latrone
El Castillo Lespugue Les Trois Upper Valdarno
Lourdes Gargas Frères Montopoli
Canecaude Pietrafitta
Bize Scopp
Ebro

Torralba, Ambrona
Tagus MADRID ROME
Tagus
SPAIN

MEDITERRANEAN SEA

SOUTHWESTERN FRANCE

■ Jovelle

◉ Périgueux

■ Rouffignac
■ La Madeleine
◆ Blanchard
● Laugerie Haute
■ Les Combarelles
■ Font de Gaume
■ Bernifal
Dordogne
Domme
■ Cougnac
■ Pech-Merle

● Bruniquel

Garonne   *Lot*

RUSSIA

POLAND

Vistula   ■ WARSAW

THE
CZECH
GUE
EPUBLIC

● Bzianka

▲ Kraków

◆ Oblazowa

● Predmosti

Brno ◆

◆ Milovice
Dolní Věstonice
Pavlov

◆ Tata   ■ BUDAPEST

SLOVAKIA

● Starunia

▲ Molodova

UKRAINE

◉ Rostov

Sea of
Azov

● Mátra

HUNGARY

Danube

RIA

ISRAEL & ETHIOPIA

Black   Sea

Alexandria ■   Ubeidiya
ISRAEL ■ JERUSALEM

EGYPT

Nile

SUDAN

SAUDI

Red
Sea

ARABIA

Afar Depression

■ ADDIS ABABA

ETHIOPIA

Y

cily

Spinagallo

0   200   400 miles

0   300   600 km

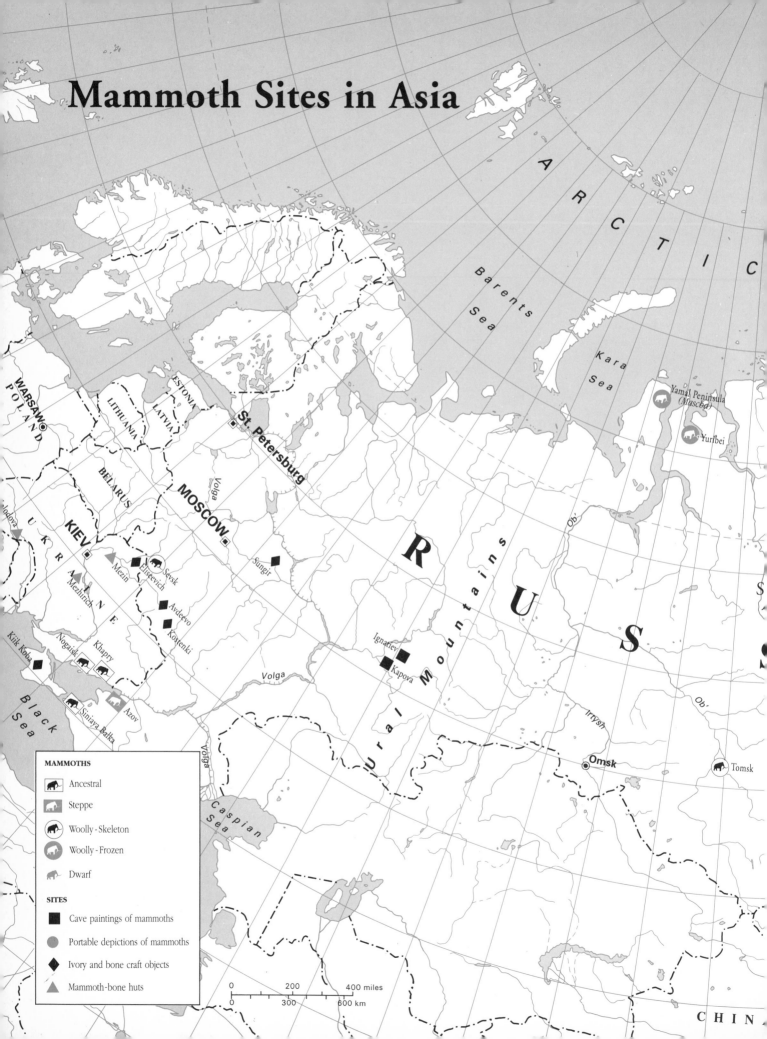

Mammoth Sites in Asia

ARCTIC

Barents Sea

Kara Sea

Yamal Peninsula (Mascha)

Yuribei

St Petersburg

POLAND
WARSAW

ESTONIA
LATVIA
LITHUANIA

BELARUS

MOSCOW

Volga

Sungir

R U S S

Ural Mountains

Ob'

KIEV

UKRAINE
Moldova

Mezin
Eliseevich
Sevsk

Avdeevo

Kostenki

Ignatiev

Kapova

Irtysh

Ob'

Nogaisk
Khapry

Kiik Koba

Siniaya Balka
Azov

Black Sea

Volga

Volga

Caspian Sea

Omsk

Tomsk

CHIN

MAMMOTHS

- Ancestral
- Steppe
- Woolly - Skeleton
- Woolly - Frozen
- Dwarf

SITES

- Cave paintings of mammoths
- Portable depictions of mammoths
- Ivory and bone craft objects
- Mammoth-bone huts

0   200   400 miles
0   300   600 km

O C E A N

Bering Sea

Laptev Sea

East Siberian Sea

Wrangel Island

Olyer Suite

Liakhov Islands

Sanga-Yurakh

Shandrin

Berelekh

Indigirka

Kolyma

Beresovka

Kirgilyak (Dima)

Taimyr

Lena River (Adams)

YAKUTIA

Sea of Okhotsk

Khatanga

Lena

Vilui

IBERIA

Lena

IA

Amur

Amur

Mal'ta

Irkutsk

Zhalainuoer

Manzhouli

Harbin

Heilongjiang, Zhaoyuan, Shan Zhan

MONGOLIA

CHINA

NORTH KOREA

BEIJING

Mammoth Sites in North America

ALASKA

Beaufort Sea

Elephant Point, Eschscholtz Bay

Old Crow

Fairbanks Creek

Anchorage

Gulf of Alaska

C A N A D A

BRITISH COLUMBIA

ALBERTA

SASKATCHEWAN

MANITOBA

ONTARIO

QUEBEC

Wellsch Valley

Olympic Peninsula
WASHINGTON

OREGON

IDAHO

MONTANA

NORTH DAKOTA

MINNESOTA

WISCONSIN

MICHIGAN

NEW YORK

VT.

Newburg

NEVADA

Colby

WYOMING

SOUTH DAKOTA

Hot Springs,
Lange-Ferguson site

IOWA

Jonesboro

INDIANA

OHIO

PENNSYLVANIA

NEW JERSEY

DELAWARE

MARYLAND

San
Francisco

CALIFORNIA

UTAH

Moab,
Bechan Cave,
Cowboy Cave

Dent

Hay Springs

NEBRASKA

Angus

ILLINOIS

Burning Tree

WEST
VIRGINIA

U N I T E D

Denver

COLORADO

Franklin
County

KANSAS

MISSOURI

Big Bone Lick

KENTUCKY

VIRGINIA

Rancho La Brea

Lamb Spring

S T A T E S

NORTH
CAROLINA

Santa Rosa
Island

Los Angeles

ARIZONA

Albuquerque

NEW
MEXICO

Miami

OKLAHOMA

ARKANSAS

TENNESSEE

SOUTH
CAROLINA

PACIFIC
OCEAN

Tucson

Blackwater Draw,
Clovis

Dallas

T E X A S

Trinity

LOUISIANA

MISSISSIPPI

ALABAMA

GEORGIA

Murray Springs, Naco,
Lehner Ranch,
Leikem, Escapule

Aucilla River

FLORIDA

Friesenhahn

Gulf of

Mexico

MAMMOTHS

Ancestral

Woolly - Skeleton

Woolly - Frozen

Columbian

Dwarf

Mastodon

SITES

Depictions of mammoths

M E X I C O

Tepexpan

MEXICO
CITY

0   200   400 miles

0   300   600 km

GUIDE TO SITES AND MUSEUMS

The following are among the most important sites from around the world containing mammoth finds ranging from complete skeletons to cave paintings. Many of these sites are no longer accessible; others are open to research parties only; but a few, marked with an asterisk, can be visited by the general public, although sometimes access may be only partial.

Aa A small river in northern France where a female woolly mammoth skeleton was excavated in the early 1900s.

Afar Depression A region of the Rift Valley in Ethiopia where fossils of the earliest elephants and mammoths, 4–5 million years old, have been recovered from deposits of the Awash Valley.

Aghnadarragh A quarry site in Northern Ireland where remains of small woolly mammoths, about 80,000 years old, were recovered in the 1970s and 1980s.

Ahlen A site in Germany where the complete skeleton of a woolly mammoth was unearthed; it is now mounted in Münster Museum.

Ambrona *see* Torralba

Angus The locality in Nebraska where a mammoth skeleton was unearthed in the early 1900s. Originally regarded as an ancestral mammoth, it is probably a variety of Columbian mammoth.

Arcy-sur-Cure A complex of nine caves in northern France occupied in the Middle and Upper Paleolithic, two of which (Grotte du Cheval and Grande Grotte) contain depictions dominated by mammoths.

Aucilla River River-bottom silts in the Florida "pan-handle" which have yielded skeletons of Columbian mammoths and, in 1993, a butchered mastodon tusk.

Avdeevo An Upper Paleolithic open-air site in European Russia. Its fossil assemblage is dominated by mammoths, and the artefacts include some portable depictions of the animal as well as numerous tools made of mammoth bone, and many tools and figurines in ivory.

Aveley A site in Essex, near London, England, where the remains of a mammoth were found above those of a straight-tusked elephant in 1964.

Azov The town near the Black Sea in southern Russia where one of the world's largest proboscidean fossils, the skeleton of a steppe mammoth nearly 15 ft (4.5 m) high, has been excavated and mounted.

Balderton A series of quarry sites in central England where mammalian fossils of the penultimate Ice Age, about 150,000 years old, were recovered from river gravels in the 1980s. The finds include hundreds of woolly mammoth molars.

Baume Latrone, La A cave near Nîmes, southern France, containing Ice Age paintings done in clay on its walls, including seven mammoths, some of which are highly stylized.

Bechan Cave and **Cowboy Cave** Two caves in Utah in which quantities of Columbian mammoth dung accumulated around 13,000 years ago.

Berelekh The northernmost Paleolithic site in the world, in northeastern Siberia. It is best known for its "cemetery" of thousands of naturally accumulated mammoth bones, as well as for a unique engraving of an elongated mammoth on a tusk.

Beresovka The river in northeastern Siberia near which a well-preserved frozen mammoth carcass was excavated in 1901 and moved in pieces to St. Petersburg, where its skeleton was mounted and its hide stuffed.

Bergharen A former gravel pit in the Netherlands where divers found a mammoth skull 40 ft (12 m) under water in 1994.

*Bernifal An Ice Age decorated cave in the Dordogne, France, containing a number of mammoth depictions as well as "tectiform" signs.

Big Bone Lick A site on the Ohio River, Kentucky, U.S.A., whose salty bog soil yielded numerous mastodon bones in the 18th century, and which has some of the latest Columbian mammoth remains in America (10,600 years old).

Bize, Petite Grotte de A cave in the Aude, southern France, containing five Paleolithic occupation layers, one of which contained a pebble bearing the engraving of a mammoth.

Blackwater Draw A series of sites in eastern New Mexico, U.S.A., where the remains of mammoths, camels, horses and bison have been found, plus extensive Paleo-Indian remains including Clovis points.

Blanchard, Abri A rock shelter in the Dordogne, southern France, occupied in the early Upper Paleolithic, best known for its abundance of mammoth-ivory work, especially its numerous beads.

Brassempouy A group of small caves in the Landes, southwestern France, occupied in the Upper Paleolithic and famous for a series of mammoth-ivory carvings including female figurines and a small human head.

Brno II An Ice Age burial in Moravia, Czech Republic, which contained the skeleton of a man accompanied by various animal bones including a mammoth shoulder blade and two tusks, as well as a remarkable "marionette" made of ivory.

Brown Bank An area of the North Sea between eastern England and Holland whose bed is rich in bones of fauna of the last Ice Age, including woolly mammoths.

Bruniquel A series of rock shelters in southwestern France, occupied toward the end of the Ice Age. One of them yielded an antler spear-thrower carved into the form of a mammoth.

Burning Tree A site in Ohio, U.S.A., which yielded an almost complete mastodon skeleton dating to about 11,500 years ago, with the remains of the animal's last meal in its stomach, and living intestinal bacteria within the stomach contents.

Bzianka A site in Poland where a 14,000-year-old woolly mammoth skull with abnormal tusks was unearthed.

Canecaude A cave in the Aude, southern France, with a number of Upper Paleolithic occupations, the last of which contained a fine antler spear-thrower carved into the form of a mammoth.

*Castillo, El A major cave site in northern Spain, occupied throughout the Paleolithic and containing numerous Ice Age engravings and paintings, including one outline of a mammoth.

Chabot A small cave in the Ardèche, southern France, also called the Grotte des Mammouths because of the Ice Age engraved friezes of mammoths and other animals it contains.

Cherny Yar A Russian site where a skull of an early woolly mammoth was recovered.

Chilhac *see* Senèze.

Clovis One of the Blackwater Draw sites in New Mexico, Clovis was originally a spring-fed pond where at least 15 mammoths have been found, 6 of them associated with stone points.

Colby An old stream channel in Wyoming, U.S.A., dating to 11,200 years ago, where parts of at least seven Columbian mammoths were found stacked into piles and associated with artefacts including stone points and a granite chopper.

*Combarelles, Les A long, narrow cave in the Dordogne, France, containing hundreds of Paleolithic engravings, including 37 of mammoths.

Les Combarelles

Condover A commercial quarry in Shropshire, England, where one adult and four juvenile woolly mammoth skeletons were discovered in a kettle-hole in 1986.

*Cotte de St. Brelade, La A Paleolithic cave site on Jersey, Channel Islands, containing thousands of artefacts and the stacked bones of 20 mammoths and 5 rhinos.

*Cougnac A decorated Ice Age cave in the Quercy region of France containing paintings including giant deer, mammoths and ibexes.

*Cromer Forest-bed A complex geological formation exposed along 30 miles (48 km) of coast in Norfolk and Suffolk, England, containing a rich fossil assemblage ranging from about 1.7 million to 500,000 years ago. Hundreds of molars of steppe mammoths and ancestral mammoths have been collected over the past 150 years, from localities including Happisburgh, Mundesley and West Runton.

Deep Water Channel An area of the North Sea between Britain and the Netherlands, from which Early and Middle Pleistocene fossils, including *M. meridionalis* and *M. trogontherii*, have been dredged.

Dent A Paleo-Indian site in Colorado, U.S.A., where the first Clovis points were found in 1932, and which provided the first unequivocal evidence in America for the association of projectile points with mammoth remains.

Dolní Věstonice A major open-air Upper Paleolithic site in Moravia, Czech Republic, whose fossils are dominated by mammoth bones, and which has produced a wealth of tools and carvings in ivory, including a famous human head.

Domme A cave in the Dordogne, France, also known as the Grotte de Saint-Front or Grotte du Mammouth because of the large bas-relief carving of a mammoth high up on its wall.

Durfort A site in central France from which the skeleton of an ancestral mammoth was recovered in the late 19th century. It is now displayed at the Muséum National d'Histoire Naturelle, Paris.

Eastern Scheldt A marine inlet in the Netherlands from which numerous mammalian fossils have been dredged, including teeth of ancestral mammoths.

Edersleben A site in eastern Germany where a complete skeleton, identified as that of a steppe mammoth, was excavated.

Elephant Point, Eschscholtz Bay The site of the first reported find of a mammoth carcass in Alaska, U.S.A., made by L.S. Quackenbusch in 1907.

Eliseevich An Upper Paleolithic open-air site on the Russian Plain, with mammoth-bone huts, and also containing a limestone carving of a mammoth and a female figurine in ivory.

Escapule A site in Arizona, U.S.A., where a butchered mammoth skeleton was found associated with stone points. Some archaeologists have suggested that it represents an escapee from a slaughter at nearby Lehner Ranch.

Fairbanks Creek The site of the most famous mammoth find in Alaska, U.S.A., where the face, trunk and foreleg of a mammoth calf were uncovered in 1948.

Figuier, Le A cave in the Ardèche, southeastern France, with Paleolithic occupations and a few figures on the walls, including stylized mammoths.

*Font de Gaume An Ice Age decorated cave in the Dordogne, France, containing about 230 figures, dominated by bison, but with a noteworthy series of mammoths, sometimes associated with "tectiform" signs.

Franklin County Deposits of wind-blown sand near Campbell, Nebraska, U.S.A., in which a huge skull of a Columbian mammoth, now displayed at the University of Nebraska Museum, was found in 1915.

Friesenhahn Cave A cave in Bexar County, Texas, U.S.A., where numerous juvenile remains of Columbian mammoths were found alongside other Late Pleistocene fossils, including those of scimitar-tooth cats.

*Gargas A large cave in the French Pyrenees with considerable Paleolithic occupation and a great deal of art on its walls, including some engraved mammoths.

Geissenklösterle A cave in southwestern Germany containing Paleolithic occupations and important ivory figurines from the very early Upper Paleolithic.

Gönnersdorf An extensive late Upper Paleolithic open-air site in northwestern Germany, best known for its 400 engraved stone plaques, including at least 62 mammoth figures.

Hay Springs A site in Nebraska, U.S.A., where remains of early Columbian mammoths, possibly identifiable as *M. imperator*, have been excavated.

Heilongjiang, Zhaoyuan, Shan Zhan A silt bed in Harbin, China, where a woolly mammoth skeleton, the most complete in China, was found. It is dated to around 21,000 years ago.

*Hot Springs A sinkhole deposit in South Dakota, U.S.A., discovered in 1974, where the remains of at least 50 Columbian mammoth skeletons have been excavated.

Ignatiev A decorated Ice Age cave in the southern Urals, Russia, containing several depictions of mammoths on its walls.

Ilford An area of northeast London, England where numerous mammalian fossils, including many mammoth and straight-tusked elephant remains, have been recovered from 200,000-year-old deposits of the River Thames.

Indigirka River A large river basin in northeastern Siberia where the frozen remains of a very young woolly mammoth, 29,000 years old, were recovered in 1992.

Jonesboro A site in Indiana, U.S.A., where the complete skeleton of a Columbian mammoth, now mounted in the American Museum of Natural History, New York, was discovered in 1903. It was originally named as a separate species, *M. jeffersonii*.

Jovelle A cave in the Dordogne, France, containing five archaic, deep engravings of mammoths as well as other animals.

Kapova Cave A major cave in Bashkortostan, in the southern Urals of Russia, with Upper Paleolithic occupation and about 40 paintings of animals and signs on its walls, including at least seven mammoths.

*Kent's Cavern A large cave near Torquay, southwestern England, alternately occupied by hyenas and humans in the Late Pleistocene. One of the first localities to demonstrate the coexistence of humans and extinct animals, it has yielded many artefacts and fossils including woolly mammoth.

Khapry A locality north of the Sea of Azov, southern Russia, where the Liventsovka quarry has yielded abundant early remains of the ancestral mammoths around 2–2.5 million years old, which have been named by some authors *M. gromovi*.

Khatanga A frozen mammoth carcass found in 1977 on the left bank of the Bolshaya Rassokha River, Siberia, and dated to more than 45,000 years ago.

Kiik Koba A Middle Paleolithic cave site in the Crimea, Ukraine, which contained two Neanderthal burials.

Kirgilyakh A tributary of the Kolyma River, where baby mammoth Dima was discovered in 1977.

Kniegrotte An Upper Paleolithic cave site in eastern Germany, whose artefacts include some unique ivory carvings.

Kolyma, Middle The site on the bank of the Bolshaya Baranikha River, Siberia, where a deformed and wrinkled scrap of mammoth trunk, 11 in (28 cm) long, was found in 1924.

Kostenki A major group of Upper Paleolithic open-air sites on the Don River in European Russia, containing large quantities of mammoth bones, including the remains of mammoth-bone huts and bone-filled pits. The sites have also yielded numerous tools and carvings in ivory.

Kraków, Spadzista Street A site in southern Poland where the traces of a mammoth-bone hut have been found.

Lamb Spring A Paleo-Indian site in Colorado, U.S.A., where about 40 mammoths and many other species were found, together with a stone tool and a cobble brought in by humans.

Lange-Ferguson site A Paleo-Indian site in South Dakota, U.S.A., where an adult and juvenile mammoth were possibly killed and certainly butchered using tools made from a mammoth shoulder blade.

Laugerie Haute An important Upper Paleolithic rock shelter in the Dordogne, France, containing a wealth of material including many art objects.

Lehner Ranch A site in Arizona, U.S.A., where 13 Clovis points were found with the remains of 13 young Columbian mammoths, regarded by some archaeologists as evidence for slaughter of a family group.

Lehringen A Middle Paleolithic open-air site in Germany best known for the discovery of a broken yew-wood spear between the ribs of a straight-tusked elephant skeleton.

Leikem A site in Arizona, U.S.A., where an individual mammoth skeleton was found associated with stone points. Some archaeologists have suggested that it represents an escapee from a slaughter at nearby Lehner Ranch.

Lena The Adams mammoth's frozen carcass was discovered at the mouth of the Lena River, Siberia, in 1799; it was removed to St. Petersburg in 1806.

Lespugue A series of small cave sites in the French Pyrenees containing Upper Paleolithic occupations; one of them yielded a famous ivory female figurine.

Liakhov Islands A small male adult mammoth was recovered from the Liakhov Islands, off the north coast of Siberia, in 1901–3, and its skeleton was subsequently given to the Muséum Nationale d'Histoire Naturelle, Paris.

Lourdes A town in the French Pyrenees containing a number of Upper Paleolithic caves, one of which, Les Espélugues, yielded a wealth of art objects, including a fine horse carved in mammoth ivory.

Madeleine, La A large late Upper Paleolithic rock shelter in the Dordogne, France, containing an abundance of art objects including an engraving of a mammoth on a piece of ivory, the discovery of which in 1864 finally proved the contemporaneity of humans and extinct animals.

Mal'ta An Upper Paleolithic open-air site in south-central Siberia, best known for its numerous art objects, including ivory figurines.

Marche, La An Upper Paleolithic cave site in the Vienne region of central France which yielded over 1,500 engraved stone slabs, including some remarkable depictions of mammoths.

Mátra A site in Hungary where the skeleton of a woolly mammoth was unearthed.

Mayenne-Sciences A cave in northwestern France, also known as the Grotte du Mammouth because the Ice Age drawings on its walls include two mammoths.

Mezhirich An Upper Paleolithic open-air site in Ukraine, best known for its five mammoth-bone huts and its painted mammoth skull.

Mezin An Upper Paleolithic open-air site in Ukraine, containing a number of mammoth-bone huts and a series of painted but battered mammoth bones which some believe may represent a set of musical instruments.

Miami A Paleo-Indian site in Texas, U.S.A., where at least five mammoths were found in association with Clovis artefacts.

Milovice An Upper Paleolithic open-air site near Dolní Věstonice in Moravia, Czech Republic, where the remains of a mammoth-bone hut have been discovered.

Moab A town in Utah, U.S.A., close to which exists a petroglyph image of a mammoth or mastodon hammered into a rock face.

Molodova A group of Paleolithic open-air sites in western Ukraine, where there is evidence for Middle Paleolithic mammoth-bone huts.

Montopoli A river deposit near Florence, Italy, where some of the earliest European remains of ancestral mammoths have been recovered.

Mosbach A huge sand quarry on the Rhine River in Germany, where thousands of fossils, including numerous remains of the steppe mammoth, have been excavated from river deposits over the past 100 years.

Murray Springs A Paleo-Indian open-air site in Arizona, U.S.A., where artefacts including a mammoth-bone shaft-wrench are associated with mammoth remains which were probably from animals that were scavenged rather than killed.

Naco An open-air site in Arizona, U.S.A., where eight Clovis points were found within an adult mammoth skeleton.

Newburgh A site in New York State, U.S.A., where Charles Peale and family unearthed two mastodon skeletons in 1801.

Nogaisk A site in southern Russia where the complete skeleton of an ancestral mammoth was excavated. It is now mounted in the Zoological Museum in St. Petersburg.

Norwich Crag An extensive deposit of shelly sands overlying the Red Crag in eastern England, containing fossils of ancestral mammoths dating to around 2.4 to 1.8 million years ago.

Obere Klause A site in southern Germany best known for its late Ice Age engraving of a mammoth on a piece of ivory.

Oblazowa An Upper Paleolithic cave site in southern Poland which contained a boomerang made from a mammoth tusk – the world's oldest boomerang.

Old Crow A river basin in the Yukon Territory, Canada, which has yielded thousands of Pleistocene fossils, including fossils from the woolly mammoth and earlier mammoth species.

Olyer Suite A complex series of deposits in the Kolyma region of northeastern Siberia in which the earliest remains identifiable as steppe and woolly mammoths have been found.

Olympic Peninsula A site in Washington State, U.S.A., where a mastodon had a bone or antler point embedded in a rib.

Oulen An Ice Age decorated cave in the Ardèche region of France, containing engravings and paintings including several mammoths.

Paviland An Upper Paleolithic cave site in southern Wales that contained the earliest known British burial, erroneously called the "red lady", which was accompanied by objects of mammoth ivory.

Pavlov An Upper Paleolithic open-air site in Moravia, Czech Republic, near Dolní Věstonice, which contained numerous artefacts in mammoth bone and a tusk bearing complex engraved motifs which some interpret as a map or landscape.

*Pech-Merle A major Ice Age decorated cave in the Quercy region of France containing about 60 animal figures including some remarkable mammoths drawn in black.

Pietrafitta A lignite mine in central Italy which has yielded a rich Early Pleistocene fauna, including 15 crushed skeletons of the ancestral mammoth, *M. meridionalis*.

Pindal, El An Ice Age decorated cave by the sea in northern Spain, best known for its mammoth painted in red outline with a "heart" inside.

El Pindal

Polch A site near Koblenz, Germany, where a partial skeleton of a very old woolly mammoth individual was excavated.

Praz Rodet A site in Switzerland where a very late woolly mammoth skeleton, only 12,000 years old, was recovered in the early 1970s.

Předmostí A Paleolithic open-air site in Moravia, Czech Republic. The Upper Paleolithic occupations are characterized by huge quantities of mammoth fossils (about 1,000 individuals), and a collective grave was covered by mammoth bones. The site is also rich in bone and ivory tools, and in portable art, including a mammoth carved in ivory and a stylized woman engraved on a tusk.

*Rancho La Brea Area of Los Angeles, California, U.S.A., where thousands of animals, including Columbian mammoths and mastodons, met their death by being caught in tar seeps.

Red Crag An extensive deposit of shelly marine sands underlying parts of eastern England, containing fossils dating to between about 3.2 and 2.4 million years ago. These include some of the earliest European mammoths of the species *M. meridionalis*.

*Rouffignac A huge Ice Age decorated cave in the Dordogne, France, containing hundreds of painted and engraved figures on its walls and ceilings, heavily dominated by well over 100 mammoths.

Sanga-Yurakh River A river in Yakutia that was the site of the discovery of a frozen female mammoth carcass which was recovered in 1908.

Santa Rosa One of the California Channel Islands off Berkeley, U.S.A., where remains of the dwarf mammoth *M. exilis* have been found.

Scoppito (L'Aquila) Site in central Italy from which a huge ancestral mammoth skeleton was excavated, now housed at the castle of Aquila.

Senèze and **Chilhac** Two sites in central France from which skulls of the ancestral mammoth have been recovered, dating to around 1.9 million years ago.

Sevsk A sand quarry in Bryansk Province, Russia, where a natural "cemetery" of mammoths was found in 1988, the biggest known in Europe. The finds are notable for the seven almost intact skeletons of all ages, including three babies, that may have formed a single herd or family.

Shandrin A tributary of the Indigirka where a mammoth skeleton was unearthed in 1972 containing the digestive organs and stomach contents.

Siegsdorf A site in Bavaria, Germany, where Europe's largest woolly mammoth skeleton, nicknamed Oscar, was discovered in 1975.

Siniaya Balka A site on the Taman peninsula near the Black Sea, southern Russia, which has yielded abundant remains of late ancestral mammoths about a million years old, showing advanced features foreshadowing the steppe mammoth.

Spinagallo A cave in southeastern Sicily where remains of the world's smallest dwarf elephants have been found, possibly evolved from the *Palaeoloxodon* line.

Stanton Harcourt A gravel pit in Oxfordshire, England, where remains of fauna 200,000 years old, including 13 mammoth tusks, have been recovered in ancient deposits of the River Thames.

Starunia A site in western Ukraine, Poland, where rhinoceros carcasses and a mammoth were naturally pickled in a petrochemical seep and surrounded by a mineral wax.

Steinheim A site in central Germany where the large skeleton of an early woolly mammoth was excavated in the early 1900s. It is now exhibited in the Stuttgart museum.

Sungir An Upper Paleolithic open-air site in European Russia. Europe's northernmost Paleolithic site, best known for its spectacular burials. The three skeletons were accompanied by numerous ornaments and art objects, including ivory spears, bracelets, figurines and about 10,000 beads.

Süssenborn Riverine deposits in eastern Germany from which many steppe mammoth teeth have been recovered, including the first to be named as *M. trogontherii*.

Taimyr The valley of the Mammoth River, in the northwest Taimyr Peninsula, Siberia, was the site of the 1948 discovery of an exceptionally complete woolly mammoth skeleton which has become the type specimen for the species.

Tata A Middle Paleolithic open-air site in Hungary whose fossil assemblage is dominated by mammoths, and which is best known for a carved and polished segment of mammoth molar.

Tattershall Thorpe A site in central England yielding a rich fossil assemblage probably dating to the penultimate Ice Age, including numerous woolly mammoth teeth.

Tegelen A lake deposit in the Netherlands containing a rich fossil assemblage about 1.7 million years old, including the ancestral mammoth *M. meridionalis*.

Tepexpan A site in Mexico which has provided one of the most southerly indications of Columbian mammoths in North America. The remains were associated with stone implements.

Tomsk A site in western Siberia where the broken bones of a young mammoth were found with a fireplace and many stone tools.

Torralba and **Ambrona** Two large Lower Paleolithic lakeside sites in Spain, containing the partially dismembered remains of many animals, particularly scores of straight-tusked elephants, together with stone artefacts. Most animals came to be at the site through natural causes, but some may have been killed or butchered by humans.

Trinity River Alluvial deposits near Dallas, Texas, U.S.A., where numerous Columbian mammoth remains have been recovered from sand and gravel pits since the 1920s. At least 15 skeletons and 13 skulls have been reported.

Trois Frères, Les A major Ice Age decorated cave in the French Pyrenees, containing hundreds of wall engravings, including a particularly fine mammoth in the "Sanctuary".

Ubeidiya A lower Paleolithic site in Israel including remains of the ancestral mammoth about a million years old.

Upper Valdarno An area of the Arno Valley near Florence, Italy, which has yielded abundant fossils of ancestral mammoths, including those that were first named as "*Elephas*" *meridionalis* in 1825.

Vilui A river site west of the Lena River, in northeastern Siberia, where a single molar represents the easternmost finding of the ancestral mammoth in the Old World.

Vogelherd A Paleolithic cave site in southwestern Germany, where the very early Upper Paleolithic layers contained carved ivory animal figurines including some of mammoths.

Voigtstedt A site in the Thüringian region of Germany from which some of the latest remains of ancestral mammoths, around 600,000 years old, have been recovered.

Wellsch Valley A site in Saskatchewan, Canada, containing some of the earliest mammoth remains (ancestral mammoths) in North America, about 1.5 million years old.

West Runton River deposits in Norfolk, England, which have yielded a rich interglacial fossil assemblage about 600,000 years old and a skeleton of an early steppe mammoth. Part of the Cromer Forest-bed.

Wrangel Island An island in the Arctic Ocean off northeastern Siberia where remains of dwarf woolly mammoths only 7,000–3,700 years old have been discovered.

Yamal Peninsula The site of the discovery in 1988 of the baby mammoth Mascha, the westernmost Siberian frozen carcass.

Yuribei A river in the Gydanskij Peninsula, Siberia, along which, in 1977, a small adult female mammoth was discovered, the latest frozen specimen found so far, dating to 10,000 years ago. Its gastrointestinal tract was packed with a grassy mass, and the other internal organs were entirely preserved.

Zhalainuoer A coal mine in Inner Mongolia, China, which has yielded China's largest mammoth skeleton as well as 28½ lb (13 kg) of mammoth dung dating to around 33,400 years ago.

A selection of museums around the world with mammoths on display

BELGIUM
Brussels Koninklijk Belgisch Instituut voor Natuurwetenschappen (woolly mammoth skeleton, skulls and other fossils)

BRITAIN
Cardiff National Museum of Wales (robotic life-size model)
Ipswich Ipswich Museum (bones and teeth; life-size model)
Jersey The Jersey Museum (mammoths from La Cotte)
London Natural History Museum (skull, teeth and bones)
Norwich Norwich Castle Museum (skeleton of steppe mammoth)

CANADA
Edmonton Provincial Museum of Alberta (skeletons and other remains of woolly and Columbian mammoths)
Ottawa Royal Ontario Museum (fossils)

CZECH REPUBLIC
Brno Anthropos Museum (life-size woolly mammoth model; skeleton; remains from Paleolithic sites)

FRANCE
Chilhac Chilhac Museum, Auvergne (skulls and other remains of ancestral mammoths)
Lyon Musée Guimet d'Histoire Naturelle (steppe or woolly mammoth skeleton)
Paris Muséum National d'Histoire Naturelle (skeleton of ancestral mammoth)
Le Thot, Dordogne Centre de Recherches et d'Art Préhistorique (robotic model)

GERMANY
Bottrop Museum für Ur- und Ortsgeschichte (various mammoth remains)
Mainz Naturhistorisches Museum (remains of steppe mammoth)
Münster Geologisches-paläontologisches Institut (skeleton of woolly mammoth; skull of steppe mammoth; other fossils)
Sangerhausen Spengler Museum (skeleton of ancestral or steppe mammoth)
Steinheim an der Mürr Urmensch-Museum (skeleton of early woolly mammoth)
Stuttgart Staatliches Museum für Naturkunde (skeleton of early woolly mammoth; other fossils)

ITALY
Aquila Aquila Castle (skeleton of ancestral mammoth)
Florence Museo di Geologia e Paleontologia dell'Università di Firenze (skeletons and skulls of ancestral mammoths)
Rome Museo di Paleontologia e Geologia dell' Università di Roma (skeletons of dwarf mammoths; skulls of woolly mammoths)

POLAND
Kraków Institute of Systematics and Evolution of Animals (pickled woolly mammoth remains, skulls and other fossils)

RUSSIA
Moscow Paleontological Museum (skeleton of woolly mammoth; other fossils)
St. Petersburg Zoological Institute (frozen remains and skeletons of woolly mammoths)
Yakutsk World Museum of the Mammoth (frozen remains, skeletons and other fossils of woolly mammoth)

SWITZERLAND
Basle Naturhistorisches Museum (skull and other remains of ancestral mammoth)

U.S.A.
Denver Denver Museum of Natural History, Colorado (skeletons and skulls of Columbian mammoths)
Fairbanks University of Alaska Museum (various fossils)
Gainesville Florida State Museum of Natural History (ancestral and Columbian mammoths)
Hot Springs Hot Springs Mammoth Site, South Dakota (excavation of Columbian mammoths)
Lincoln University Museum, Lincoln, Nebraska (Columbian mammoth skeleton; other fossils)
Los Angeles Natural History Museum of Los Angeles County, California (Rancho La Brea tarpits, life-size models and skeleton of Columbian mammoths)
New York American Museum of Natural History (skeleton of Columbian mammoth; frozen Alaskan baby; other remains)
Springfield Illinois State Museum (mastodon skeleton, various mammoth fossils)
Washington, D.C. National Museum of Natural History (various fossils)

BIBLIOGRAPHY

In each section, the most important references are marked with asterisks.

GENERAL

Agenbroad, L.D. and B.R. Barton *North American Mammoths: An Annotated Bibliography* Mammoth Site, Hot Springs, South Dakota, 1991
*Agenbroad, L.D., J.I. Mead and L.W. Nelson (eds.) *Megafauna and Man: Discovery of America's Heartland* Mammoth Site, Hot Springs, South Dakota, 1990
Augusta, J. and Z. Burian *A Book of Mammoths* Paul Hamlyn, London, 1962
Carrington, R. *Elephants* Basic Books Inc., New York, 1959
Cohen, C. *Le Destin du Mammouth* Editions du Seuil, Paris, 1994
*Garutt, W.E. *Das Mammut* Mammuthus primigenius (*Blumenbach*) Franckh'sche Verlagshandlung, Stuttgart, 1964
*Guthrie, R.D. *Frozen Fauna of the Mammoth Steppe. The Story of Blue Babe* University of Chicago Press, Chicago, 1990
*Haynes, G. *Mammoths, Mastodonts, and Elephants: Biology, Behavior, and the Fossil Record* Cambridge University Press, Cambridge, 1991
Joger, U. and U. Koch *Mammuts aus Sibirien* Darmstadt, Hessisches Landesmuseum, 1994
Kurtén, B. and E. Anderson *Pleistocene Mammals of North America* Columbia University Press, New York, 1980
Mol, D., L.D. Agenbroad and J.I. Mead *Mammoths* Mammoth Site, Hot Springs, South Dakota, 1993
*Mol, D. and H. van Essen *De Mammoet. Sporen uit de Ijstijd* Uitgeverij BZZTôH, 's-Gravenhage, 1992
Shoshani, J. (ed.) *Elephants* Weldon Owen Pty. Ltd., New South Wales, 1992
Silverberg, R. *Mammoths, Mastodons and Man* World's Work Ltd., Kingswood, 1970
Stuart, A.J. *Pleistocene Vertebrates in the British Isles* Longman, London, 1982
*Surmely, F. *Le Mammouth, Géant de la Préhistoire* Editions Solar, Paris, 1993
Sutcliffe, A.J. *On the Track of Ice Age Mammals* British Museum (Natural History), London/Harvard University Press, Cambridge, Mass., 1985
Vereshchagin, N.K. and A.N. Tikhonov *Exterior of the Mammoth* Yakutsk Republican Commission for the Study of Mammoths, 1990 [in Russian]

1 ORIGINS

GENERAL LIST: Garutt, Kurtén and Anderson, Mol and van Essen, Shoshani
Aguirre, E.E. "Revisión Sistemática de los Elephantidae por su Morfología y Morfometría Dentaria", *Estudios Geológicos 24*, 1968, 1969: 109–67; *25*: 123–77, 317–67
Azzaroli, A.A. "Evolutionary patterns of Villafranchian elephants in central Italy", *Mem. Atti. Accad. Naz. Lincei, Sci. fiz., mat. and nat., ser. 8, 14*, 1977: 149–68
Caloi, L., T. Kotsakis, M.R. Palombo and C. Petronio "The Pleistocene dwarf elephants of Mediterranean islands" in Shoshani and Tassy
Dubrovo, I.A. "A history of the elephants of the Archidiskodon – Mammuthus phylogenetic line on the territory of the USSR", *Journal of the Palaeontological Society of India 20*, 1977: 33–40
Frenzel, B., M. Pécsi and A.A.Velichko (eds.) *Atlas of Paleoclimates and Paleoenvironments of the Northern Hemisphere. Late Pleistocene – Holocene* Gustav Fischer, Stuttgart, 1992
Kalb, J.E. and A. Mebrate "Fossil elephantoids from the hominid-bearing Awash Group, Middle Awash Valley, Afar Depression, Ethiopia", *Transactions of the American Philosophical Society 83*, 1993: 1–114
Lister, A.M. "Proboscidean Evolution", *Trends in Ecology and Evolution 4*, 1989: 362–63
———— "Mammoths in miniature", *Nature 362*, 1993: 288–89
*———— "History and taxonomy of the mammoth lineage in Eurasia" in Shoshani and Tassy
*Maglio, V.J. "Origin and evolution of the Elephantidae", *Transactions of the American Philosophical Society 63*, 1973: 1–149
Osborn, H.F. *Proboscidea, vol. 2* American Museum of Natural History, New York, 1942

Roth, V.L. "Dwarfism in elephants in the Californian Islands" in Shoshani and Tassy
Sher, A.V. "On the history of mammal fauna of Beringida", *Quartärpaläontologie 6*, 1986: 185–93
Shoshani, J., J.M. Lowenstein, D.A. Walz and M. Goodman "Proboscidean origins of mastodon and woolly mammoth demonstrated immunologically", *Paleobiology 11*, 1985: 429–37
*Shoshani, J. and P. Tassy (eds.) *The Proboscidea: Trends in Evolution and Palaeoecology* Oxford University Press, Oxford, 1994
Tassy, P. and J. Shoshani "The Tethytheria: elephants and their relatives" in *The Phylogeny and Classification of the Tetrapods, vol. 2* (ed. M.J. Benton), Clarendon Press, Oxford, 1988: 283–315
Vartanyan, S.L., V.E. Garutt and A.V. Sher "Holocene dwarf mammoths from Wrangel Island in the Siberian Arctic", *Nature 362*, 1993: 337–40

2 MAMMOTHS UNEARTHED

GENERAL LIST: Agenbroad and Barton, Garutt, Kurtén, Stuart, Sutcliffe
*Agenbroad, L.D. and J.I. Mead (eds.) *The Hot Springs Mammoth Site: A Decade of Field and Laboratory Research in Paleontology, Geology and Paleoecology* Mammoth Site, Hot Springs, South Dakota, 1994
Anthony, H.E. "Nature's deep freeze", *Natural History 58*, 1949: 296–301
*Digby, B. *The Mammoth and Mammoth-Hunting in North-East Siberia* Witherby, London/Appleton, New York, 1926
Harris, J.M. (ed.) *Terra 31 (1)*, 1992 [special issue on Rancho La Brea]
Herz, O.F. "Frozen mammoth in Siberia", *Ann. Rep. Smithsonian Inst. for year ending June 30 1903*, 1904: 611–25
Leroi-Gourhan, A. "Le mammouth dans la zoologie mythique des Esquimaux", *La Terre et la Vie* 2e semestre, 1, 1935: 3–12
Lister, A.M. "The Condover mammoth site: excavation and research 1986–93", *Cranium 10*, 1993: 61–67
Mashchenko, E.N. "Structure of a mammoth herd from the Sevsk late Pleistocene locality (Russia, Bryansk region)", *Proc. Zoological Inst. St Petersburg 246*, 1992: 41–59 [in Russian]
Mol, D. "Het ijstijdlandschap van de zuidelijke Noordzee", *Grondboor en Hamer (Nederlandse Geologische Vereniging) 45 (1)*, 1991: 9–14
Mol, D., A. Verhagen and H. van Essen "De mammoet en de prehistorische mens van Siegsdorf", *Cranium 5 (1)*, 1988: 57–64
Nelson, L.W. *Mammoth Graveyard: A Treasure-Trove of Clues to the Past* Mammoth Site, Hot Springs, South Dakota, 1988
*Pfizenmayer, E.W. *Siberian Man and Mammoth* Blackie and Son, London and Glasgow, 1939
Stock, C. *Rancho La Brea: A Record of Pleistocene Life in California* 7th ed. Natural History Museum of Los Angeles County, Los Angeles, 1992
*Tolmachoff, I.P. "The carcasses of the mammoth and rhinoceros found in the frozen ground of Siberia", *Transactions of the American Philosophical Society 23*, 1929: 1–76
Vereshchagin, N.K. "The Berelekh 'cemetery' of mammoths", *Proc. Zoological Inst., Leningrad 72*, 1977: 5–50 [in Russian]
*Vereshchagin, N.K. and V.M. Mikhelson (eds.) *The Magadan Baby Mammoth* Nauka, Leningrad, 1981 [in Russian]

3 THE NATURAL HISTORY OF MAMMOTHS

GENERAL LIST: Guthrie, Haynes, Vereshchagin and Tikhonov
Allison, N. "Evidence of mastodont's last meal: bacteria still working after 11,000 years", *Mammoth Trumpet 6 (4)*, 1991: 1–6
Bricknell, I. "Palaeopathology of Pleistocene proboscideans in Britain", *Modern Geology 11*, 1987: 295–309
*Buss, I.O. *Elephant Life: Fifteen Years of High Population Density* Iowa State University Press, Ames, 1990
*Kubiak, H. "Morphological adaptations of the mammoth: an adaptation to the arctic-steppe environment" in *Paleoecology of Beringia* (eds. D.M. Hopkins et al.), Academic Press, New York, 1982: 281–89
Mead, J.I., L.D. Agenbroad, O.K. Davis and P.S. Martin "Dung of Mammuthus in the arid southwest, North America", *Quaternary Research 25*, 1986: 121–27
Roth, V.L. "Fabricational noise in elephant dentitions", *Paleobiology 15*, 1989: 165–79

*Sikes, S.K. *The Natural History of the African Elephant* Weidenfeld and Nicolson, London, 1971

Spiegeleire, M.A. de "Figurations paléolithiques et réalité anatomique du mammouth (*Mammuthus primigenius*): essai d'interprétation", *Bull. Soc. belge Anthrop. Préhist. 96*, 1985: 93–116

Suzuki, N., A. Tikhonov, N.K. Vereshchagin and T. Hamada "Extracted heart from the frozen baby mammoth in Siberia", *Scientific Papers of the College of Arts and Sciences, Univ. Tokyo, 42*, 1992: 63–78

Ukraintseva, V.V. *Vegetation Cover and Environment of the "Mammoth Epoch" in Siberia* Mammoth Site, Hot Springs, South Dakota, 1993

4 MAMMOTHS AND HUMAN CULTURE

GENERAL LIST: Augusta and Burian

Bader, O.N. *La Caverne Kapovaïa, Peinture Paléolithique* Nauka, Moscow, 1965

*Bahn, P.G. and J. Vertut *Images of the Ice Age* Windward, Leicester/ Facts on File, New York, 1988

Berdin, M.O. "La répartition des mammouths dans l'art pariétal quaternaire", *Travaux de l'Institut d'Art Préhistorique de Toulouse 12*, 1970: 181–367

Bibikov, S.N. *The Oldest Musical Complex Made of Mammoth Bones* Naukova Dumka, Kiev, 1981 [in Russian]

Bosinski, G. "The mammoth engravings of the Magdalenian site Gönnersdorf (Rhineland, Germany)" in *La Contribution de la Zoologie et de l'Ethologie à l'Interprétation de l'Art des Peuples Chasseurs Préhistoriques* (eds. H-G. Bandi et al.), Editions Universitaires, Fribourg, 1984: 295–322

*Bosinski, G. and G. Fischer *Mammut- und Pferdedarstellungen von Gönnersdorf* Steiner, Wiesbaden, 1980

Capitan, L., H. Breuil and D. Peyrony *La Caverne de Font-de-Gaume aux Eyzies (Dordogne)* Monaco, 1910

——— *Les Combarelles aux Eyzies (Dordogne)* Masson, Paris, 1924

*Gladkih, M.I., N.L. Kornietz and O. Soffer "Mammoth-bone dwellings on the Russian Plain", *Scientific American 251 (5)*, 1984: 136–43

Hahn, J. *Kraft und Aggression. Die Botschaft der Eiszeitkunst im Aurignacien Süddeutschlands?* Archaeologica Venatoria 7, Tübingen, 1986

Haynes, C.V. and E.T. Hemmings "Mammoth-bone shaft wrench from Murray Springs, Arizona", *Science 159*, 1968: 186–87

Jorda Cerda, F. "El mamut en el arte paleolitico peninsular y la hierogamia de Los Casares" in *Homenaje al Prof. M. Almagro Basch I* Min. de Cultura, Madrid, 1983: 265–72

*Klein, R.G. *Ice Age Hunters of the Ukraine* University of Chicago Press, Chicago, 1973

Kozlowski, J.K. and H. Kubiak "Late Palaeolithic dwellings made of mammoth bones in South Poland", *Nature 237*, 1972: 463–64

Liubin, V.P. "The images of mammoths in Palaeolithic art", *Sovyetskaya Arkheologya*, 1991: 20–42 [in Russian]

*Pales, L. and M.T. de St Pereuse *Les Gravures de La Marche: IV, Cervidés, Eléphants et Divers* Ophrys, Paris, 1989

*Semenov, S.A. *Prehistoric Technology* (transl. M.W. Thompson) Adams and Dart, Bath, 1964

Soffer, O. *The Upper Paleolithic of the Central Russian Plain* Academic Press, Orlando, 1985

Thompson, B. "Where have all the mammoths gone?", *Patina* (Utah), June 1993, in 2 parts: 1–21 and 1–23

Valde-Nowak, P., A. Nadachowski and M. Wolsan "Upper Palaeolithic boomerang made of a mammoth tusk in South Poland", *Nature 329*, 1987: 436–38

5 EXTINCTION

GENERAL LIST: Agenbroad, Mead and Nelson, Carrington, Guthrie, Haynes

Billiard, G. "Y a-t-il encore des mammouths vivants?", *Bulletin de la Société Préhistorique française 44*, 1947: 41–43

Budyko, M.I. "On the causes of the extinction of some animals at the end of the Pleistocene", *Soviet Geog. Review and Translation 8*, 1967: 783–93

Conybeare, A. and Haynes, G. "Observations on elephant mortality and bones in water holes", *Quaternary Research 22*, 1984: 189–200

Dansgaard, W. et al. "Evidence for general instability of past climate from a 250-kyr ice-core record", *Nature 364*, 1993: 218–20

Eiseley, L.C. "Myth and mammoth in archaeology", *American Antiquity 11 (2)*, 1945: 84–87

Fisher, D.C. "Mastodon butchery by North American Paleo-Indians", *Nature 308*, 1984: 271–72

Fisher, J.W. "Observations on the Late Pleistocene bone assemblage from the Lamb Spring site, Colorado" in *Ice Age Hunters of the Rockies* (eds. D.J. Stanford and J.S. Day), Denver Museum of Natural History and University Press of Colorado, Niwot, 1992: 51–81

Frison, G.C. "Cultural activity associated with prehistoric mammoth butchering and processing", *Science 194*, 1976: 728–30

——— "Clovis tools and weaponry efficiency in an African elephant context", *American Antiquity 54*, 1989: 766–78

Frison, G.C. and L.C. Todd *The Colby Mammoth Site: Taphonomy and Archaeology of a Clovis Kill in Northern Wyoming* University of New Mexico Press, Albuquerque, 1986

Hagelberg, E., M.G. Thomas, C.E. Cook, jr., and A.M. Lister "DNA from mammoth bones", *Nature 370*, 1994: 333–4

Haynes, C.V. "Elephant-hunting in North America", *Scientific American 214*, 1966: 104–12

——— "Geoarchaeological and paleohydrological evidence for a Clovis-age drought in North America and its bearing on extinction", *Quaternary Research 35*, 1991: 438–50

Haynes, G. "Age profiles in elephant and mammoth bone assemblages", *Quaternary Research 24*, 1985: 333–45

*——— "Late Pleistocene mammoth utilization in northern Eurasia and North America", *Archaeozoologia 3*, 1989: 81–108

Heuvelmans, B. *On the Track of Unknown Animals* 2nd ed., Hart-Davis, London, 1962

*Martin, P.S. and R.G. Klein (eds.) *Quaternary Extinctions. A Prehistoric Revolution* University of Arizona Press, Tucson, 1984

Mithen, S. "Simulating mammoth hunting and extinction: implications for the Late Pleistocene of the Central Russian Plain" in *Hunting and Animal Exploitation in the Later Palaeolithic and Mesolithic of Eurasia* (eds. G.L. Petersen et al.), 1993: 163–78

Mosimann, J.E. and P.S. Martin "Simulating overkill by Paleoindians", *American Scientist 63*, 1975: 304–13

Narr, K.J. "Des Mammuts Ende: Aussterben oder Ausrottung?" *Jahrbuch des Bernischen Historischen Museums 63/4 (1983/4)*, 1985: 225–39

Owen-Smith, N. "Pleistocene extinctions: the pivotal role of megaherbivores", *Paleobiology 13*, 1987: 351–62

*Saunders, J.J. "A model for man-mammoth relationships in Late Pleistocene North America", *Canadian Journal of Anthropology 1 (1)*, 1980: 87–98

Scott, K. "Two hunting episodes of Middle Palaeolithic age at La Cotte de Saint-Brelade, Jersey (Channel Islands)", *World Archaeology 12*, 1980: 137–52

Soffer, O. "Upper Paleolithic adaptations in central and eastern Europe and man/mammoth interactions" in *From Kostenki to Clovis, Upper Paleolithic – Paleo-Indian Adaptations* (eds. O. Soffer and N.D. Praslov), Plenum, New York, 1993: 31–49

Stanford, D., R. Bonnichsen and R.E. Morlan "The Ginsberg experiment: modern and prehistoric evidence of a bone flaking technology", *Science 212*, 1981: 438–40

Strong, W.D. "North American traditions suggesting a knowledge of the mammoth" *American Anthropologist 36*, 1934: 81–88

*Stuart, A.J. "Mammalian extinctions in the Late Pleistocene of northern Eurasia and North America", *Biological Reviews 66*, 1991: 453–562

——— "The failure of evolution: Late Quaternary mammalian extinctions in the Holarctic", *Quaternary International 19*, 1993: 101–7

INTERPRETING THE EVIDENCE

GENERAL LIST: Guthrie, Haynes, Stuart, Sutcliffe

Lister, A.M. "Sexual dimorphism in the mammoth pelvis: an aid to gender determination" in Shoshani and Tassy

*Lowe, J.J. and M.J.C. Walker *Reconstructing Quaternary Environments* Longman, London, 1984

Pääbo, S. "Ancient DNA", *Scientific American*, Nov. 1993: 60–66

INDEX

AUTHORS' ACKNOWLEDGMENTS

Many friends and colleagues have provided invaluable help in the form of documentation, pictures and information during the writing of this book. We would particularly like to thank: Larry Agenbroad, Gennady Baryshnikov, Gerhard Bosinski, Bernard Bredow, Ian Bricknell, Alan Bryan, Jane Callander, Paul Callow, Lucia Caloi, Claudine Cohen, Russell Coope, George Corner, Andrew Currant, Rob Driscole, Irina Dubrovo, Francesco d'Errico, Hans van Essen, George Frison, Asya Lvovna Gabysheva, Vadim Garutt, Morris Goodman, Dale Guthrie, Mariana Gvozdover, Erika Hagelberg, Adrien Hannus, Jon Hather, Gary Haynes, Vance Haynes, Gordon Hillman, Flavius Ikome, Ann Inscker, Ken Joysey, Kathy Judelson, Ralf Kahlke, Jon Kalb, Alice Kehoe, Wighart von Koenigswald, Thijs van Kolfschoten, Henryk Kubiak, Peter Lazarev, Phyllis Lee, Rod Long, Alexander Marshack, Paul Martin, Eugene Mashchenko, Geoffrey McCabe, Jim Mead, Simon Mikhailov, Steven Mithen, Dick Mol, Joe Muller, Adam Nadachowski, William Nawrocki, Kate O'Sullivan, Gilles Pacaud, Shirley-Ann Pager, Jean Plassard, Philip Powell, Nikolai Praslov, Louise Roth, Dominique Sacchi, Robert Sattler, Jeffrey Saunders, Kate Scott, Nick Shackleton, Viacheslav Shchelinsky, Andrei and Anna Sher, Vladimir Shirokov, Jeheskel Shoshani, Anthony Stuart, Antony and Una Sutcliffe, Richard Tedford, Alexei Tikhonov, Pat Troy, Pawel Valde-Nowak, Nikolai Vereshchagin, Yvonne Vertut and Jesse Warner. We are also grateful to the following colleagues for permission to base graphs on their original work: W. Dansgaard and colleagues (pp.134–135), Vadim Garutt (pp.149–150), Fiona Grün (p.147), Dale Guthrie (p.38), Erika Hagelberg and colleagues (pp.138–139), Steven Mithen (p.136), Kate Scott (p.129), Nick Shackleton and colleagues (p.26), Andrei Sher (p.74) and M.A. de Spiegeleire (p.149). Modelling (p.117) was by Cynthia Henriques. Paul Bahn was able to visit the cave of Kapova thanks to Olga Boiko, Nick Evans, Viacheslav Kotov, Nigel Lewis and Erika Rauschenbach. Adrian Lister's trip to the Yakutian mammoth exhibition at Dinard was made possible by Gilles Pacaud. We are grateful to Jean Auel for writing the preface; to our agent Sheila Watson; and, for guiding the book from synopsis to finished product, Antony Mason and the rest of the Marshall Editions team. To anyone whom we may inadvertently have omitted, we extend our sincere apologies.

ILLUSTRATION CREDITS

David Ashby 21*r*, 65*t*, 68–69; Bounford Chapman Associates 12*t*, 16*t*, 25*br*, 26, 27*b*, 28*t*, 30*t*, 35*t*, 45, 53, 74*b*, 78, 79, 121*t*, 134–135; Bill Donohue 64–65, 66–67, 82–83, 84–85; Andrew Farmer 94–95, 104–105, 149, 150; Gary Hincks 20–21, 38–39, 54–55; Mark Iley 120–121, 122–123; Mainline Design 138–139; Oxford Cartographers 152–156; Richard Phipps 12–13, 14–15, 16–17, 28–29, 32–33; Sue Sharples 83*b*, 148; Ann Winterbotham 15*t*, 38*b*, 54*b*, 67*t*, 85*t*, 124–125; Michael Woods 5, 12*b*, 15*b*, 16*b*, 22–23, 25*bl*, 27*t*, 28*b*, 31*b*, 32*b*, 137*b*

PICTURE CREDITS *l* = left; *r* = right; *t* = top; *c* = centre; *b* = bottom

1 Paul Bahn; 2/3 M.O. and J. Plasssard; 6 The Natural History Museum, London; 7 Alexander Marshack; 10/11 Anup Shah/Planet Earth Pictures; 18*t* Douglas Faulkner/Oxford Scientific Films; 18*b* Paul McCullagh/Oxford Scientific Films; 22 P. Kumar/Planet Earth Pictures; 23 Jon Kalb; 24 Dick Mol; 25*t* Adrian Lister; 25*b* ENEL S.p.a. (Italy); 27 Daniel J. Cox/Oxford Scientific Films; 31 Dr. R. Tedford/American Museum; 34 Daniel J. Cox/Oxford Scientific Films; 35*l* Nikita Ovsianikov; 35*r* Courtesy of The University of Nebraska; 36/37 The Mammoth Site of Hot Springs, South Dakota, Inc.; 40 Matthieu Scandella; 40/41 The Mansell Collection; 41*t* The Peale Museum; 41*b* Matthieu Scandella; 42/43 Andrei Sher; 43 The Natural History Museum, London; 44 Torquay Museum; 45*t* Dr. V.E. Garutt; 45*b* Novosti; 46*t* World Museum of Mammoths, Yakutia; 46*b* V.M. Khabri; 47 Andrei Sher; 48 A.V. Lozhkin; 49*t* Dale Guthrie; 49*b* Novosti; 50 N.K. Vereshchagin; 51*t* Courtesy of Gary Haynes and the Hwange Research Trust; 51*c* Pavel A. Nikolskiy; 51*b* Dick Mol; 52*t* Northern Arizona University; 52*b* Larry Agenbroad; 53 The Mammoth Site of Hot Springs, South Dakota, Inc.; 56/57 Courtesy of the George C. Page Museum; 57 Kate O'Sullivan; 58*t* A.J. Sutcliffe; 58*b* *The Telegraph*; 59 Flip Schulke/Planet Earth Pictures; 60 Thijs van Kolfschoten; 61*t* Adrian Lister; 61*b* Dick Mol; 62/63 M.O. and J. Plassard; 68 Paul Bahn; 68/69 Mike Newton; 69*l* N.K. Vereshchagin; 69*r*/70*t* Mike Newton; 70*bl* Lon E. Lauber/Oxford Scientific Films; 70*br* Mike Newton; 71*t* Masahiro Iijima/Ardea; 71*b* Muséum National d'Histoire Naturelle, Paris; 72*l* Courtesy of Gary Haynes and the Hwange Research Trust; 72*r* Torquay Museum; 73*l* Naoki Suzuki; 73*r* Morris Goodman; 75*t* Muséum Autun; 75*cl* A.J. Sutcliffe; 75*cr* Neil Davies/A–Z Botanical Collection; 75*bl* Jon Hather; 75*br* A.J. Sutcliffe; 76*t* E. Mead; 76*c* Paul Martin; 76*bl* Gordon Hillman; 76*br* Jon Hather; 77*tl* Naoki Suzuki; 77*tr* Paul Bahn; 77*b* M.O. and J. Plassard; 78*t* Adrian Lister; 78*b* Institute of Palaeontology, University of Bonn, G. Oleschinski; 78/79 Mike Newton; 80*tl* Page Museum/Finley Holiday Films; 80*tr*/*b* Muséum Autun; 81*t* The Natural History Museum, London; 81*blr* Museum Autun; 81*bc* Adrian Lister; 86*t* M.O. and J. Plassard; 86/87*b* Steve Turner/Oxford Scientific Films; 87 Jean Vertut; 88 John Bracegirdle/Planet Earth Pictures; 89*t* Mike Newton; 89*b* Dr. C. Vance Haynes; 90*t* Mike Newton; 90*bl* Adrian Lister; 90*br*/91*t* Mike Newton; 91*b* Oxford University Museum; 92/93 Paul Bahn; 95 Réunion des Musées Nationaux; 96*t* Muséum National d'Histoire Naturelle, Paris; 96*b* Jean Vertut; 97 Franz Steiner Verlag Wiesbaden GmbH, Stuttgart; 98*l* Franz Steiner Verlag Wiesbaden GmbH, Stuttgart; 98*t* Dominique Sacchi; 98*c* Alexander Marshack; 98*br* Dominique Sacchi; 99*l* Prähistorische Staatssammlung, Museum für Vor- und Frühgeschichte, München; 99*r* Franz Steiner Verlag Wiesbaden GmbH, Stuttgart; 100*t* Paul Bahn; 100*b*/102 Jean Vertut; 103*t* E. Mead; 103*b*/104 Paul Bahn; 106 Dominique Sacchi; 108 Alexander Marshack; 109 Paul Bahn; 110 Dr. L. Adrien Hannus; 111*t* Alexander Marshack; 111*b* The Natural History Museum, London; 112 Dr. Pawel Valde-Nowak; 112/113 Matthieu Scandella; 113/115 Alexander Marshack; 116*l* Mike Newton; 116*r* Yakutsk Art Museum; 117*t* N.K. Vereshchagin; 117*bll*/*br* Mike Newton; 118/119 Jean Vertut; 126*t* Denver Museum of Natural History; 126*b* Arizona State Museum, The University of Arizona; 127*t* Denver Museum of Natural History; 127*b* Arizona State Museum, The University of Arizona; 128 Réunion des Musées Nationaux; 129*t* Stamps illustrated courtesy of the Jersey Post Office; 129*c* Kate Scott; 129*b* Adrian Lister; 130*tl*/*c* Réunion des Musées Nationaux; 130*b* Adrian Lister; 131*t* N. Praslov; 131*b* Adrian Lister; 132/133*t* Lon E. Lauber/Oxford Scientific Films; 132/133*b* Yuri Shibenev/Planet Earth Pictures; 137*t* Nikita Ovsianikov; 137*b* The Mansell Collection; 139*tl* Department of Tourism, Dordogne; 139*tr* Paul Bahn; 139*b* Geoff Tompkinson/Science Photo Library; 151 Hulton Deutsch Collection. If the publishers have unwittingly infringed copyright in any of the illustrations reproduced, they would pay an appropriate fee on being satisfied of the owner's title.